William Penn

PROFILES IN POWER

General Editor: Keith Robbins

. . . .

WILLIAM PENN

Mary K. Geiter

An imprint of **Pearson Education**

Harlow, England · London · New York · Reading, Massachusetts · San Francisco
Toronto · Don Mills, Ontario · Sydney · Tokyo · Singapore · Hong Kong · Seoul
Taipei · Cape Town · Madrid · Mexico City · Amsterdam · Munich · Paris · Milan

Pearson Education Limited
Edinburgh Gate
Harlow
Essex CM20 2JE
England

and Associated Companies throughout the world

Visit us on the World Wide Web at:
http://www.pearsoneduc.com

First published 2000

ISBN 0 582 29901 2 CASED
ISBN 0 582 29900 4 PPR

British Library Cataloguing-in-Publication Data
A catalogue record for this book is available from the British Library

Library of Congress Cataloging-in-Publication Data
A catalog record for this book is available from the Library of Congress

10 9 8 7 6 5 4 3 2 1
04 03 02 01 00

Typeset by 35 in 11/13pt Janson
Produced by Pearson Education Asia Pte Ltd.
Printed in Singapore

CONTENTS

For OL

PREFACE

This book is about the political life of William Penn and is the result of questions which were raised when I examined the influence of English politics upon the establishment of Pennsylvania. Obviously Penn figured prominently in the creation of the colony, but I was more interested in its investors and the events surrounding its beginnings. Far from losing sight of the proprietor, however, I started to look at him also as an investor and at his place in English society. It became apparent to me that he was more than what most historians had, so far, made him out to be. The hagiography that surrounded his life steeped him in Quakerism and everything he accomplished was attributed to his faith. Anything else, which seemed not to fit with this explanation, was put down to one of those 'mysteries' about the man. The result, in America though not in Britain, was the building of an enigma and an icon and any attempt to challenge that view was seen as an attempt to belittle the man's greatness. While I understood the sanctity of Penn's Quakerism among some scholars, I did not expect an attempt to suppress evidence. But this is exactly what happened when I submitted documentary proof of Penn's Jacobitism to a leading American journal and the article was rejected. Happily, it was accepted by another academic journal, in Britain, which was not encumbered by such prejudice.

As a Pennsylvanian, I was, at first, dismayed to find a man at variance with the idealistic interpretation given him over the years. However, through living and studying in England for many years, my American view of Penn was stripped away and was replaced with a British perspective. Consequently many of the mysteries surrounding my subject became explainable. My investigation of Penn's life soon led me to realize that there were crucial questions which, in my view, had never been satisfactorily answered. Who or what kind of man was Penn before he donned the mantle of the Society of Friends? Was his pacifist persuasion enough to explain his ambitions and achievements and troubles? Were his successes really simply because he was the friend of kings? Were his failures simply due to his naivety concerning human nature and finances?

I came to realize through a fresh examination of Penn that a key to understanding his role is that he was a member of the ruling elite. Thus his position in society influenced his outlook as much if not more than did his religion. He was someone who thought in the broader religious terms of dissent, which put his Quaker faith into the context of nonconformity. Indeed, historians have argued that his political activities conflicted with his Quakerism, creating tensions, but that is not necessarily true. Because of his broad religious outlook, he was able to rationalize his political involvement. He wanted a more tolerant society, but that did not necessarily mean a wholly egalitarian one. He could and did act arbitrarily. Still, Penn looked at the big picture. Such a combination of qualities enabled him to make his dreams of political attainment come true. He was able to create a successful political and religious experiment. Besides his plans for a more equitable society, his dream of expanding English influence in North America from its east coast to the Gulf of Mexico is testament to his vision, a vision which is echoed in the American dream.

. . . .

ACKNOWLEDGEMENTS

I have been guided by sound advice and encouragement from a number of people throughout the research and writing of this book. The staff of numerous libraries and archives in Britain and the United States have my immense gratitude for their help, if not a huge salary increase, which they more than deserve. The Cambridge University Library, the London Public Record Office, the British Library, and numerous local archives in the United Kingdom have been very kind and helpful. On the other side of the Atlantic, I am grateful to the Historical Society of Pennsylvania, the Library Company of Philadelphia, and the Huntington Library for their assistance. Also, the staff of Swarthmore College was gracious enough to allow me to explore their collections without first making an appointment.

If I had to name all of the people who took time from their own interests to listen to me and to give me their insights, the result would be a book-length list of acknowledgements. Unfortunately, I must be brief. First, my most loyal companion, Buddy, who patiently listened to my rants and, at times, cries of despair; all the while encouraging me to take breaks and get fresh perspective by going for walks. My family who, though not as patient as Bud, nevertheless withstood my selfish quest to the point of putting up with my long absences, punctuated by whirlwind appearances. I missed them more than they will ever know.

Time passes and so do people dearest to one. My mother, father, and grandmother saw the beginnings of my endeavour, but, heartbreakingly, they were not here for its completion. Still, they must know. Nevertheless, life continues and with it new joys in the persons of a daughter-in-law and grandson. What they will make of my obsessions, only time will tell.

Expressing my ideas and views to people who understood the period was essential to clarifying points of my work. During the early years of my project, the Cambridge seminars in American and English history, run by Tony Badger and John Morrill respectively, were encouraging forums in which I could air my findings on Penn and Pennsylvania. Later, Stephen Saunders Webb was good enough to read a chapter of my work and advise me on my errors, providing hints on how to improve my subject. I am also grateful to Woody Holton, who listened to my ramblings and who livened up my otherwise desperate year as temporary lecturer.

My greatest appreciation and obligation during this journey is to my closest companion and mentor, Bill Speck, who provided me with the tools to pursue the political life of Penn from a fresh perspective. His modesty belies his inestimable knowledge of the British political arena of the period. Without his contributions to scholarship in this area, the story of the creation of the North American colonies would have remained incomplete. But the greatest lessons he passed on were the excitement of exploration, an open mind, and the endeavour to write true history.

LIST OF ABBREVIATIONS

APS	American Philosophical Society
BL	British Library, London
CSP Colonial	*Calendar State Papers Colonial*, multi-volume, in progress (London, 1860–)
CSP Domestic	*Calendar State Papers Domestic*, 85 vols (London, 1857–1972)
DNB	*Dictionary of National Biography*
FLL	The Library of the Religious Society of Friends, London
HMC	*Historical Manuscripts Commission*
HSP	Historical Society of Pennsylvania
PRO	Public Record Office, London
PWP	Richard S. Dunn and Mary Maples Dunn (eds), *The Papers of William Penn*, 4 vols (University of Pennsylvania Press, 1981–86)

CHRONOLOGY

1644	(14 Oct.) Born in London
1656–60	Penn family at Macroom Castle, County Cork, Ireland
1660	Matriculates at Christ Church, Oxford
1661	Leaves Christ Church
1662	Goes to France
1664	(Aug.) Returns to London
1665	(Feb.) Enters Lincoln's Inn to study law
1666	(Feb.) Goes to Ireland to manage father's estates
1667	Defends Quakers at Cork
	(Nov.) Returns to England a Quaker
1668	Writes *Sandy Foundation Shaken*
	(Dec.) Imprisoned for blasphemy
1669	(Feb.) Writes *No Cross, No Crown*, and *Innocency with her Open Face*, while in the Tower
	(July) Released from Tower
	(Sept.) Leaves for Ireland
1670	Writes *A Seasonable Caveat Against Popery* and *The Great Case of Liberty of Conscience*
	Arrested for preaching
	(Sept.) The Penn–Meade trial
1672	(4 April) Marries Gulielma Springett and moves to Rickmansworth, Hertfordshire
1675	Writes *A Treatise of Oaths* and *England's Present Interest Discover'd*
1676	(July–Sept.) Arranges division between East and West New Jersey. Defends West Jersey's jurisdictional rights
1677	Journeys to Holland and Germany

1679	Publishes *England's Great Interest in the Choice of this New Parliament* and *One Project for the Good of England*
	Campaigns for Algernon Sidney's election to parliament
1681	Receives the charter for Pennsylvania
	Writes *Some Account of the Province of Pennsilvania*
1682	Goes to Pennsylvania
1683	First assembly meeting in Philadelphia
1684	Returns to England to defend Pennsylvania boundary from Maryland's claims
1685	Charles II dies
	James II's accession
1686	Publishes *A Persuasive to Moderation*
	Travels to Netherlands and Germany
1687	Publishes *Good Advice to the Church of England*
	Participates in the campaign to pack parliament
1688	William of Orange lands at Torbay
	James flees to France
1689	Warrant issued for Penn's arrest
1690	The Battle of the Boyne
	Publishes *Some Proposals for a Second Settlement of Pennsylvania*
1692	New York's governor, Benjamin Fletcher, appointed governor of Pennsylvania
	Penn loses Pennsylvania charter
1693	Writes *Essay Toward the Present and Future Peace of Europe. By the Establishment of a European Dyet, Parliament and Estates*
1694	Receives back Pennsylvania charter
	Death of Gulielma Penn
1696	Marries Hannah Callowhill
	Affirmation Bill passed into law
1697	Writes *A Briefe and Plaine Scheame*
1699	Arrives in Pennsylvania
1701	Returns to England
1703	Begins serious negotiations to sell Pennsylvania to the Crown
1708	Imprisoned for debt owed to Philip Ford and family
	Released from prison after the Churchills and Quaker business friends pay debt
1710	Pennsylvania election results in Penn's favour
1712	Suffers first stroke
	Makes new will naming Harley and Poulet executors
1713	Hannah takes charge of estate due to Penn's incapacitation
1718	Dies and is buried at Jordans, Buckinghamshire

Chapter 1

INTRODUCTION

Benjamin West's painting of *William Penn's Treaty with the Indians* depicts a man who is in the middle period of his life. His girth reflects his prosperity. His manner is a gracious one, exhibited by the open gesture of his hand. His deportment reflects the pacific nature of his sect. The Quaker leader and founder of Pennsylvania looks benignly upon the natives to whom he is proffering an exchange for land and the promise to coexist peaceably with one another. All is well and the future of the colony looks good.

This image has influenced interpretations of Penn's life down to the present day. William Penn's biographers, from Joseph Besse to Harry Emerson Wildes, bolster the image of a benign and benevolent patriarch who presided over his fledgling colony and made peaceful pacts with the native Americans in that corner of the world.[1]

In fact, he was credited with being the only white man whose treaties with the Indians were made without swearing oaths and were never broken.[2] Always depicted as a Quaker first, Penn's actions and decisions emanated from a spiritual light within. Melvin Endy emphasizes that one object remained clear in Penn's mind and that was his spiritual purpose.[3] This religious purpose has been combined with the idea of experimentation by Edwin Bronner, whose book was entitled *William Penn's Holy Experiment.*[4] Thus Penn's biographers have stressed the religious element in his career, which has become firmly entrenched in American textbooks on the subject.

However, if we look a little closer at the picture, there are clues to another side of the man. The clues emanate from the painter's own background. West was born in Pennsylvania to parents with Quaker connections. His maternal grandparents went over to Pennsylvania in 1682 with William Penn. Therefore it is reasonable to assume that West heard, at first hand, stories about the Proprietor. By the time

1

West painted the picture for Penn's son Thomas, he was living in England and aware of the political struggle between the Penn family and the Pennsylvania government. West had also moved from painting portraits to illustrating historical events of significant importance. He had just completed *The Death of Wolfe* when he was commissioned to paint the treaty at Shackomaxon. Both subjects were historically important and politically significant. Thus West combined what he knew of Penn with the political moment to create a stylized version of the Quaker leader. To be sure, the scene reflects the promise of harmony between the savage and civilized worlds. The painting also shows the potential of the new colony, with ships arriving in the background and buildings being erected. The Penn family wanted to emphasize the positive contribution of their father but they also wanted to remind the colonists of the political clout of the family.

At the centre of the picture stands someone who is without a doubt in charge. Here was a man whose dress was not quite the simple attire of a follower of the Society of Friends. There are the silk stockings, the frill of the cravat, and a slightly exaggerated brimmed hat. His size belies the reality of his age: he was, in fact, only 38 years old and much more svelte. His inflated girth was meant to represent paternalism and power. In essence, the picture shows Penn acting in the capacity of a potentate rather than that of a plenipotentiary.

Contemporary accounts of Penn show a man who was a polished and effective speaker, one who could converse well in Latin and French. John Aubrey, a contemporary, described the youthful Penn as lively, yet sensitive. Descriptions of his propensity towards spirituality are mainly based upon Penn's own account of his life. Other contemporary accounts variously describe Penn as witty, courtly, haughty, very athletic, above average height, a good swordsman. The portrait of the young Penn upon his return from Europe certainly suggests these qualities. His long flowing hair and bright eyes set in a soft frame depict a young man about to embark upon a career in the military. One contemporary, in fact, described Penn as the most handsome, best-looking, and the liveliest gentleman she had ever seen. Even after his convincement, the Quaker term for conversion, his dress was less severe than the usual dress of the Friends.[5] One undoubted aspect of his personality emerges, and that is an energetic and somewhat aggressive character. He never really lost his supercilious approach, particularly when his will was being thwarted. Neither did he forget his own status. In 1683 he objected to Lord Baltimore addressing him as 'William Penn Esquire' and 'the said Penn', and not by his full title as proprietor of Pennsylvania. 'Indeed his carriage all along shows he came to defie me,' he grumbled, 'not treat me like either Neighbour or Gentleman.'[6] In 1709 he complained about assemblymen in Pennsylvania who were challenging his authority. How long would they have lived in England, he asked of three of humble origins, before they would have been members of assembly and justices of the peace? 'Have they forgot their low circumstances? I have not.'[7]

By reminding Friends in Pennsylvania of their low social status, Penn was drawing attention to the fact that he was something of an anomaly as a gentleman Quaker. The social origins of English Quakers are a matter of dispute among historians. Some argue that they were mainly urban tradesmen and craftsmen, others that they were rural farmers and yeomen, while yet others maintain that they were even more lowly in origin than these. Yet all agree that few were of gentry origin. Penn was almost unique in coming from the ruling class.[8]

The Society of Friends was founded by George Fox towards the end of the English civil wars under the regime of Oliver Cromwell. The term Quaker was a derisive one which was taken from Fox's admonition to his followers to tremble at the word of the Lord. The sect emerged out of the cauldron of religious experiments that boiled over after the established Church of England was dismantled. Breaking with the orthodox religions, the central tenet of the Society of Friends was the belief that the light within oneself was all that was needed for revelation and salvation. In its early period, Quaker outlook had not solidified into a consistent orthodoxy. Although Fox advocated pacifism, plain dress, speech, repugnance to swearing oaths, and the eschewing of political activity or becoming too worldly, all these were not necessarily practised by all who considered themselves Friends. Although Cromwell complained of the threat posed by pacifist Quakers during wartime, there were Quakers willing to use violence. For William Penn, the whole notion of pacifism created tension between his beliefs and his political decisions. It would not be inaccurate to suggest that while the Quaker philosophy suited Penn, particularly in his youth, as he acquired power and prominence he did not necessarily suit it.

That he was a pacifist made his relationship with the country's elite appear, at first sight, baffling. However, the fact that he was born into a family that already had entrée into court circles helps to explain some of the mystery that surrounds his life. His father, Sir William Penn, an active admiral under Cromwell and Charles II, was a man of means. His Irish and English estates yielded a vast amount of money. Upon his father's death, Penn inherited a handsome sum of £1,500 per annum and his income was further enhanced by his marriages.[9] His first wife, Gulielma Springett, brought £10,000 to the union and his second marriage to Hannah Callowhill brought him £3,000 a year. For all his protestations that he would rather live a simple life with little money than that of a wealthy London merchant, he continued to live a life of, if not sumptuousness, certainly comfort compared to most of his fellow Quakers. Even though he was later to jeopardize his financial well being, Penn never lived a life of penury.[10] Illustrative of his elevated position in society was his protestation of charges brought against him for having meetings at his home at Worminghurst Place, not as a Quaker but as a gentleman of rank. Not only did he protest against the two JPs who reported him, but Penn used his connections, evidence of his social influence, by writing to the earl of Middlesex and Dorset objecting to such offensive behaviour.[11] This incident was not the only time Penn exercised his social clout to gain a political point. Shortly before his father's death, young William, imprisoned for sedition, allowed himself to be bailed in order to visit his dying father. Upon Sir William's demise, Penn designed his father's tomb complete with his military accomplishments emblazoned on the wall of St Mary Redcliffe in Bristol. The monument was not only a gesture to the memory of his father, it was a social statement.

Penn's circle of powerful friends testifies to his own influential position in English society. His correspondence reveals time and again intimate friendships with the leading politicians of the age. Although Penn's authority in Pennsylvania was so considerable that Voltaire described him as sovereign of the colony, his power was based on his significance in English politics. His stature in the counties was impressive enough for politicians to look to him for support in elections because it was felt that he could deliver the dissenting vote. For Penn, as we shall see, was not only a prominent Quaker but a leading dissenter. He became a spokesman for the dissenting interest, comprising Presbyterians, Independents, Baptists, and other non-Anglican sects besides Quakers which had sprung up in the upheavals of the civil war and Interregnum. At first they lacked strict doctrinal orthodoxy. People went from one sect to another, experimenting with their beliefs. Sir William Penn, himself a Presbyterian, was willing to listen to preachers of different faiths. Thus he allowed Thomas Loe, an Irish Quaker, into his home in Ireland in 1655. Young William Penn was exposed to that kind of eclecticism from an early age. The religious convictions he reached in the 1660s were born out of his formative years under the Cromwellian regime. The freedom with which non-Catholics could practise their beliefs meant that he was exposed to a variety of sects flourishing in those years. Many were in a state of doctrinal flux. Labels such as Quaker and Seeker were not precise terms at the time. Quakers did not adopt pacifism, for instance, until after the Restoration, when George Fox promulgated the peace testimony. Even then not all Friends renounced violence. As we shall see, Penn himself contributed to the development of Quaker beliefs.

By the time of his convincement, however, the Quakers were already distinguishable from other sects by several characteristics. One was their lack of deference, exemplified by their refusal to pay hat honour to their superiors. Penn himself kept his hat on even in the presence of Charles II, which led that good-humoured monarch to bare his head in riposte. Another was their dislike of a ministry and churches, or 'steeple houses' as they termed them. Their own organization was based on an impressive system of 'meetings', which held the Society of Friends together at local, regional, national, and even international levels. Besides such obvious manifestations there were doctrinal distinctions, although Friends were resistant to the adoption of a formal creed. Their concept of God differed from the vengeful Jehovah of the Puritans, stressing His love for His creatures. They believed that God's love expressed itself in every human being by an inner light.

Since this is a monograph of Penn as a politician at or near the centre of power, the aim of this study is to address the major political issues surrounding him. For that reason, relatively little space is given to his religious activities except when they impinge upon politics and his role as political leader in England as well as in North America. This will doubtless annoy those to whom Penn is an icon rather than a historical figure, but to keep within the remit of this series the risk must be run.

Penn is not an immediately obvious candidate for a 'profile in power'. He was not a monarch like Elizabeth I or James II, or a dictator like Mussolini or Stalin. He was not even a prime minister such as Gladstone or Walpole. Unlike other politicians of the period who played a major role in parliament, Penn was debarred from the House of Commons by dint of being a Quaker. But parliament was by no means the only political arena in which politicians operated. Indeed, there were powerful influences operating at court in the shape of ministers and councillors who surrounded the monarch. These men were an integral part of the political scene at a time when the royal prerogative was still a formidable factor in politics. Thus the corridors of power connected the court and the ministerial offices in Whitehall. Penn became a familiar figure in those corridors, especially during the reign of James II, from the time he petitioned for the Pennsylvania charter in 1680 until he was incapacitated by a stroke in 1712. This was six years before his death in 1718. During those years he dealt either directly with the Crown or with those politicians who acted as the monarch's power brokers. He was a skilful courtier who knew how to make himself useful to the Stuarts and their favourites, among whom for a while, under James II, he could count himself. This was because he knew what made these men tick, and in many ways shared their outlook on politics and their views on the political problems facing men in power in the late seventeenth and early eighteenth centuries.

Up to Penn's involvement with colonial endeavours, his main political activities were aimed at full toleration for his fellow dissenters. His political clout only increased with the death of his father and his subsequent inheritance. As a prominent dissenter and a leader of the Quaker sect, Whitehall took him seriously as one who could deliver the vote of the nonconformists.

Penn also played the major role in the formative years of the development of Pennsylvania. There he clearly exercised more power than he did in England. For that reason the book has been divided into two parts to distinguish his experience in England and Ireland from his proprietorship of Pennsylvania. The distinction is to some extent artificial since, as we shall see, his authority in the colony reflected his status in the mother country. Although we know him chiefly through his connection with Pennsylvania, Penn would not have seen himself that way. He was an Englishman first and, as head of the Penn family, he bore dynastic responsibility. The decisions he took regarding his assets arose from his awareness of his position in society. It would be a mistake to assume that Penn's decisions regarding the colonies were separate from his activities in England. They were inextricably linked and, if we view the Quaker from that perspective, hitherto unresolved questions surrounding Penn's actions and his life can be elucidated. Once those aspects are illuminated, Penn's role as a political force can be fully appreciated. Penn viewed his colony from an imperial perspective always with a view to England's greatness. As he wrote to Robert Harley, 'Let us be treated like Englishmen and not lose our domestick advantages for cultivating of wildernesses so much to the honour and wealth of the crown.'[12] To understand Penn, it is vital to appreciate the imperial context in which he operated. Understanding of one side of the Atlantic is not enough.

*   *   *

People are not born knowing the context of late Stuart politics. Yet it is necessary to appreciate the political environment in which Penn operated in order to understand how he came to exercise power. The rest of this introduction provides the background to his activities as a politician.

The civil wars and their aftermath in the central decades of the seventeenth century left a legacy which was to inform English politics well into the next. The execution of Charles I and the creation of the Republic were accompanied by the dismantling of the Church of England and the rise of radical sects. The social hierarchy was challenged with the aboli-tion of the House of Lords and the proliferation of radical groups such as the Levellers, the Diggers, the Ranters, and the Quakers who saw the removal of the monarchy as a hopeful social transformation. The Diggers, or 'true levellers', led by William Everard and Gerrard Winstanley, advocated communal sharing where there would be no such thing as private property. The Ranters bucked religious traditions and moral conventions by pushing to the extreme the notion that God dwelled within the person. As such, they considered themselves exempt from mundane moral law, thereby incurring the charge of antinomianism. Though not as radical in their moral precepts as the Ranters, the Quakers nevertheless were seen as extreme enough to become a target for persecu-tion even by the Parliamentary regime. Nevertheless, the new repub-lican society denoted a more egalitarian approach than that of the Stuart monarchs, and with it there emerged a time of relatively free expres-sion.[13] As new sects emerged from the cauldron of the civil wars they became distinguished by different creeds. With the exception of the Presbyterians, they rejected the Thirty-Nine Articles of the established Church, not wanting such precepts to guide them. The Presbyterians, while agreeing with most of the Articles, objected to three or four which they claimed had no scriptural sanction. They particularly objected to the episcopal hierarchy, and favoured a form of church government organized from below rather than from above. The Independents were just that. They had no central authority to appeal to. They were the first sect to preach the virtues of religious toleration and to try to reach an accommodation with other Protestant sects. Toleration, however, remained an elusive goal in the Interregnum. This was because, in the years between the civil wars and the Restoration of Charles II, the sects were engaged in political strife. Many Baptists became Fifth Monarchy Men who sought to usher in the reign of King Jesus by violent means. Even the Quakers continued to be seen as a threat to social stability.

From the outset, Charles II's restoration to the throne of England marked a change in the social and political climate of the country from its time under Cromwell. Outwardly, Charles's reign appeared as flamboyant as the years under Cromwell seemed austere. Indeed, Charles's coronation procession embodied all that was anathema to the former regime. Superficially at least, the king became the model for excess, with what seemed to be a constant round of parties, gambling, and carnal licence. Underneath it all, however, there was a move to bring England back into the conservative mould. The question was how to avoid plunging the country into anarchy and chaos again. Men and women of all political and religious persuasions yearned for a settlement which would last. The trouble was that they had different solutions to the problem, which meant that England came perilously close to a repetition of the mid-century upheaval in the Glorious Revolution of 1688. It was regarded as 'glorious' partly because it avoided the complete breakdown of the country's institutions which had occurred in the 1640s and 1650s. Even so, it failed to settle the kingdom entirely, the decades following it being notorious for political instability.

Among the myriad suggestions put forward after 1660 for a permanent solution, three can be said to have commanded the most serious support. One solution was based upon the assumption that the country had slipped into the catastrophe of civil war and revolution because power had slipped from the Crown and Church to parliament and the radical religious sects. The answer was to strengthen the monarchy and the establishment and to weaken if not to crush their rivals. This was the programme of the majority in what became known as the Cavalier Parliament, and their successors, the Tories. They tried to restrict office holding in local and national government to Anglicans. Thus the Corporation Act of 1661 and the Test Act of 1673 confined posts in borough corporations or under the Crown to those who communicated with the established Church. Opposed to this approach were those who felt that absolute monarchy and a monolithic Church had violated traditional liberties. Limited monarchy and religious toleration, therefore, would guarantee liberty and make revolution unnecessary. This was the view of the 'Country' opponents of the Court in the Cavalier Parliament and their heirs, the Whigs. From 1679 until 1714 with the death of Queen Anne, the last of the Stuart monarchs, there emerged the 'first age of party'. This was due to the coalescing of identities over critical issues. It was given impetus by frequent elections, starting with the years between 1679 and 1681, when three parliamentary elections were held. During this period, variously termed the Restoration Crisis or the Exclusion Crisis, efforts were made to curb the prerogative powers of the king. One of the ways in which the Crown's prerogative power was threatened was through the attempts to bar the duke of York, heir to the throne, from inheriting his brother's crown. The result was that groups which hitherto had been loose coalitions solidified into something much more identifiable. The terms Whig and Tory emerged from being derogatory labels applied to Catholic bandits in Ireland and the Presbyterians in Scotland to denote political parties. They distinguished Tories, who upheld the divine right of monarchs, the indefeasible hereditary right of kings, and the rights of the Church of England as by law established, from Whigs committed to a limited monarchy, a Protestant succession and a broader toleration of religious beliefs except for Catholicism.

Besides these Cavalier/Tory and Country/Whig approaches to the questions left unresolved at the Restoration there were other solutions to the problem of securing a permanent settlement. Perhaps the best known was that of the 'trimmer', the marquis of Halifax. He found the answer in the law, harking back to the great common lawyers like Sir Edward Coke who, in James I's reign, had maintained the sovereignty of the law over that of the king's prerogative and the king in parliament. The law would restrain kings who attempted to rule arbitrarily and subjects who were bent on anarchy. But while appeals to the mystical majesty of the law were fine in theory, in practice the law could be manipulated by the Crown for its own ends.

A more pragmatic approach was adopted by men who trimmed between the Cavalier/Tory, Country/Whig solutions in other ways. They felt that a settlement could be served on the basis of a consensus. People could accept the religious pluriformity which had emerged in the civil wars and Interregnum provided it did not threaten political and social stability. However, such acceptance could not be expected from parliament. Parliaments of all kinds, from the Long Parliament to the Cavalier Parliament, had thrown up majorities which time and again had displayed intolerance and a penchant for asserting their own religious preferences. Thus the Long Parliament had abolished episcopacy, proscribed the Book of Common Prayer and required the use of the Directory of Public Worship. The Rump had set up triers and ejectors to test the orthodoxy of parish clergymen. The Barebones Parliament had supported the excesses of the Fifth Monarchists. The Protectorate parliaments had Presbyterian majorities intolerant of minor sects. The most blatant example of this was shown in 1656 when punishment was meted out to the Quaker James Naylor for riding through Bristol on a donkey emulating the second coming of Christ. For this blasphemy, he was put to the lash, pilloried, and had his tongue bored through.[14] As a result of parliament's intolerance and bigotry, the executive was looked to as a more promising instrument for effecting a consensus. Even under the Protectorate a sort of compromise had emerged which resulted in a regime regarded as the most tolerant of religious minorities of any up to that time. It even witnessed the return of the Jews to England. After the death of Cromwell, hopes of achieving a similar consensus centred on the king.

Charles II cultivated these hopes in the Declaration of Breda which helped restore him to his father's throne. In it he offered an indulgence for tender consciences which did not 'disturb the peace of the kingdom'. This was precisely the kind of religious compromise which the advocates of consensus sought. The fact that their hopes withered on the vine was not their fault. Rather the responsibility lay at the feet of the restored Anglicans backed up by the vindictive majority in the Cavalier Parliament. This parliament passed a series of laws, over the next few years, requiring conformity to the Church of England. The Act of Uniformity upheld subscription to all Thirty-Nine Articles. Many clergymen installed in Anglican livings during the Interregnum refused to subscribe and became the first nonconformists. They were not allowed to set up rival congregations to those of the establishment. Further laws prohibited seditious meetings of dissenting conventicles, and made conventicle meetings illegal within a five-mile boundary around incorporated towns. Collectively misnamed by historians the Clarendon Code, these laws were a warning bell to those who thought toleration would flourish under the new regime. Charles himself continued to hope for a religious settlement which would accommodate tender consciences. Twice he issued Declarations of Indulgence to effect this, on each occasion earning a rebuke from the Anglicans in the House of Commons.

The earl of Clarendon, the architect of the restoration of Charles II, shared this view at the time. He was anxious to settle the restored monarchy on the broadest possible basis. It was only later when he fell from power that he adopted the stance of a disgruntled high Anglican. Yet if he changed his mind others did not. The goal of religious toleration held out by the Crown remained an aim of Clarendon's successors, such as his son Laurence, earl of Rochester, Robert Spencer, earl of Sunderland, and Sidney, Lord Godolphin. But the growing polarization of groups inhibited their plans and forced them to include this new equation in their strategy. The emergence of parties gave the Crown and its servants a problem. The object was to control the government as well as parliament. But the desire of the Crown was to prevent party rule. The solution, in part, was to create a buffer of servants who were able to offset party dominance in government. By doing so, the Crown could maintain its hegemony. These 'managers' or 'power brokers' were the key to success. From 1679 onward, these men occupied vital positions which were connected with the monarch, whether in the royal closet, cabinet, or privy council. They shared a common vision. They were prepared to compromise and, if necessary, override any allegiance to party to achieve their goals, primarily the rise of the English empire.

The men surrounding the Crown did not advocate religious toleration out of sheer altruism or even merely to secure political stability. They saw in it the key to economic growth and prosperity. Looking abroad they saw France enjoying the fruits of such a regime under Louis XIV until his disastrous revocation of the Edict of Nantes in 1685. The United Provinces of the Dutch Republic also seemed to offer a model of tolerance coupled with spectacular commercial success. Charles's brother and successor, James II, was to identify himself with such a model when he asserted in his Declarations of Indulgence that he had always been against 'imposing upon conscience in matters of religion' since it was contrary 'to the interest of government, which it destroys by spoiling trade'. As we shall see, Penn's views were close to those of the king. He had scruples, however, about James's desire to include his fellow Catholics within the scope of the Declaration. Other dissenters baulked at this idea, suspecting the king's motives. The result was that James alienated most of his subjects, Tories as well as Whigs, who joined together to welcome William of Orange's invasion and the subsequent revolution.

After the revolution, however, the former fissures reopened. Tories were reluctant to recognize the claims of dissenters for toleration. The so-called Toleration Act of 1689 extended only minimal concessions to Protestant non-Anglicans. Thus, while it granted those who believed in the Trinity the right to worship separately from the Church of England, it specifically upheld the Corporation and Test Acts, thereby maintaining the Anglican monopoly of offices in local and national government. It also required non-Anglicans to continue to pay tithes to the established Church, a grievance which dissenters in general, and Quakers in particular, felt strongly. The Friends also objected to the continued insistence upon the swearing of oaths, and campaigned for the right to affirm instead. As we shall see, Penn became closely involved in this campaign, and achieved temporary relief for his fellow Friends in the Affirmation Act of 1696, though this was not made permanent until 1722. Thus the religious disputes which divided Tories from Whigs continued to be central to English politics well into the eighteenth century, beyond the death of William Penn.

* * *

There are problems in dividing Penn's life between his affairs in England and in North America. Penn would never have considered these activities as separate but as overlapping, with one emanating from the other. Nevertheless, for convenience Chapters 2 to 6 discuss his activities in England, while Chapters 7 to 11 concern his dealings with Pennsylvania. Chapter 2 narrates his early years and his development as the leader of the dissenting interest, and analyses his participation in late Stuart politics. Chapter 3 describes how he obtained the charter for Pennsylvania. Chapter 4 examines his role in the reign of James II, when he exercised power in England. Chapter 5 investigates his alleged Jacobitism in the early 1690s. Chapter 6 demonstrates how he managed to retain the proprietorship of his colony despite attempts to deprive him of it under William III and Queen Anne. Chapter 7 surveys his colonizing activities in the middle colonies. Chapter 8 explains the various constitutions he devised for Pennsylvania and Delaware. Chapter 9 shows how he dealt with relations between his colony and other powers in the region, such as native North Americans and adjacent colonies. Chapter 10 relates his exercise of power as governor of Pennsylvania. The last chapter traces his final years and discusses the legacy that Penn left behind.

. . .

NOTES AND REFERENCES

1. Joseph Besse, *A Collection of the Works of William Penn* (London, 1726); Harry Emerson Wildes, *William Penn* (New York, 1974).
2. Voltaire, *Lettres Philosophiques*, ed. Gustave Lanson, 2 vols (1915), I, p. 48.
3. Melvin Endy, *William Penn and Early Quakerism* (Princeton, 1973), p. 348.
4. Edwin Bronner, *William Penn's Holy Experiment* (New York, 1962).
5. Leigh Hunt, *The Old Court Suburb*, 2nd edn, 2 vols (London, 1855), pp. 285–93.
6. Richard S. Dunn and Mary Maples Dunn (eds), *The Papers of William Penn*, II, p. 498.
7. *PWP*, IV, p. 661, Penn to Logan, 14 Oct. 1709.
8. See David Hackett Fischer, *Albion's Seed: Four British Folkways in America* (Oxford, 1989) pp. 434–5 n.; Bill Stevenson, 'The Social Integration of Post-Restoration Dissenters, 1660–1725', in Margaret Spufford (ed), *The World of Rural Dissenters 1520–1725* (Cambridge, 1995), pp. 360–87.
9. Oliver Lawson Dick (ed.), *Aubrey's Brief Lives* (Penguin, 1962), pp. 300–2.
10. Richard S. Dunn, 'Penny Wise and Pound Foolish: Penn as a Businessman', in Richard S. Dunn and Mary Maples Dunn (eds), *The World of William Penn* (University of Pennsylvania, 1986), pp. 37–54.
11. *PWP*, I, p. 515, Penn to the earl of Middlesex and Dorset, 17 Nov. 1677.
12. *HMC Portland*, III, 601, Penn to Harley, 30 Jan. 1699.
13. J.A. Sharpe, *Early Modern England: A Social History 1550–1760*, 2nd edn (Arnold, 1997), pp. 251–2.
14. J.F. McGregor and B. Reay (eds), *Radical Religion in the English Revolution* (Oxford University Press, 1988), pp. 158–9.

Chapter 2

DISSENTER AND POLITICIAN

It is a truism that politics and religion were inextricably linked under the later Stuarts. Religious toleration, for example, was a political issue throughout the era. It was a central concern of a Quaker like William Penn and a king like James II. But Quakers and kings rarely moved in the same circles. Penn was unique as a Quaker who brought the concerns of dissenters into the sphere of the court. To appreciate how he moved between the world of nonconformity and the world of high politics it is appropriate to separate his role as dissenter from that of politician.

· · ·

DISSENTER

William Penn was born on 14 October 1644. His father, Sir William Penn, was a Presbyterian, and his mother was a Dutch Calvinist. So the future Quaker was born into a dissenting family. He was a dissenter first and a Quaker second not only by chronology but also by conviction. Consequently, Penn's Quakerism must be set in the larger context of dissent. This larger view may be the explanation for James II's sceptical attitude towards Penn's Quaker proclivities when the king commented, 'I suppose you take William Pen[n] for a Quaker, but I can assure you he is no more so than I am.'[1] This is comprehensible only when we look at Penn's formative years, which span a period of religious toleration and diversity under Cromwell to intolerance and attempted uniformity under Charles II. By the time Anglicanism was fully restored and dissent was repressed, Penn was in the full throes of adolescence, and did what most young people do: he rebelled. He reacted first as a student and later as a Quaker convert.

Although the political climate of the 1640s and first half of the 1650s was unstable, nevertheless normal life went on. For Penn, this meant his developmental years took a conventional route. As the eldest son, he followed the usual path as heir to his father's estates. Thus he was educated in the typical manner of the gentry, being sent to a private school and later to university. After university many young men took a tour of Europe, peace permitting. Upon their return, young gallants supposedly came back slightly more polished and worldly, ready to assume their place in society. Penn was no different from his peers. He went to the Continent and returned somewhat of a dandy dressed in the French style. Further instruction in law helped to round out his skills and prepared him to take his place in society. His conversion to Quakerism, however, prevented him from fulfilling the role expected by his family, that of taking up a political career. While he did not follow the traditional route, by becoming, for example, a member of parliament, he did become a major figure in English politics. Paradoxically his development as a dissenter was to become the means by which he achieved greatness.

William spent his early childhood in the vicinity of London. His education was fairly typical of his social class, being schooled at home until the age of 11. Penn has been variously described as 'bookish', yet there are few accounts of his temperament. What we do have to go on is the type of education that he was given. From the age of 11 he began his formal training at Chigwell Academy near Wanstead in Essex. Established in 1629, the academy comprised two schools within the same building. One school concerned itself with more practical applications such as reading, writing, and mathematics. The other was more classically orientated, teaching Latin and Greek. It has been assumed that Penn was taught in the latter school.[2] Such an assumption has little foundation. Penn was indeed a classical scholar, but he was also a pragmatic man whose father was more inclined to the practicalities of life. Sir William, ambitious for his son, recognized the importance of being able to manage estates. Also, given the political environment in which the young Penn was being educated, it seems highly likely that he would be given instruction for more practical applications. Only after the fall of the Protectorate, and the impending Restoration of the monarchy, can we say for certain that Penn's education took a more classical turn.

Penn entered Oxford University in 1660 as a gentleman commoner. More specifically, he attended the citadel of Anglicanism, Christ Church. Under the deanship of John Fell, Christ Church became the pre-eminent place for anyone seeking to get a foothold in the new regime. It was there that Penn acquired his knowledge of classical scholarship.[3] Although

Penn was to spend less than two years at Christ Church, he came into contact with men who would become political allies. Robert Spencer, later earl of Sunderland, was also at Oxford, and, although he would matriculate as a nobleman above Penn's lower status, he and Penn became well enough acquainted to travel through Europe together. There were also men who would influence his thinking in other ways which would enhance his religious and political outlook. John Locke was then a censor at Christ Church and most probably tutored Penn in Greek.[4] While it could not have been through any acquaintance with Locke that Penn acquired a radical political philosophy at this time, since Locke was then still conservative in his thinking, nevertheless Penn would have developed a rigorous style of debate that would serve him later. The ideas of the more radical Locke of the 1680s possibly influenced Penn's concept of colonization. Later in the 1690s Locke's importance would be seen in the development of colonial policy. As the significant weight behind the development of the Board of Trade and the recoinage policy, Locke's position had considerable impact upon Penn's career.[5]

It was also during his days at Oxford that Penn most likely listened to the former vice-chancellor, dean, and well-known Puritan theologian, Dr John Owen. This experience is usually seen as a turning point in Penn's religious leanings, but he came from a dissenting background, and therefore it would not have been unreasonable to be instructed by somebody sympathetic to dissent, in this case the vice-chancellor, who had not yet been dismissed from the college.

Owen was dismissed, however, shortly after the new government was installed. Because of the restrictive laws against dissent, many clergy were deprived of their livings because they could not in conscience fulfil the requirements of adherence to the restored Anglican Church, such as participation in the sacrament, oaths of allegiance, supremacy, non-resistance, and a declaration against the validity of the Solemn League and Covenant. William's father, previously Presbyterian and recent convert to the Church of England, saw no problem in obeying the new set of laws. He was a pragmatic man and a survivor. Meanwhile, young William was confronted with the decision to wear the surplice, a vestment denoting the intention to take holy orders, as part of the renewed religious conformity.[6] His reaction was to write his objections, for which he claimed he was 'banished'. In fact, there is no evidence that he was actually 'sent down'.[7] A more reasonable assumption is that he was only ever intended to use his time in college as a first step into society. Families usually sent their sons to university in order to make contacts in the wider world. These contacts, hopefully, would benefit them in later life in business as well as politics.

William was sent to Europe, ostensibly to get him out of the political controversy that was arising from the continuation of the Clarendon Code, which now included prohibition of the gathering of five or more nonconformists for worship. While in France, Penn attended the Protestant Academy of Saumur. This would not have been seen as an act of rebellion against his father, for Sir William almost certainly did not object to his son going to the Academy, and possibly even recommended William to attend it. There Penn was under the tutelage of Moise Amyraut, one of the leading Calvinist theologians of the day. Although Penn's studentship was short, because Amyraut died in 1664, it became a watershed in his religious and political outlook.

Moise Amyraut played a key role in promoting religious toleration in France. He was well connected, not least with the political and religious influences at the Catholic court of Louis XIV. His views on Protestant moderation found favour with moderate Catholics. The Edict of Nantes allowed Protestants to practise their faith, hence the Academy. It was in this environment that Amyraut was able to rationalize the acceptance of the divine right of kings with the tenets of Calvinism and conclude with the philosophy of non-resistance. Amyraut's philosophy of non-resistance and the illumination of the mind and will, or the inner light, greatly influenced Penn's religious outlook. It not only helps to explain his attraction to the Quaker life, but also his later political position. With his feet planted firmly in Amyrauldian thought, Penn was able to rationalize and actively support James II's policies for toleration of Catholics.[8] Consequently, Penn was labelled as a papist himself.[9] The influence of Amyraut's views on toleration also helps to explain why Penn shifted his allegiance from James II to William and Mary after the Glorious Revolution.

Penn's first theological tracts, *Truth Exalted* and *The Guide Mistaken and Temporizing Rebuked*, published in 1668, reflect Amyrauldian thought.[10] While the latter work is the more polemical in its reply to other dissenters, such as Jonathan Clapham and his rationalization for conforming to the Act of Uniformity, both assert the inward light and the possibility of universal salvation.[11] In *Truth Exalted*, the young Penn challenged the doctrines of Catholics and Protestants alike for not being based on the Bible. 'What Scripture ever made a Pope', and where do the Scriptures 'own such persecutors', were some of the questions which Penn asked in order to illustrate how far professed Christians had moved away from their beginnings. Like Amyraut, Penn demanded that men look within themselves for the light, where they would find the resolution to their differences. Quoting from the Bible, Penn asserted Christ was the true light and that every man was capable of receiving salvation through his inner light: 'by no other way did I ever receive the knowledge of the least evil, or ability to conquer it, than in this universal Light'.[12] *The Guide Mistaken* furthers Penn's ideas on salvation by defending his stand against conformity, and comes ever closer to the issue of the Trinity, three persons in one God. 'The Scriptures do not warrant that division into, and appellation of three persons,' Penn maintained, and queried whether or not we should take this on faith. Written in the same year, *The Sandy Foundation Shaken* logically followed Penn's doubts on the Trinity and tested the grounds for the rejection of the divinity of Christ. If the Trinity was not valid, as he implied, was Christ of divine essence? 'If God, as the Scriptures testifie, hath never been declar'd or believ'd, but as the Holy ONE, then will it follow, that God is not a Holy THREE, nor doth subsist in THREE distinct and separate Holy ONES.' Again, Amyraut's brand of Calvinism reflected this concern with Trinitarian doctrine. Penn came close to expressing Unitarian views in this tract. The immediate reaction was that he was charged with Socinianism, of denying the doctrine of the Trinity. Although he quickly backed off from this approach, following a spell in the Tower and the publication of a new tract, *Innocency with her Open Face*, which mollified the authorities by saying that he was misinterpreted over the issue of divinity, the label of deist stuck to him for much of his life.

His writings on dissent, from his first exuberant tract *Truth Exalted* in 1668, to his final thoughts on life in general in *More Fruits of Solitude* in 1702, provide a map of his philosophical development.[13] Penn authored over 40 works, most of which dealt with his ultimate goal of toleration in general. The only exception for toleration which Penn made was in the case of Roman Catholics, as stated in his 1670 tract *A Seasonable Caveat Against Popery*, but that is muted in later years. Nevertheless, his works represent stages in his life, spanning the early years of religious zeal to modifying his views in light of political expediency, and finally to that stage most people reach when one becomes more philosophically resigned to the realities of life.

* * *

After Penn returned to England in 1664, his father found a mature son who was ready to take on the responsibilities of an heir. William spent some time learning law at the Inns of Court in London, a valuable foundation for anyone embarking on a life involving business, not least in pressing his father's Irish claims. He left there, possibly because of the plague, sometime in the spring of 1665. Meanwhile, a second war had broken out between the Dutch and English, and in March Penn was actively involved in the effort, acting as messenger running between the court and the flagship the *Royal Charles*. His position was no doubt due to the influence of his father, the admiral, who was based at the Navy office in London. By July Penn was cutting his teeth in the local politics of Buckinghamshire. As one of the commissioners for charitable uses, he determined cases brought on by complaints of abuse of charitable trusts.[14] Essentially, the commissioners for charity were a body established through Elizabethan statute and later modified through Jacobean law. The body was under the jurisdiction of the Church of England. Through the bishop's chancellor, the commissioners were appointed to investigate complaints, empanel juries, and hand down decisions on alleged abuses.[15] Given his empathy with the dissenting element, though he was not himself a dissenter at this point, Penn must have felt suited to the job. This position also gave Penn the experience he later applied so ably in his own and other Friends' defence of the promotion of toleration. It is interesting to envisage Penn before his time as a Quaker, acting as a justice of the peace. As a JP he would have had to be a communicant Anglican. He would have taken an oath for office. Moreover, at this time he would be establishing his influence in the locality which would serve him later in national politics during the period between 1679 and 1681.

For the present, Penn's responsibilities included time in Ireland. While he was there, he gained formative experiences in commercial and polit-ical activities as well as in his spiritual life. In later years, he referred to the area outside Philadelphia as 'our English pale', an expression used by the Anglo-Irish gentry about the area surrounding Dublin.[16] Ireland was the first testing ground for Penn as a young man to use his political and social *savoir-faire*. On the first, he rather stumbled, as in the case of his arrest in Cork when he tried to play the barrack-room lawyer with the mayor of Cork. He clumsily tried to go over the head of a magis-trate by appealing to Ireland's lord justice and family friend, only to be told off. There is little known of his social refinement at this time. Descriptions of him are of someone still sporting a wig and fancy attire, something he acquired during his sojourn on the Continent. There is a hint that he enjoyed the company of a lady. He was rather quick to exert himself physically, as in the case of his part in the suppression of a mutiny at Carrickfergus and his ejection of a soldier at a Quaker meeting in Cork.

Though his visits in 1666, 1669, and 1698 marked different phases in his own life, it was his visit beginning in 1666, as a young man, that became a major turning point in his religious development. Although the time of Penn's conversion to Quakerism is imprecise, we do know that in the autumn of 1667 Penn attended a Quaker meeting in Cork and was subsequently brought before the magistrate for being present at what was termed a 'riotous and tumultuary assembly'.[17] The story unfolds that while observing a meeting of the Friends, Penn noticed that a soldier, who was also attending, was creating a disturbance, whereupon Penn forcibly ejected the man from the room. The soldier returned with reinforcements who then hauled the Quakers, including Penn, before the magistrate. It is that event which is considered the crucial moment because the date of his conversion roughly coincides with it. Although not a Quaker at this juncture, Penn's arrest and subsequent treatment by the magistrate must have influenced his sympathies. He returned to England to a chagrined parent who probably despaired at the thought of his only son and heir becoming an outcast to society. In the long run, and paradoxically, it was his position as one of the leaders of dissent which pushed Penn to the forefront of society. Along with other contemporaries in the higher social echelons, such as Robert Barclay, a Scottish Quaker, he was able to influence and move the Society of Friends further down the path of religious freedom and political inclusiveness.

Penn's conversion also marked a crucial point in the path towards consolidation in Quaker principles. It had begun at the Restoration with George Fox's decision to lay down the sword of violence and write the *Peace Testimony*. The *Testimony* was in answer to Charles II's Declaration of Breda, which granted toleration for those who would not disturb the peace of the kingdom. In this document Fox saw a chance for ingratiating the Friends with the restored monarchy. Even though Fox's *Testimony* went some way to distinguish the peace-loving Quakers from other radical groups, there was still no systematic philosophy for the sect to follow. That was provided later in 1676 by Robert Barclay in his *An Apology for the True Christian Divinity*. This became the template for the ordering of Quaker doctrine. Penn began to formulate some kind of philosophy as early as 1669. In his work *No Cross, No Crown*, he set out the rules for behaviour. He rejected hat honour, titles, and the vanity of apparel, and promoted the use of thee and thou when addressing one another, regardless of status. Penn listed scriptural reasons for the rejection of outward vanities, observing, 'Honour was from the beginning, but hats, and most titles, here of late; therefore there was true Honour before hats or titles, and consequently true honour stands not therein.' Furthermore, he quoted James 2: 1–11, urging people to look further than man's outward appearance, and not to accept any man just 'for his gay cloathing, rich attire, or outward appearance'. As Penn became more involved in the politics of dissent, he found it increasingly difficult to maintain the standard he set in this work. Nevertheless, it was the first coherent guide on Quaker behaviour. Later, when he was confronted with the responsibility of running a colony marked by its religious tolerance, Penn found himself hard put to sustain these rules, particularly his support for eschewing oaths in favour of affirming.

Penn was able to further the Quaker cause through his forceful polemics and by practical applications in parliamentary elections. Although Penn's earlier writings included defences of the Quaker way, his first foray into political activism on behalf of dissent came with the onset of the new Conventicle Act in 1670. The new law prohibited sects such as Quakers from gathering for worship which was not according to the liturgy and practice of the Anglican Church. In response to this, and during another sojourn in Newgate prison, Penn wrote *The Great Case of Liberty of Conscience*, which was directed to the consideration of King Charles II. The thrust of the tract was the immorality of persecution, which was against reason and nature. 'For my own part,' he boldly proclaimed, 'I publickly confess my self to be a very hearty Dissenter from the establish'd religion of these nations.' His leading role in dissenting circles, thus made him a prominent political figure.

Penn's protest against the Conventicle Act did not spare him from being arrested under it for what the authorities claimed was sedition. But, unlike his earlier imprisonments, where he modified his views, this time he was determined to defend them in court. A fellow Quaker, William Meade, was also arrested with Penn and together they defended their positions. Their arguments were based on the rights of Englishmen which were being threatened by the Act. In what became celebrated as the Penn–Meade trial an important precedent was established. At the conclusion of the trial a verdict of not guilty was delivered for which the jury was imprisoned by the mayor of London. The order was overturned by the chief justice, thereby establishing the future autonomy of juries. The action by the mayor, however, raised the spectre of arbitrary power that had not been seen since the reign of Charles I, and it heightened political tensions. It also brought Penn widespread respect for his able championing of dissent. From this point, Penn was taken seriously by the Crown as well as parliament as somebody who could influence the dissenting element in society. This was particularly true during the political crises from 1679 to 1681, during the attempt by James II to introduce religious toleration in the 1680s, and in the early years of colonial development.

In 1671 Penn was again arrested, this time for being in breach of the Five Mile Act by holding forth at Spitalfields, and was carted off to prison. This time he was severely restricted from publishing tracts he wrote in jail. This experience made him realize that preaching and publishing tracts were not enough. More direct action was taken when he helped to compose a petition to parliament calling for toleration for dissenters.

Although the petition was unsuccessful it marked yet another turning point in Penn's career. He was gradually becoming a leading political spokesman for dissent. By 1687, under James II, he had become the most influential dissenter in politics. His writings during this period are essentially political. His contributions to James's *Declaration of Indulgence* in 1687 and 1688 place Penn at the height of his powers. From this height, he was sought out as an intermediary to the king. He was of the inner circle as one of James's closest advisers. Until the Glorious Revolution in 1688 and James's downfall and flight to France, Penn enjoyed a position that his father never dreamed his son would ever attain.

After the Revolution, Penn fell from favour with a thud. The new regime of William and Mary looked upon the Quaker as a part of a larger threat to the country's security. He was accused of conspiring against the new regime. For this he was imprisoned and lost his colony. Penn had to claw his way back to political influence, and his reinstatement was mainly due to the passage of time during which King William was able to secure his English throne. Penn's ability to sway dissent in England and his influence over his colonists in Pennsylvania were also factors in his return to power. His ability to bring about a Quaker settlement with the new regime resulted in another milestone in his efforts to secure toleration for dissent through the enactment of the Affirmation law. However, though he regained his colony and reinstated himself in the political environment, he never attained the pinnacle of influence in England that he enjoyed under James.

In the last years of his life, during the reign of Queen Anne, Penn worked to put the Affirmation Act on a permanent basis. But, other than writing a tract against the Anglican effort to penalize Occasional Conformity at the outset of the reign, he seems to have distanced himself from any overt religious activity.

· · ·

POLITICIAN

Penn's accomplishments did not rest solely in his religious convictions. As important as his religion was, equally influential on his career were the mercantile inheritance and political connections of his family. His maternal background comprised Dutch and Irish merchants while his paternal side combined trade and the sea. His grandfather, Giles Penn, was a sea captain trading in the Mediterranean, and later consul at Sale' in Morocco. William's uncle George rose to the rank of envoy to Spain during Charles II's reign, only to die before he could take up his post and recoup the loss of £12,000 in goods which he sustained under the Spanish regime. Penn's father, Sir William, became executor of his brother's estate, which in turn devolved to the son, who continued to press for the reimbursement of the loss in the reign of Queen Anne.[18] However, Sir William continued in the family business, spending his youth on board ship with his father and his adulthood as captain in the new Republican government. Under Cromwell, he was part of the flotilla that guarded the Irish Sea from the threat of the king's ships and, after the execution of Charles, he provided the pivotal support during Cromwell's Irish campaign. His effective seamanship won him a promotion to vice-admiral. After the campaign, Penn's previous experience in the Mediterranean suited him perfectly in his role of chasing the remnant royal forces in that area. His reward for his efforts was the confiscated Irish lands of Macroom near Cork. This acquisition was also, in part, due to his petition on behalf of his wife, who lost property there during the civil wars.

But it was the expedition to Hispaniola in the West Indies as part of Cromwell's great design to defeat Spanish dominance in the New World that proved Sir William's undoing, and no doubt served as a lesson to his son on the fragility of political alliances. William's father and General Robert Venables were given orders to take Hispaniola, but failed to do so, although they captured Jamaica. Upon their return to England, they were thrown into the Tower of London on what amounted to a charge of treason against the Republic. Although he was later released and retired to his estates in Ireland, the action against Admiral Penn created an insecurity that must have affected the young William at the threshold of puberty.

Penn's family background clearly influenced his religious and political views which led to his youthful rebellion at Oxford and his withdrawal from the university. When he went to the Academy at Saumur, as we have seen, he came under the profound ideological influence of Moise Amyraut. After his return to England, however, he continued to perform the duties of a scion of a landed family, taking a place in the commission of the peace for the county of Buckinghamshire. This familiarized him with the world of the landed elite in the localities from which his conversion to Quakerism would later exclude him.

Another experience which affected Penn's political as well as his religious views was his visit to Ireland in 1666. There too he took on the role of a landed magnate and a military representative of his father. Politically and religiously, the settlement of Ireland did not necessarily reflect the split in England between a monarchy that represented a tolerant viewpoint and a parliament which was suspicious of any divergence from the Anglican stand. For one thing, Ireland had its own legislative body based in Dublin, albeit under English rule. Although it became clear that the new English parliament elected in 1661 was in no mood to go along with the king's views on toleration, the Irish parliament was different. It was made up of Protestant peers and commons with Catholic links. This kind of relationship factored into the Act of Settlement for Ireland in 1662 in which provisions were made for 'innocent Catholics' in the recovery of lands lost under Cromwell. Indeed, the first viceroy under the new regime, James Butler, newly created duke of Ormond, had many familial links to Catholicism. He therefore epitomized the Stuarts' consensus attitude whereby he could accommodate other religious groups while maintaining the Protestant interest.[19] Although the Irish parliament was virtually devoid of Catholics, apart from one papist peer, there was an attempt to comprehend Catholics within the new government by means of a remonstrance which distinguished loyal papists from disloyal ones. Although the remonstrance was defeated, the reinstituting of a hierarchy within the Catholic Church in Ireland is indicative of increased toleration at that time. Dissenting sects were less appreciated, but on the whole tolerated. Their commercial contributions as merchants and traders were acknowledged as vital to Ireland's economy.

The Act of Settlement also affected soldiers and adventurers particularly. Prior to the restoration of Charles II, Admiral Penn acquired land in Ireland, partly through his wife and partly as a consequence of Cromwell's cleansing of the Catholic interest in Ireland. Unfortunately for the Admiral, the Restoration meant that there were priorities for the king over those of Sir William. As a result some of the lands he acquired during the Interregnum had to be given up.[20] Charles did not forget Penn's part in his restoration, however, and so he replaced the lost property with extensive estates in Shangarry, Kinsale, and Cork. Kinsale, fourteen miles from Cork, was a crucial seaport for the victualling of the Navy, as well as an entrepôt for trading beef and butter to the West Indies and tallow and hides to England.[21] In recognition of the growing importance of Kinsale, a new fort was being built. There was also a repayment for Sir William's loan of money to the king, in the granting of rent from Crown lands in Ireland to the amount of £1,356. 14s. 2d.[22]

The fact that Sir William was in charge of Kinsale was also indicative of his own importance in Irish affairs. Moreover his involvement meant liaising with other Irish magnates. James Butler, first duke of Ormond, was a staunch loyalist to the English Crown, to the point of going into exile with Charles II. He remained lord lieutenant of Ireland until 1669, and again from 1677 to 1685. Roger Boyle, first earl of Orrery, who was less constant during the 1640s, was nevertheless instrumental in the restoration of Charles II. The Boyle family was the pre-eminent family of Ireland. During the Cromwell years and the Restoration period, they were crucial figures in Ireland's politics. Perhaps the most eminent or at least most famous of that family was Robert, who was known for his scientific experiments. But, for the moment, Orrery was a leading figure in the Irish settlement and was therefore instrumental in sorting out the Penn estates. There is some allusion to a much deeper involvement between the Penns and Boyles that goes back to earlier days in Europe, when Orrery was a student under the tutelage of a Mr Markham. There is a suggestion that Markham was a relative of the Penns on the paternal side of the family.[23] Like Ormond, Orrery sided with Charles I, and he was active in the suppression of the Irish Catholic rebellions of 1642 and 1643. Later, he went over to Cromwell and it is probably at this time that he and the elder Penn crossed paths as soldiers of the Commonwealth.

One of the seven commissioners appointed to oversee the resettlement of Irish lands was John Churchill, and it was probably at this point that Sir William was introduced to him. Young William continued the association with Churchill's son, the future duke of Marlborough, who was to help him over the problems of Pennsylvania.

The Southwells were another major landowning family, especially around Munster. Their connection with the Penns stemmed back to the period under Cromwell. Robert Southwell was a leading figure at Kinsale, and his son, also named Robert, succeeded him as vice-admiral of Munster in 1677. Long before that, in 1664, he had been made clerk to the privy council for Irish affairs, a post he held until 1679. As clerk, Southwell was responsible for introducing into the government at Dublin the wishes of the privy council. Penn's letters to him in the middle of the 1670s denote a growing sense of knowing whom to approach in the corridors of power. A letter to Southwell in November 1676 hints at a favour which was being exchanged, and in a letter of June 1677 Penn's method is clear when he acknowledges that 'you great men can best prevail upon one another'.[24] Later, from 1690 to 1702, Southwell served as Irish secretary. Like Boyle, he became a member of the Royal Society.

Penn's relationship with these Irish magnates is crucial to understanding the foundations of his Irish experience, which influenced his plantation in Pennsylvania. His associates in Ireland would continue to be an invaluable part of his political and social life into the eighteenth century and his venture into North America.

At the age of 21 William Penn was sent to Ireland to settle the family claims. While he was there, two activities have attracted the attention of historians trying to unravel Penn's motives for converting to Quakerism: his military involvement; and his business activities. It is difficult to reconcile these with his involvement with the Quaker meeting at Cork where he was arrested, but if we look at his *modus operandi* as his father's deputy and the economic situation in the area, his conversion, while important, is nevertheless not the only factor relevant to a discussion of his coming of age.

In May 1666, while in northern Ireland, Penn became involved in suppressing a mutiny at Carrickfergus in County Antrim, another seaport with an English garrison. The place erupted when the men, who had been unpaid for nine months, took over the castle. Penn showed his skill in helping the earl of Arran and the duke of Ormond to put down the revolt. In gratitude Ormond wrote to Sir William, recommending that his son take command of the garrison at Kinsale. Penn's father refused, not because he thought that his son could not handle the responsibility: after all, William had seen action from the bow of a ship in the second Dutch War. It would be natural, therefore, for him to seek promotion in the military sphere. Quite simply, Sir William planned to retire to his Irish estates in the near future and live off the revenue from them, together with the income from his post as commander of the garrison at Kinsale. As for young William, he was given the role of victualler at Kinsale, a position in keeping with his business responsibilities there. In no way, therefore, did his father's refusal to allow him direct military participation represent a turning point in Penn's life. Military activity at this point in time did not mean a divergence from Quaker beliefs, since Penn was probably not a Quaker when the question arose.

His conversion to Quakerism, as we have seen, is generally accepted as having occurred in 1667 when he attended a meeting in Cork. Yet, if we look closely at his role in Ireland and his father's position at that time, perhaps his reasons for being at that meeting were more complex than any curiosity about some dissenting practice.

Trade in Ireland was expanding. Up to 1665, 74 per cent of Irish exports went to England, but by 1683 this had dropped to 30 per cent. The bulk of the Irish goods, such as beef, butter, lamb, fish, and horses, found new markets either on the Continent or in the colonial West Indies. Imports such as tobacco, woollen cloth, grocery, ironware, silks, linen, and hops indicated a growing economy. For this, the essentials were ports, and a peaceable society. Instrumental to this stability was the satisfaction of the merchants. In the case of Cork, the Quaker merchants were economically influential.[25] Acting as a deputy to his father, who was not only on the naval board but in charge of the ports of Cork and Kinsale, Penn had a duty to make sure there was no social unrest that would disrupt the citizens, and particularly the trade in that area. While Penn's attendance at the fateful meeting does not indicate his conversion, it was, however, consistent with his duties as well as his philosophical outlook. After all, he grew up within a family which was open to, and invited into their home, preachers of different persuasions. Thus, if indeed his old acquaintance, Thomas Loe, was speaking that day, Penn would understandably attend in remembrance of their meeting during his childhood. The motives behind his ejection of the disruptive soldier were therefore twofold. He was aware of the longstanding animosity of the mayor, Christopher Rye, towards dissenters, and quite possibly the soldier had been sent to create a disturbance as an excuse to rout the Quakers. Penn, witnessing what was afoot, decided to try to thwart the plan, thereby preventing an injustice and placating an economically vital section of the merchant community.

The incident also illustrates Penn's budding political astuteness. His correspondence with the Irish magnates such as Ormond, Orrery, and Southwell does not only reflect his own role in Irish affairs, the long association between their families, and a common desire for stability in Ireland: Penn skilfully used their positions in society to achieve his particular desires. The main protagonists during the period from 1660 to the end of the decade were the duke of Ormond, the earl of Orrery, and Robert Southwell. Like Penn, they had experienced other societies where tolerance of religious practices did not threaten those governments. Penn's letter to Orrery, at the time of his imprisonment at Cork, reveals the common bond between the likes of Orrery and Penn. Penn appealed to Orrery's intimate experience of other countries where diversity of faith and freedom of conscience were not conducive to the disruption of society. He reminded Orrery of the earl's own past solicitation for freedom of conscience.[26]

Although Penn rightfully challenged the mayor's basis for arresting the Quakers, nevertheless, the mayor referred to the Proclamation handed down by the privy council which prohibited seditious meetings. The Conventicle Acts of 1664 and, later, 1670 were not extended to Ireland. After the Restoration, Ireland had its own legislative identity, albeit under English rule so that the government in Dublin had the power to enact its own laws as long as they were compatible with those in England.

Penn's appeal to Lord Orrery rather than to the lord lieutenant Ormond reflects an awareness of where the power at court lay at any given moment. At the time of Penn's arrest, Ormond was viceroy, but was falling victim to factions at court over the Restoration settlement of

Ireland. By contrast, at least for the moment, Orrery was on the rise. As president of Munster, he was able to take initiatives in legal and administrative matters in the area in order to keep some degree of economic stability. His role as a lord justice for Ireland meant that Penn knew where to appeal for direct pressure to be put upon the local magistrate. Unfortunately for Penn, he got what amounted to a warning not to try to usurp the law of the land.[27]

The Irish years were a prelude and a training ground for William. His experiences there gave him the expertise for future business ventures and it was the political arena in which he honed his disputatiousness. His writings and the Penn–Meade trial during the decade of the 1670s show a zeal which was gradually maturing into a sophistication which indicates the astute politician he was to become. The Meade trial in 1670 and his third imprisonment in 1671 coincided with new legislation attacking dissenters. Penn now sought direct political action by petitioning parliament for relief for dissenters.

Penn was increasingly being seen as the spokesman for a growing economic section of society, in England as well as Ireland. By 1677, there were at least fourteen substantial Quaker merchants in London alone. These, together with Quaker merchants and tradesmen throughout England and Ireland, represented a sizeable contribution to the economic growth of the country.[28] As noted, Penn's commercial connections were not limited to Quakers. In fact, it was his broader dissenting relationships which increased his political attraction, so much so that Penn was the leading spokesman for toleration when he presented evidence to a committee of the House of Commons debating the use of recusancy laws against Quakers.[29]

Penn's marriages were also a testament not only to his religious philosophy but to his social position. His first marriage, to Gulielma Maria Springett, whom he courted for three years before they married in 1673, linked him with an influential London family. The stepdaughter of Isaac Penington, a notable London merchant, when she married William, she also held considerable lands in Kent and Sussex. The pair had known each other since the 1660s and it seems to have been a love match. One of the earliest known letters shows an affection which went beyond mere friendship.[30] At the same time their relationship was based upon common interests and background. Both came from families of good standing and both were Quakers. The marriage ended with Gulielma's death in 1694.

Penn's second marriage, only two years after the death of his first wife, was a love match as well as a dynastic arrangement. By the time Penn married Hannah Callowhill in 1696, he was approaching middle age while she was in her mid-twenties. The attraction of a young girl for an older man was not a mysterious event, then or now, but his affection for her found expression in the most romantic terms: 'My best love embraces thee, wch springs from that fountaine of love & life, wch time, distance nor disapointments can ever ware out.'[31] At the same time, another motive lay in their family background. The Callowhills were merchants in Bristol. Penn's marital connections with influential families were reinforced by his sister's marriage to Anthony Lowther, member of parliament for Appleby in 1679. Lowther came from a prominent London merchant family. By the time of Penn's death, he had become an inextricable part of the political life of England, networked to everyone who was anyone in politics and business. Even after his debilitating stroke in 1712, his influence was enough to fend off creditors and political enemies who were looking for the chance to seize his estates in England and America.

Penn's networking with prominent English politicians paid dividends when he obtained the grant of his colony in 1681. One of the most useful was Robert Spencer, second earl of Sunderland, whom he had met while they were students at Oxford in 1660. They both left the university under a cloud, but, more importantly, they shared similar viewpoints towards religious toleration. Now Sunderland was in a position of power, as privy councillor and secretary of state. Penn was to appeal to him for favours. Laurence Hyde, earl of Rochester, was another connection at court, perhaps even more useful to him than Sunderland. Rochester and his brother, Henry, second earl of Clarendon, accompanied Charles into exile with their father. Rochester spent time in Europe as envoy and by the end of the decade became first lord of the treasury and a privy councillor. A third prominent politician was Sidney Godolphin. His career was intricately involved with that of Rochester. Both were employed by Charles II as diplomats in the late 1670s. Godolphin purchased the post of master of the robes from Rochester and served under him as a commissioner of the treasury. In 1680 these three men, all known to Penn, formed a ministry satirically dubbed the 'Chits' on account of their youth and relative inexperience.

It was Penn's relationship with such men, who were able to influence policy and act as brokers between the court and parliament, that gave him access to power. If he wanted a favour, it was accomplished through the mediation of these managers. These court managers were men of broad experiences, too broad to be hog-tied to a narrow view of the Church. For this reason they were neither Whig nor Tory but Court politicians. They took their lead from the king, not from party leaders whether Whig or Tory.

Penn started his political career in 1679 aligned with opponents of the Crown such as the republican Algernon Sidney. He supported Sidney's attempts to enter parliament at Guildford in the first election held that year and at Amersham and Bramber at the second, and backed the son of a Cromwellian major-general at Bramber when Sidney withdrew.[32] Penn had sufficient influence in the county of Sussex to support Sir John Fagg, another Cromwellian officer, against the dominant interest of the Pelhams. Though Sir John Pelham topped the poll, his victory was commented on by his sister-in-law, the mother of the earl of Sunderland. The Dowager Countess of Sunderland's contemptuous remark that 'Penn did what he could to help Fagg and hinder my brother, Pelham, who had not one gentleman against him', is more than socially revealing.[33] That Penn was worthy of mention illustrates the extent of his interest in the county of Sussex. His electoral activities on behalf of candidates in the Exclusion Crisis display the natural interest of his gentry family more than the campaigning of a dissenting leader on behalf of the Whigs. Penn himself was never a Whig. The electoral tract he wrote at that juncture, *England's Great Interest*, did not support exclusion. Rather it advocated Country measures against the Court. His disaffection with courtiers such as the earl of Danby arose from his frustrated efforts to petition for a colonial charter in those years. Whereas throughout Danby's ministry he had been knocking on a closed door, after the earl's fall the 'Chits' opened it and beckoned him in. Penn's connections at court with managers like Sunderland and Rochester now began to pay off. He dropped his Country acquaintances and became a Court politician himself. He never looked back, always thereafter identifying his interests with those of the Crown's managers. The politicians with whom Penn associated himself would change over time. What they had in common was loyalty to the Court rather than to a party. In 1681 he finally obtained his long-sought charter for Pennsylvania, thanks to the help of the 'Chits'.

In 1685, during the reign of James II, Penn rose to the pinnacle of his career and he did so with little contradiction to his convictions. While he relented in his attack concerning toleration towards Catholics, he maintained his position as a monarchist. Towards the end of James's brief reign he was favoured as one of the king's closest advisers, intimately involved in the campaign to relax the penal laws against Catholics and dissenters. Although he was caught off balance in 1689 after James fled the country, Penn was able to adjust his political dress after realizing what he had to lose, at least his estates, at most his life, if he did not come to terms with the new regime. With the collapse of the monarchy in 1688, and the takeover by James's daughter and son-in-law, Mary and

William, Penn's powers evaporated, albeit temporarily. The problem over religious toleration remained unsolved. Although the Bill of Rights, passed at the outset of the new regime, set down a Protestant succession and guarded the Church against legal abuse by a monarch, and the Toleration Act of 1689 allowed for separate worship as long as belief in the Trinity was upheld, there was still a requirement to conform to the established Church in order to participate in politics. There were still limits to political participation for some dissenters, such as the Quakers, who could not abide the Test Act, which required the holders of public office to swear an oath. For Penn, this was doubly troubling because he was now viewed as a supporter of James and, as such, his liberty was threatened, rendering him politically ineffective for a time. He even lost his proprietorship of Pennsylvania temporarily. With the death of Mary in 1694 the proscription was relaxed, and he mended fences with William sufficiently to regain his colony.

From the mid 1690s to the death of Queen Anne, Penn was no longer *persona non grata* at court. Once again he was able to cultivate people like Sidney, now Lord Godolphin, John Churchill, earl and later duke of Marlborough, John, Lord Somers, and Robert Harley. These powerful connections enabled him to stave off a threat to his proprietorship of Pennsylvania mounted by the Board of Trade.

Penn's dealings with Court managers, from the Chits of 1680 to the 'triumvirate' of Marlborough, Godolphin, and Harley in Anne's reign, might suggest that the course he took throughout his political career was devious. In fact it was completely consistent. The Crown was the fountain of power. Its patronage could flow through different channels at different times. The fate of favourites was well known to be precarious, their tenure temporary. This could be due to the fickleness of monarchs or the changing situation in parliament. To retain the favour of the Crown, which Penn sought, and had to seek in order to retain his proprietorship of Pennsylvania, inevitably involved sensing the signs of changing fortunes of Courtiers. Penn was an extremely sensitive weather vane, picking up the slightest breeze of change at court. The ministers whom he first courted, and then discarded for another set of favourites, bore him no grudges. They were well aware that they were the mere conduits through which the Crown's patronage flowed. They could be employed one year, dismissed the next, and then employed again. When those who sought access to the monarch did so through them when they were in office, turned to others when they were out, and then returned to press their suits again when they were back in favour, this was a routine part of the political process. Hence Penn's ability to retain the good graces, and even the firm friendship, of an apparently bewildering variety of politicians of all political hues, from the Tory earl of Rochester to the Whig Junto. But those he felt most comfortable with were not party politicians but managers for the monarch, those who acted as brokers between the Crown and those who sought its favours. These were, principally, the second earl of Sunderland, Lord Godolphin, the duke of Marlborough, and, above all, the man he came closest to, Robert Harley, earl of Oxford.

· · ·

NOTES AND REFERENCES

1. Gilbert Burnet, *A History of His Own Time*, 6 vols (Oxford, 1833), IV, p. 140, Dartmouth's quote.
2. Catherine Owens Peare, *William Penn* (New York, 1957), pp. 14–15.
3. E.G.W. Bill, *Education at Christ Church, Oxford, 1660–1800* (Oxford, 1988) provides the best account of the college of Christ Church.
4. Hargreaves-Mawdsley W.N., *Oxford in the Age of John Locke* (University of Oklahoma, 1973), pp. 98–115.
5. Peter Laslett, 'John Locke, the Great Recoinage, and the Origins of the Board of Trade: 1697–1698', *WMQ*, 3rd ser., 14 (1957), pp. 370–402.
6. Harry Emerson Wildes, *William Penn* (London, 1974), pp. 27–8.
7. Anthony A. Wood, *Athenae Oxoniensis* (London, 1691), II, pp. 105–54.
8. Amyraut backed English Presbyterians in 1649 in condemning the execution of Charles I. The Westminster Assembly went along with Amyraut. Sir William Penn, a Presbyterian, would have sided with this line of thinking.
9. Burnet, *History*, IV, p. 140.
10. William Penn, *The Guide Mistaken and Temporizing Rebuked: A Brief Reply to Jonathan Clapham's Book, Intituled, A Guide to the True Religion* (London, 1668).
11. Clapham, who was an Independent turned Presbyterian, argued against separation of Church and State and eschewed arguments in favour of salvation for the likes of Penn.
12. *Truth Exalted* (1668).
13. For a convenient edition of his tracts see Hugh S. Barbour (ed.), *William Penn on Religion and Ethics: The Emergence of Liberal Quakerism*, 2 vols (Lampeter, 1991).
14. Huntington Library MS HE 40, Thomas Herbert's book on the Commissioners for Charitable Uses.
15. *The Compleat Justice* (London, 1633), p. 213, Bishop and his Chancellour and three Justices of Peace have power to examine how money for relief of the poor appointed by the statute is bestowed, and to call to account detainers thereof.

16. CO 5/1261, Proprietary colonies 1701–2, 8A, fo. 24, Penn to the Lords of Trade, 2 July 1701.
17. *PWP*, I, p. 51, Penn to Orrery, Nov. 1667.
18. Granville Penn, *Memorials of the Professional Life and Times of Sir William Penn*, 2 vols (London, 1833), II, p. 311; Granville Penn, *The Case of William Penn Esq. Executor of Sir William Penn 1712–13* I, p. 555.
19. J.G. Simms, 'The Restoration 1660–85', in T.W. Moody, F.X. Martin and F.J. Byrne (eds), *A New History of Ireland*, 3rd edn, 3 vols (Oxford, 1991), III, p. 421.
20. See ibid., p. 422 for a concise explanation of the reallocation of land during the 1660s.
21. *PWP*, I, p. 40, n. 3.
22. Bodleian Rawlinson MS c. 986, Margaret Penn's petition to the Crown, n.d.
23. *DNB, sub* Markham.
24. BL Add. MS 12098, fo. 14, Penn to Southwell, 1 Nov. 1676; *PWP* microfilm 2:444, Penn to Southwell, 14 June 1677.
25. R.F. Forster, *Modern Ireland 1600–1972* (Penguin, 1988), pp. 123–31, esp. p. 131: the Act for encouraging Protestant strangers into Ireland which resulted in the immigration of Huguenots and Quakers into Cork; Simms, 'The Restoration'; Moody *et al.* (eds), *A New History of Ireland*, III, pp. 441–3.
26. *PWP*, I, p. 51.
27. *PWP*, I, p. 53. Orrery was removed from power in 1671–72 after a dispute with Ormonde. His removal was also due to his less than sympathetic attitude towards the Catholics, at a time when Charles II was embarking upon a new Catholic policy with the treaty of Dover in 1670.
28. See Mary K. Geiter, 'Affirmation, Assassination, and Association: The Quakers, Parliament and the Court in 1696', *Parliamentary History*, 16 (1997), p. 280; *The Little London Directory of 1677: The Oldest Printed List of the Merchants and Bankers of London* (London, 1863); *HMC Ormonde*, VII, p. 121, 30 Aug. 1683.
29. Mark Goldie, 'James II and the Dissenters' Revenge: The Commission of Enquiry of 1688', *Historical Research*, 66 (1993), p. 69; Whiting, p. 175; A. Grey (ed.), *Debates of the House of Commons*, 10 vols (1769), V, pp. 250–5; Gough, II, pp. 433–5.
30. *PWP*, I, p. 85.
31. *PWP*, III, p. 413, Penn to Hannah Callowhill, 10 Sept. 1695.
32. R.W. Blencoe (ed.), *Diary of the Times of Charles II by the Honourable Henry Sidney*, 2 vols (1843), pp. 114–17.
33. Ibid., p. 123.

Chapter 3

FOUNDING FATHER

In 1701 William Penn informed the earl of Dorset why he had taken the trouble to launch the colony of Pennsylvania. 'I took it for a great debt & meritorious, which cost me almost to solicit it, the whole ministry of the duke of Leeds. I could have bought it for 1200lbs. I took it in lieu of all further hopes of 20,000lbs which my demands came to or very near in [16]81.'[1] The reference to the ministry of the duke of Leeds is to the years 1674 to 1679 when Thomas Osborne, who was elevated to the dukedom in 1694, was earl of Danby and lord treasurer. Thus Penn had started to solicit for the grant seven years before it was conceded. The bulk of the debt, some £16,000, was owing to his father, Sir William Penn, who died in 1670. Penn was to repeat this claim many times in subsequent years. Certainly the Crown's relationship with Admiral Penn played a part in the launching of the colony. The charter itself speaks of the king's having a regard for his memory and merits.[2] And Penn informed a friend that Charles II himself had named the colony Pennsylvania 'in honour to my Father'.[3]

Yet the notion that Pennsylvania arose out of the Crown's indebtedness to Penn's father is generally dismissed as a mere pretext. Instead the launching of the colony tends to be given a religious explanation. It is usually assumed that the Quaker leader sought a religious refuge for fellow Friends who were being persecuted under Charles II – that he embarked on a 'holy experiment' – and this notion concerning the foundation and first decades of Pennsylvania remains the conventional wisdom on the colony's origins. In this view the establishment of the colony was the work of a single individual with a religious purpose, and the grant of a charter was a solution to certain of the king's religious and financial problems. Charles II gave William Penn land in America partly to get rid of troublesome dissenters and partly in payment of a debt owed to the Quaker's father; while Penn's main motive was to 'secure a refuge for his co-religionists'.[4]

But in fact the Quakers were not being persecuted in England at the time. On the contrary, when Penn petitioned for the charter in 1680 they, along with other dissenters, were enjoying a respite from persecution. In November 1680 a toleration bill was introduced into the House of Commons which, had it passed, would even have allowed Quakers to affirm instead of taking an oath, the result of which would have been direct political participation. The bill only fell when the king prorogued parliament.[5] The explanation for the granting of the charter lies therefore not in the legal status of the Quakers, but in the complex relationship between dissent in general and Penn's role in the politics of the period in particular. The fact that Penn had been obliged to wait seven years for it suggests that Danby, who had no time either for dissenters or for proprietary colonies, had not responded sympathetically to his solicitation. The crisis that brought about Danby's fall in 1679, however, also produced an opportunity for Penn to press his case. In it he emerged as a spokesman not just for his fellow Quakers but for all Protestant dissenters whose cause was taken up by the Crown's opponents in the Exclusion Crisis.

The crisis arose from the reaction to the Popish Plot of 1678, when Catholics were alleged to be implicated in a conspiracy to assassinate the king so that his Roman Catholic brother James could succeed him. The succession of a papist to the throne filled Protestant Englishmen with alarm, as they felt that a Catholic king would act arbitrarily to undermine their liberties. Some were prepared to avert that fate by sponsoring bills in parliament to exclude James from the succession. Their opportunity came in 1679 when Charles II at last dissolved the Cavalier Parliament and called a general election for the first time since 1661.

The second tactic the king employed was the reorganization of the privy council. The new council was divided into three main sections, dealing respectively with Ireland, Tangiers, and trade and plantations. The division of the council reflects the importance of the three areas in England's quest for empire. The creation of the committee for trade and plantations is indicative of the growing importance of colonies to the Crown. The king's choice of appointments to it was motivated by his desire to neutralize the opposition and to gather around him men whose primary goal was to extend England's power. Importantly, for Penn, the members of the committee, many of whom he personally knew, were power brokers whose role would be crucial in the obtaining of a charter for his colony.

As president of the privy council, Charles appointed his chief opponent, the earl of Shaftesbury, hoping to neutralize his influence. Shaftesbury was a virulent opponent of popery and the ringleader in the investigation into the Popish Plot, but he was also one of the proprietors of the colony of Carolina. Being on the council meant influence in decisions taken in England's growing empire. He was also one of twenty privy councillors who had mercantile interests, and whom Penn would use in his efforts to promote the cause of toleration and the acquisition of a new colony. Shaftesbury proved, however, to be a liability to the king and was dismissed six months later in October. He was replaced by John Robartes, earl of Radnor, who favoured toleration for dissenters. Radnor was also a personal friend of Penn, and later was helpful in limiting the bishop of London's influence in the drawing up of the charter.

Twenty councillors served on the privy council's committee of trade and plantations in the months between 14 June 1680 and 24 February 1681, during which the petition for the Pennsylvania charter was introduced and its final draft read. Christopher Monck, second duke of Albemarle, was a Carolina proprietor and later became governor of Jamaica. Henry Compton, bishop of London, by his very office was concerned with securing and developing Anglicanism in the colonies. Thomas Chicheley was MP for Cambridge during the Exclusion Parliaments and was master of the Grocer's Company in London.[6] Some of the committee's members at this crucial juncture played a more active part than others in procuring Penn's charter. Lord Conway, one of the secretaries of state, is usually seen as being of vital importance because his wife was allegedly a Quaker and in touch with Penn, and was related to the Finch family, who had links with commerce.[7] Lord North, whose family was heavily involved in the City and the Levant Company, played a significant role in the shaping of the Pennsylvania charter.

Other members of the committee for trade and plantations were also influential. Penn's friend from his youth, Robert Spencer, earl of Sunderland, is sometimes seen as the most involved in the processing of the charter since he introduced the petition on behalf of Penn on 1 June 1680. He was also principal secretary of state. Nonetheless, he came out in favour of the Exclusion bill in the second parliament, and was dismissed shortly after its dissolution in January 1681, before the charter was finally issued.[8] It appears that, in the later stages of the process, Penn was also assisted by two constant attenders of the committee: Leoline Jenkins and Henry Hyde, earl of Clarendon. Jenkins, secretary of state, was devoted to furthering the Crown's interests in the colonies. He was MP for Oxford University in the last two Exclusion Parliaments, and was a strong adherent of the Crown against the Exclusion bills. Clarendon's role was perhaps even more crucial, as he was in close touch with his brother Laurence Hyde, whose influence in the government was at its height when the colonial charter was issued. Laurence and Henry, brothers-in-law to the duke of York, were staunch royalists and strong Anglicans. Henry was a commissioner for trade and searcher of customs. Laurence, who followed Thomas Osborne, earl of Danby, as first lord of the treasury, became involved in trade as governor of the Merchant Adventurers Company after 1684.[9] His post on the treasury commission is a crucial consideration when assessing the king's motives and actions during the period.[10] Thus Hyde's awareness of the financial potential of the American colonies, combined with the opportunity to strategically seal the seaboard plantations against foreign encroachment, helps in an understanding of the establishment of Pennsylvania. He was aware that Penn had been angling for a colonial grant during the Danby ministry, but had so far failed to acquire one. At that time, the Crown was embroiled in the Anglo-Dutch wars which resulted in the acquiring of New York in 1674. The temper of the parliament was not then conducive to granting tracts of land for private ownership, much less to a dissenter. The grant of New York to the duke of York was not the same case because, as he was the heir to the throne, it was considered a potential Crown colony. The eventual granting of a charter for Pennsylvania can only be explained by the changing political situation. The onset of the crisis to the monarchy and the dissolution of the Cavalier Parliament allowed Penn an opportunity to use his political muscle to further his desires for toleration and his economic interests.

The first election in eighteen years brought Penn into the parliamentary arena. As a Quaker he could not stand for parliament himself, since he could not swear the required oath of allegiance and supremacy. But he could back someone who was as dedicated to bringing toleration to fruition. His choice of Algernon Sidney was based upon friendship and a common political viewpoint. Penn had known Sidney for some years and saw him as a politician who could be an asset to the Friends. It was Sidney's religious toleration rather than his radical republicanism which drew Penn to support his candidature at Guildford. Sidney, a contemporary of Penn's father, had backed the Parliamentary side in the civil wars, fighting at Marston Moor. He was never wholly reconciled with the Restoration government. His attempts to get into parliament were the result of the political crisis and not a long-term career plan. His temperament was volatile, and his radical ideology was out of step with the Crown. Indeed, until this moment he did not see his stay in England as being permanent.

At the polls Sidney was unsuccessful, but with Penn's help he petitioned against the member, Thomas Dalmahoy. Parliament, however, was prorogued before the petition could be reported in committee, and then dissolved to make way for another election. Once again Sidney decided to stand, this time in either Amersham or Bramber. This was a calculated move on the part of Penn and Sidney. The latter's familial connection with the Pelhams of Bramber would guarantee votes for him, but Amersham was his primary choice. At Amersham, Penn could use his family influence to secure the return of his candidate. Indeed, it was, as Jonathan Scott has put it, 'the nearest thing in England to a Quaker borough, its Quaker interest shared between two powerful local families closely connected to Penn: the Peningtons and the Childs'.[11] The result was a double return of Sir William Drake and Sidney. A series of prorogations followed these elections to the second Exclusion Parliament, starting in October 1679 and ending with the Houses finally meeting in October the following year. Until then, the double return could not be resolved. During this time there were moves by the king and his councillors to swing support in their favour or, failing that, to neutralize the opposition. It was also during this period, between October of 1679 and some time in the new year, that Penn was either approached with, or thought of, the idea of governing the land west of New Jersey and across the Delaware River. Meanwhile, the king noted Sidney's return, saying cynically that he would prove an honest man. This indicated that Charles was closely scrutinizing the returns. When parliament did meet, Sidney's petition was heard, with the result that the election was voided. At the ensuing by-election Sidney stood again, but this time without success. It was also without Penn's support. Parliament was prorogued in January 1680 and in June the king gave the go-ahead for processing a grant to Penn for the largest tract of land on the eastern seaboard of North America. Penn, no doubt, had integrity. The king also knew he had a price.

By abandoning Sidney, Penn did not necessarily abandon his principles. Nor did he back away from politics. It is true that he made mention to Sunderland that he felt things were getting violent but this was probably because of his experience at one of the polls where he was rudely turned away. Penn, in fact, did not withdraw from politics. The elections were over for the moment, and therefore he could not remain active in that sphere. However, he continued to write political tracts advocating liberty of conscience, although these were somewhat more tempered than previous tracts. In a petition to parliament, Penn concentrated on the economic deprivation of the Society of Friends because of their faith. He argued, on behalf of the Quakers, that because they were being treated under the law the same as Catholics, the subsequent fines and distraints were hurting their trades.[12] This was followed by a proposal to remedy the problem. Although the month is not certain, the *Declaration or Test* by Penn almost certainly followed the petition.[13] The result was that a bill was drafted to distinguish between Protestant dissenters and Catholic recusants. The Commons passed a resolution to give some relief to Protestant dissenters from the penal laws.[14]

Meanwhile, a new political group was gaining influence. During the period between November 1679 and June 1680, Sunderland, Sidney Godolphin, and Laurence Hyde formed the nucleus of policy making. 'The Chits', as they were known, formed the new inner circle of the king's cabinet.[15] Between the three, Penn's support was assured. Certainly Sunderland was the one who introduced Penn's petition for a plantation in the New World. Godolphin, at this point, was on the coat-tails of Sunderland and therefore would have a similar political outlook. His abilities in finance were appreciated particularly at a time when the king was experiencing money difficulties.[16] His relationship with Penn would develop over the years as he rose in his career. However, Hyde, as head of the treasury commission, was more intricately involved in the royal finances. The financial question lay at the heart of deciding whether or not to call parliament.[17] Hyde's advice had more impact on the king than either Sunderland's or Godolphin's.[18] He would be well aware of the importance of revenue from the colonies.[19] He would also appreciate the significance of those merchants in the City who wanted more freedom in trading, and who were linked to the opposition. Hyde was also a friend of Penn and was in as strong a position as Sunderland, if not a stronger one, to support his cause at court.

The granting of Penn's charter became part of a larger plan on the part of the 'Chits' to counter the threat to the monarchy by appeasing those elements in the City which were sympathetic to the Crown's opponents. Between the prorogation of the second parliament and its reconvening in the autumn of 1680, petitions flowed in demanding that it meet. None concerned the king more than the London petition, which included approximately 16,000 signatures. Among those signatures were the members of the various companies in the City, including Levant Company members who became investors in the Pennsylvania venture.[20]

The merchants, both the supporters and the opponents of the Court, shared a common fear of French competition. This fear lay behind their concerns about the effect which foreign policy decisions had on English commerce. One of the ways in which the king mollified part of the opposition in 1680 was to enforce by proclamation the statutory embargo on French trade. Another was to take the opportunity to negotiate for them, through Hyde, a new avenue of trade by granting a new colony in North America. The decision to grant it to Penn as a proprietor stemmed from the political situation. The alternatives, to create a Crown colony or to grant one to a trading company like the Virginia or Massachusetts

Bay companies, were apparently never seriously considered. The creation of a Crown colony would have been a highly sensitive hostage to fortune since it would pass to the king's brother James should he succeed, an eventuality which lay at the very heart of the Exclusion Crisis. To hand over the control of the new colony to merchants who, in the political climate then prevailing, could not be trusted was out of the question also. The other means by which a colony had traditionally been settled was through a proprietorship. Yet Charles required a proprietor who had experience as well as integrity, but who was not fully aligned with the City Whigs. Penn was an ideal choice for the king. He was connected with the City merchants, and yet his own religious philosophy appeared to be more tolerant than some of the more radical sects in the country. However, a proprietorship, to make economic sense, had to be kept under control.[21]

Also, Penn needed the duke's permission to annex the Delaware territory, which became known as the three lower counties, to Pennsylvania. Without these endorsements, the charter could not go forward.

Penn was anxious to have as much control as possible over his colony and the privy council was just as anxious to safeguard the Crown's rights. There was a third element, the rights of the neighbouring proprietors. The duke of York, proprietor of New York, was anxious to keep control of the fur trade route up the Delaware River into New York. This meant ensuring the boundaries around Pennsylvania were made explicit. At the southern end of the new colony, Lord Baltimore, proprietor of Maryland, was equally concerned that his borders were not encroached upon. Penn knew he had to have an outlet to the Atlantic, otherwise his trade would be stymied by duties imposed by whoever had control of the waterways. Thus, he needed the Delaware passage for his goods shipped from Philadelphia and he needed a secondary outlet from the interior. This meant that Penn needed to secure from the duke of York the rights to the Delaware River, particularly the western bank where the water was deepest, enabling heavy boats to navigate safely. At this point, Penn did not have the Delaware counties. He also needed access from the Susquehanna River into Chesapeake Bay. The lower reaches of the river were within the territory granted to Lord Baltimore. There were additional reasons for having an alternative passage. Penn knew that while the initial trade would flourish along the eastern part of the colony, expansion of trade would move westward. The main water route would be down the Susquehanna and out through the Chesapeake. He also knew that the Delaware River froze in the winter, which resulted in the slowing down of trade. The Chesapeake, on the other hand, was salty and did not freeze, providing clear access for shipping.

Therefore, granting of proprietorial rights in Pennsylvania involved not only the Crown but also the king's brother, James, duke of York. Penn used the opportunity offered by the negotiations over his charter to settle issues in the adjacent territories of West New Jersey and Delaware, both of which were included in the jurisdiction of the duke as proprietor of New York. The negotiations over Pennsylvania were closely involved with the resolution of these other issues since both took place during the months between the summer of 1680 and the spring of 1681, when the charter was granted.[22] The correspondence between the duke of York, his secretary John Werden, William Blathwayt, and Penn also indicates that it was pressure from the king which eventually led to their resolution in Penn's favour and to the duke's detriment.

James had alienated the proprietorship of the territory of New Jersey to two others: George Carteret was given East New Jersey and John Berkeley West New Jersey, though Berkeley subsequently alienated his proprietorship to Quakers.[23] But the governor of New York, Sir Edmund Andros, insisted that both territories were still subject to him for purposes of government such as taxation. The inhabitants of West New Jersey objected to the imposition of taxes. Penn, on behalf of the inhabitants, petitioned the king to relieve them from duties imposed by New York. The spectre of a Catholic heir to the throne raised concern over the future of the middle colonies. New York and Maryland were governed by two Catholic proprietors; the former by James himself. This increased fears which were highlighted in Penn's petition, in which he warned that 'all men take the just moddell of goverm[en]t in New York to be the schem & draught in litle of his admin[istrati]on of old England at large if the Crown should ever divolve upon his head'.[24] The right of government to West New Jersey, making it independent of New York, was granted to the proprietors in August 1680, following the attorney-general Sir William Jones's opinion that the duke of York had given up his rights as proprietor several years earlier.[25] James at that time was *persona non grata* at court on account of the Exclusion controversy, and had been exiled first to Brussels and then to Scotland.

The duke's concession of West New Jersey's independence from New York, and with it the right of taxation, was not due simply to James's acceptance of the legal position. It was also brought about by the political circumstances of the time. These concessions to the West New Jersey proprietors gave the king an opportunity to conciliate some of his opponents. This was made clear by the duke's secretary, Sir John Werden, who thought that the concession could be ascribed only to royal pressure: he and others reckoned that the duke was 'trepaned' into releasing the government of West New Jersey.[26]

When the charter for Pennsylvania was being sought, Penn was also seeking to acquire the three counties on the west bank of the Delaware River south of the new colony which belonged to the duke. The granting of the three lower counties by the duke to Penn in 1681 was again due to pressure from the Crown and not, as is usually argued, an act of generosity on the part of James. Indeed, Werden advised against the grant of the three counties, predicting that it would be detrimental to New York's trade. Yet the privy council recommended that Penn should apply to the duke of York for the Delaware territory.[27] Obtaining the western bank of the Delaware River was essential to the economic viability of Pennsylvania. The influence of Penn's London backers was most evident in securing the settlements along the Delaware Bay and River. Penn and his financiers realized that without that strip of territory the colony would not be economically viable. Two decades later, this sentiment was made clear in a petition by the Philadelphia merchants in which they noted that Pennsylvania was not readily accessible by water and only the acquisition of the Delaware made possible Philadelphia's success as a trading centre.[28] As a contemporary explained, although the New Jersey side of the Delaware was navigable, while it 'is also safe to navigate the river with large vessels, the deepest water is however on the west side'.[29] The acquisition of the western bank would enable access to and from Philadelphia, which would be about one hundred miles inland. It must also be free from duties, which at the moment New York could claim.

One way in which Penn could resolve the difficulty over getting the land along the western bank of the Delaware would be to approach the duke directly. James was in exile in Scotland, but he was not inaccessible. Penn used his connection with his friend, the Scottish magnate and fellow Quaker Robert Barclay, to persuade him to speak on his behalf to James.

Initially, Penn requested the rights to the lower counties. But James made it clear from the beginning that it was not in his power to allocate rights to government. Although he governed the lower counties *de facto*, James had no official authorization to that effect: its granting lay in the power of the king alone.[30] The duke knew full well that granting the region in question would cut severely into the revenue of New York. Already the relinquishing of New York's rights over West New Jersey had caused financial hardship, and to concede any more territory would be financial suicide for the duke. Sir John Werden approached the proposal for the Delaware counties cautiously, recommending against their grant to Penn.[31] He asked, 'If this be what Mr Pen would Have? I presume the R[igh]t Hon[oura]ble the Lords of the Committee for Trade

& Plantations, will not encourage His pretentions to it, because of what is above mentioned; which shewes plainly the Duke's Right Preferable to all others, (under His Maj[es]tys Good likeing) though it should not prove to be strictly with the limitts of the Duke's Pattent.'[32] With this advice in mind the duke ordered his agent in his colonies, John Lewin, to find out exactly what 'estate rents and revenues profitts and perquisites which of any sort of wright belong and apertaine to me', and also to 'find out whether the free trade of any of the inhabitants of those places or any merchants tradeing thither now is or hath been lately obstructed or hindered and by what means'.[33]

The length of time taken to procure the charter can fully be explained only in the immediate political context. That approximately five months elapsed from petitioning for it in June 1680, to a review of its first draft in November, invites speculation. The preoccupation of the privy council with other matters has been the usual explanation.[34] At odds with this, however, is the fact that the patent was scrutinized carefully by Lord North, Creswell Levinz, attorney-general, and Henry Compton, bishop of London; thus it was given serious attention. However, this scrutiny happened after the first draft was made. Colonial petitions sometimes took from two months to two years to be considered, but this does not necessarily indicate that normal procedures were followed. The time involved can be explained in other terms if we look outside the privy council records to correspondence between people in the colonies and in England concerning the other colonies, such as East and West New Jersey, and their problems over customs duty obligations to New York. The resolution of the dispute was inextricably linked to the success of the new settlement across the Delaware. Problems over boundaries and the question of the duties were not settled until the autumn of 1680. Only then could attention be given to the terms of the charter itself.[35]

Events in parliament from October 1680 until January 1681 were also closely linked up with the activity in the committee for foreign plantations and trade, and especially with the processing of the charter. High among the committee's interests at this time was the state of the colonies.[36] Orders were given on 3 November 1680 that no governors were to return from their commands in the plantations without leave in Council because 'his Ma[jes]ty was pleased to take notice of the great p[re]judice that may arise to his service and the securitys of his colonyes by ye absence of the respective governors'.[37]

On 18 January the parliament was dissolved and writs for another election went out.[38] The dissolution and announcement that a new parliament would meet in Oxford in March 1681 was designed to wrongfoot the Whigs. Both sides knew that the parliament would not last long. Charles had even less interest in continuing the negotiations and Shaftesbury claimed the meeting would not last over three weeks. The reason for meeting in Oxford was, according to Luttrell, to 'prevent the petitioning of the City of London and the caballing of them and the Citty together'.[39] A declaration went out warning against the carrying of arms to Oxford and the route was lined with the royal guards. This was meant not only to intimidate the radical elements of the opposition against violence in Oxford, but also to serve as a warning against any thoughts about returning to London to continue the meeting of parliament if it was ended in Oxford. It was also to protect the moderates, particularly in the City of London, against any upheaval. And when news of the dissolution reached London by the following day, there were no demonstrations or rioting. The reason may have been that nobody really thought it was the final parliament. Charles had no need to call another one for some time, because he had a French subsidy, and the treaty with the Moors put off the immediate demand for financial outlay. These considerations featured in the calculation that the Oxford Parliament would not last anyway. But there is one more crucial factor and that is the other deal which was accomplished with the merchants of London. It was in their interest to avoid any disturbances. To ensure this frame of mind, between the end of the second and the third and last Exclusion Parliament, the final touches were being put to the charter for Pennsylvania. The charter was formally granted just three weeks before parliament met in March. With that, the merchants and business community could look forward to expanded and unrestricted trade. This deal could partly explain the City's relatively quiet acceptance of the dissolution.

On the surface, it appears that parliament was unmoved in the matter of exclusion and that none of the Court tactics had worked. Nevertheless, if the king failed to change men's minds over the threat of Catholic absolutism, he had succeeded in reducing the threat of civil war by compromising with the crucial elements of the City over free trade. The Order in Council to remove some restrictive customs levies on 16 February 1681 was one compromise.[40] The 'Order in Council to Encourage the Plantation Trade' is indicative of Charles's concern with the plantations and his initiation of steps to placate aggrieved traders.

The final draft of the Pennsylvania charter was agreed in February and given to Penn on 4 March 1681.[41] Its granting, along with other inducements, such as the encouraging of trade by Order in Council, ensured the demise of any threat of violence. When the new parliament assembled at Oxford on 21 March, the king hoped to pursue the question of supply, but it was clear there would be another attempt to pass a bill for exclusion. However, certain that moderate MPs would no longer be intimidated by the radical elements of the City and that prudent merchants accepted the deal over Pennsylvania, Charles dissolved parliament six days after it met and went home.

Charles had accomplished only part of his objective at the end of the Oxford Parliament, but if the crisis over exclusion was not resolved, the crisis over the Crown's prerogative was. The opposition had depended on his need for money forcing him to terms concerning the succession, but Charles outmanoeuvred them by successfully concluding a series of deals which swung support in his favour and, importantly, got rid of the threat of another civil war. Among these deals was the granting of the charter for Pennsylvania. Added to the grant was the duke of York's former province of Delaware. The Order in Council to encourage trade was an additional sop to colonial merchants.

Pennsylvania, therefore, did not owe its origins to the desire for a religious utopia. Nor was it just another colonial venture. Its genesis derived from the crisis in England which threatened the powers of the Crown. Charles saw in the rise of the opposition not only a challenge to the hereditary succession but also a potential revolutionary movement. He sought to avert the possibility of civil war by dividing his opponents, appealing to moderate elements among them to back off from the danger. Among the many methods he employed to divide their ranks was the granting of a charter for a new colony. The launching of Pennsylvania conformed with the opposition ideology that religious toleration and limited monarchy were more conducive to commercial expansion than 'popery and arbitrary power'.

The granting of the Pennsylvania charter provided the opportunity for Penn to extend his commercial interests. It also allowed him to combine his business practice with his religious belief. Thus, he opened the possibility of investment to interested parties regardless of their religious proclivities. Above all, no oaths were necessary to belong to companies involved in the adventure. Previously, taking an oath had been a requirement of becoming a member of a trading company. Over the next twenty years, the companies which emerged were founded on a more secular basis, one which, given Penn's recent admission to the Royal Society, suited his philosophy of experimentation. The first of these Pennsylvania companies, the Free Society of Traders, reflected, more than later companies, religious pluriformity and tied the Atlantic world to the Mediterranean compass. Although this company eventually failed, it paved the way for other companies to invest in Pennsylvania. The New Mediterranean Sea Company, the Susquehanna Company, and the New Pennsylvania Company, formed sometimes out of political necessity, and always with a commercial option, nevertheless maintained the spirit of toleration. They were a chance for Penn and his brethren to do what they were prohibited from doing in the English arena where company membership was limited and monopolies flourished.[42] By the end of the seventeenth century, and certainly by his death, Penn was trying to divest himself of the Pennsylvania property while holding onto the three lower counties of Delaware. The reason was that Delaware was considered the more valuable of the regions, primarily due to its water boundary, but also because its tobacco crop was a main export item.[43] That the Quakers were in the minority there explains where Penn's priority lay.

. . .

NOTES AND REFERENCES

1. *PWP*, microfilm 9:488, Penn to the earl of Dorset, 27 Aug. 1701.
2. Merrill Jensen (ed.), *English Historical Documents: American Colonial Documents to 1776*, 2nd edn (1969), IX, p. 93. The only merit specified, however, is his 'conduct courage and discretion' at the battle of Lowestoft in 1666.
3. *PWP*, II, p. 83, WP to Robert Turner, 3 Mar. 1681. Penn wanted it to be called New Wales, because he claimed his family origins were in Wales. When this was rejected, he proposed Sylvania. He even tried to bribe a secretary to change it when the king refused to drop the prefix Penn, fearing that it would be taken to apply to himself and be regarded as vanity in him!
4. Edwin Bronner, *William Penn's Holy Experiment* (New York, 1962); Richard Middleton, *Colonial America: A History, 1607–1760* 2nd edn (Oxford, 1996), pp. 161–2; cf. Alan Tully, *Forming American Politics: Ideals, Interests, and Institutions in Colonial New York and Pennsylvania* (Baltimore, 1994), pp. 27–8.
5. H. Horwitz, 'Protestant Reconciliation in the Exclusion Crisis', *Journal of Ecclesiastical History*, XV (1964), pp. 201–17.
6. B.D. Henning, *The History of Parliament: The Commons 1660–1689*, Vol. II (London, 1983), pp. 54–6. Chicheley was MP for Cambridgeshire in 1640, 1642, and 1661. He was then chosen MP for Cambridge in March and October 1679, then again in 1681, 1685, and finally in 1689. The Chicheley family was involved in Virginia, where Sir Henry was a member of the council.
7. PRO, PC, 2/68, 6: List of privy councillors for 22 April 1679; BL Add. MSS 23213–23214. Conway was not that influenced by his wife's adherence to the Quaker religion. In January 1679 he wrote to his wife that he had been given two speeches by Penn to a committee in

parliament the previous March stressing the commonality of religious principles between them. Conway did not think so, because he told his wife, 'If I should agree that theirs is better than ours, I think I should loose the use of my reason.' Conway is listed in attendance on the committee for trade and plantations on 24 February 1680/81 when the draft of the charter was discussed. However, throughout the weeks that the charter was under consideration, he appeared only once during discussions of Penn's petition.

8. John Miller, *Charles II* (London, 1991), pp. 307, 311–17. Miller describes Sunderland, along with the duchess of Portsmouth, as being moderate in nature. During this time Sunderland was one of the royal favourites and used his influence to head off what he saw as a revolt. However, by August, Sunderland was writing to Henry Sidney at The Hague, telling him that 'I take ye Duke to be undone.' BL Add. MS 32681, fo. 44, 24 Aug. 1680.

9. *DNB*, *sub* Hyde, Child. In 1676 Hyde went to Poland as ambassador extraordinary. His involvement in bringing about a compromise between the Turks and Poles was crucial. This activity, combined with his representation to the king on behalf of the Protestants, was aimed at the improvement of trade in the area; ibid., pp. 244–5. Josiah Child wrote several discourses concerning trade and during this period emphasized his view against monopolies and promoted the idea of freer trade.

10. *PWP*, IV, p. 327, [*c.* 1683], William Penn to 'My Noble Friend', most likely to the earl of Rochester, probably in the autumn of 1682. In the letter, Penn acknowledges Rochester as one of the noble persons that backed his venture, 'among whom thou wert not the least'.

11. Jonathan Scott, *Algernon Sidney* (Cambridge, 1981), p. 156.

12. *PWP*, II, pp. 50–6, 'To the King Lords and Commons in Parliament Assembled' [Oct.–Nov.] 1680; Penn presented a petition to the House of Lords on 26 November 1680, as footnoted in *PWP*; however, it was most likely that the petition was first given to parliament; *HMC Eleventh Report, Appendix, Part II, The Manuscripts of the House of Lords: 1678–1688*, pp. 201–2. Three more tracts were published which concentrated on getting relief for the Quakers from parliament: *A Particular Account of Sufferings*, [15 Nov. 1680]; *Brief Account of Sufferings*, 20 Dec. 1680; *Reasons Why the Oaths Should not be made part of the Tests*, [1680].

13. *Declaration or Test*, [1680], Wing P1272.

14. Parliament was prorogued before an Act could be passed.

15. After the prorogation of the second Exclusion Parliament in October 1680, Halifax and Sir William Temple retired from the council in disgust.

16. Roy A. Sundstrom, *Sidney Godolphin: Servant of the State* (Associated University Presses, North Carolina, 1992), pp. 29–31.

17. PRO, Baschet transcripts, Barillon correspondence, 33/3/144, 8 Jan. 1680. Hyde, in one of his rare meetings with the French ambassador,

told Barillon that he felt confident that the king could be sustained without the help of parliament.

18. BL Add. MS 17017, fos 127–36, shows that Sunderland clearly thought Hyde to be the most influential person with the king during this period.

19. Henry Roseveare, *The Treasury: The Evolution of a British Institution* (London, 1969), pp. 78–82; Roseveare, *The Treasury: 1660–1870* (London, 1973), pp. 42–4.

20. Mark Knights, 'London's "Monster" Petition of 1680', *Historical Journal*, XXXVI (1993), pp. 39–67; *London Gazette*, 13 Jan. 1680; Richard Ashcraft, *Revolutionary Politics and Locke's Two Treatises on Government* (New Jersey, 1986), pp. 174–5. Ashcraft points out the degree of radical involvement during this period by showing the extent to which non-voters became involved in politics. This does not necessarily mean, as Ashcraft suggests, that the Whigs were a highly organized group responsible for uniting people across class lines. This attempt was only partly successful.

21. Comparison of the Pennsylvania charter with that for Maryland shows that the clause in the latter giving the proprietors palatinate jurisdiction in the colony was deliberately omitted from the Pennsylvania charter.

22. *PWP*, II, pp. 103–4, Sir John Werden to William Penn, 16 July 1681; *CSP Colonial 1677–80*, no. 1565, Blathwayt to Committee, Oct.(?) 1680; ibid., no. 1544, Werden to Blathwayt, 16 Oct. 1680; *CSP Colonial 1681–85*, no. 179, Werden to Penn, 16 July 1681; *CSP Colonial 1677–80*, no. 1603, Werden to Blathwayt, 23 Nov. 1680.

23. The history of colonial New Jersey and its division into East and West before it became a Crown colony in 1702 is very complex. The best guide to these complexities is John E. Pomfret, *The Province of West New Jersey, 1609–1702: A History of the Origins of an American Colony* (Princeton, 1956).

24. William Penn, *The Case of New Jersey Stated* (London, *c.* 1680), p. 10. This case was probably published some time between September 1679, when the inhabitants first asked to be exempt from taxes by New York (*CSP Colonial 1677–80*, no. 1123, 19 Sept. 1679), and August 1680, when the duke of York accepted the opinion of Sir William Jones that New Jersey was exempt.

25. *CSP Colonial 1677–80*, no. 1123, 19 Sept. 1679; ibid., no. 1479, 6 Aug. 1680; Pomfret, *The Province of West New Jersey*, p. 112.

26. *PWP*, II, p. 115, Robert Barclay to William Penn, 23 Sept. 1681.

27. *CSP Colonial 1677–80*, no. 1409.

28. *Votes and Proceedings of the House of Representatives of the Province of Pennsylvania* (Philadelphia, 1752), I, p. 169. Delaware had seceded from Pennsylvania and tried to impose duties upon ships passing up the Delaware River.

29. HSP, MS 373, fo. 43, Peter Lindstom's Journal (1691).

30. *PWP*, II, pp. 90–1, Barclay to Penn, Apr. 1681. Barclay's letter confirms the duke's decision not to grant the Delaware area.
31. Mary K. Geiter, 'The Restoration Crisis and the Launching of Pennsylvania, 1679–81', *EHR*, CXII (Apr. 1997), pp. 313–14.
32. *PWP*, II, pp. 798, 37–8; *CSP Colonial 1681–85*, no. 2078, Werden to Sir Allen Apsely, 8 Aug. 1681. Werden strongly believed that the loss of revenue for New York was now inevitable due to the giving up of the lands on either side of the Delaware; J.R. Jones, *Country and Court, England 1658–1714* (London, 1978), p. 204.
33. HSP, Penn MS, I, fo. 3: James, duke of York to John Lewin, 24 May 1680.
34. Cf. Joseph Illick, 'The Pennsylvania Grant: A Re-evaluation', *Pennsylvania Magazine of History and Biography*, 86 (1962), pp. 379–80; Mary Maples Dunn, *William Penn: Politics and Conscience* (Princeton, 1967), pp. 78–9.
35. *An Abstract*, pp. 25–6; *PWP*, II, p. 323.
36. PRO, PCR, 2/68, p. 352.
37. PRO, PCR, 2/69, pp. 138–222.
38. *Commons Journals*, IX, pp. 699–703.
39. Narcissus Luttrell, *A Brief Historical Relation* (Oxford, 1857), II, p. 64.
40. *London Gazette*, 16 Feb. 1681, published the complete contents of the order to encourage trade in the plantations.
41. PRO, PCR, 2/69, p. 224; *CSP Colonial 1681–85*, nos. 29, 30, 32, 2070.
42. Mary K. Geiter, 'London Merchants and the Launching of Pennsylvania', *PMHB*, CXXI (Jan./Apr. 1997), pp. 101–22.
43. *PWP*, microfilm 14:536, Hannah Penn, letter to Sunderland, 1715.

Chapter 4

MINISTER WITHOUT
PORTFOLIO

In February 1685, after a short illness brought on by a stroke, Old Rowley expired. With no legitimate son or daughter to inherit the throne, his brother was next in line. During the reign of James II, Penn was to realize the highest point in his political career. He was cultivated by the king not only as a dissenter but also as a courtier. Thus he was groomed for high office in the customary way by being sent on an embassy. This was the route which courtiers such as Godolphin, Rochester, and Sunderland had taken when they were fledgling politicians. Penn was sent as an envoy to The Hague in May 1686 to sound out the attitude of the prince and princess of Orange towards the repeal of the penal laws and Test Act. In November he was appointed as a deputy lieutenant in Buckinghamshire.[1] By April 1687 he was in such high esteem at court that he assisted in the formulation of the Declaration of Indulgence. He became James's right-hand man, helping the king to regulate corporations, acting as a commissioner into the regulation of recusancy fines, and as a mediator between the king and dons of Magdalen College, Oxford. He became a general spokesman for James's policies and a door through which men had to pass to receive royal favours.[2] Penn had, at last, the chance to use his unique position to further his aims for toleration. What emerged was a pairing of king and dissenter which created the possibility for a degree of religious toleration that went beyond either one's expectation and beyond anything that England had experienced. At the same time, Penn was fulfilling his father's ambitions for him. Towards the end of James's reign he held positions of influence which rivalled the ministers of the day. There was even a rumour that he would be appointed secretary of state. A letter addressed to him around this time even greeted him as Sir William.[3]

* * *

Initially, James continued the policy of repressing dissent at home and consolidating the North American colonies across the Atlantic. Both posed problems for Penn. As a leading dissenter, he was affected by the repression. As the proprietor of Pennsylvania, he was threatened by James's American ambitions which resulted in a bid to take Penn's colony from him.

The new king was determined to relieve his fellow Catholics from the penal laws and Test Acts. At first he did not show any inclination to extend toleration to dissenters, since he perceived them as republicans and rebels. To him dissenters were those people who were involved in the abortive Monmouth rebellion in 1685 which was aimed at his overthrow. The captured rebels included Quakers as well as other dissenters, so James would not have been naturally inclined to look towards that group for support for his policy of toleration. The crisis must have evoked the horror of his earlier experiences of his father's overthrow and death at the hands of the Independents. As to the Quakers, James himself observed in July 1685, 'I have not great reason to be satisfied with the Quakers in general.'[4] By 1686, however, he was prepared to grant some relief to the Friends. Perhaps he was persuaded that as pacifists they offered no real threat to his regime. At all events, in the spring of that year some 1,200 Quakers were pardoned and released from prison. These moves represented the first official mark of favour towards Penn.

At first sight the close relationship of the king and the Quaker appears odd. Yet king and courtier did share common ground. They were both persecuted in some fashion. Both were also committed to relieving their fellow sufferers. Penn had been excluded from office, imprisoned, and fined over the years. James had suffered, like Penn, at the hands of champions of Anglican uniformity. He had been threatened with exclusion from the throne, banished from court, and his authority over the welfare of his children circumscribed.[5]

Although James was committed to ruling arbitrarily, he was also committed to liberty of conscience, particularly for his fellow Catholics. To him the two were not in conflict with one another. While James modelled his government on absolutist France, he also accepted the Edict of Nantes, which provided for an atmosphere of toleration within that country. Unfortunately, and to the embarrassment of James, Louis XIV revoked the Edict in 1685. Still, James and Penn could draw on their early experiences in France, James from the Catholic court, which allowed for toleration of the Huguenots, Penn from his experience of that liberty from the Huguenot side in Saumur. However, both could also look to Holland for a model of liberty of conscience and free trade. 'Conscience ought not to be constrained, nor people forced in matter of mere religion,' James declared in 1687. To his opponents, however, commercial success was dependent upon free government as well as upon freedom of conscience. So although the king and the Quaker moved towards universal toleration, they did so from different perspectives. However, until circumstances forced them, neither was looking for unlimited toleration. James's goal was complete toleration for his Catholic brethren, not necessarily including dissenters in that effort.

On the other hand, Penn wanted full toleration for dissenters, primarily Quakers, but, until James's reign, he had no intentions of including papists in the call for relief from persecution. After all, he did not include them in his legislation for Pennsylvania. Before James's accession, Penn railed against papists, unfortunately in print.[6] He warned that Roman Catholics were not to be trusted and argued that the recusancy laws should be modified to distinguish Quakers from Catholics. There surely must have been an uncomfortable moment when he and the new king discussed possibilities regarding a new strategy for toleration.

What had changed their minds was a combination of factors. For James, it was the failure to convince the Anglican Church of his good intentions. This was especially disastrous for him because the established Church was the traditional bulwark of the monarchy. It put into practice the belief in the divine right theory of monarchy by its active participation in the sanctification of the throne and monarch. However, when James gave Catholics commissions in the army as part of the crackdown on the rebellion, Anglican fears of popery were raised. And, far from listening to protest raised in parliament, James prorogued it in November of 1685. The king's actions only served to heighten the paranoia which swept through the country. Penn saw that it was now foolish to continue to omit Catholics from his pleas for toleration with a Catholic king on the throne, and that he had to moderate his stand on papists if he was going to have any hope of getting legislative relief for dissenters. For this he was accused of promoting the cause of Catholics, when a pro-Catholic pamphlet was circulated with his name on it as author. Penn denied the charge vigorously. However, he did defend his stand on a much broader toleration than before in *A Persuasive to Moderation*.

Legislative relief for dissenters had implications for the colonies. Without toleration their religious freedoms would be jeopardized. So while Penn was building bridges with the new regime, he also had a wary eye on the future of his colony.

James's move to put the colonies under the Crown had already begun under his brother, Charles, in 1684 with writs of *quo warranto* being issued against Massachusetts and Bermuda, challenging their authority to operate outside the navigation laws and particularly accusing the former of inhibiting religious toleration.[7] The new regime, under James, subsumed Connecticut, New Hampshire, and Rhode Island, as well as Massachusetts and ultimately New Jersey and New York, into what became known as the Dominion and Territory of New England. But a change in emphasis in colonial policy was occurring under James. Where previously the main motivation had been the increase of commerce, now there was a shift towards more military and strategic considerations. Although there was peace with France, it was at best tenuous. The friction between the two countries centred on the allegiance of the five Indian nations. So, though England and France agreed to respect each other's boundaries and trade, the issue over actual trading with the Indians was not clear.[8] Skirmishes between Indians and settlers were a consequence and served to fuel the tension. Even so, it took James until January of 1687 to arrange a one-year peace deal with Louis XIV. James directed his governor-general, Edmund Andros, to treat with the five nations for the release of any French prisoners.[9]

Meanwhile, writs of *quo warranto* continued to be issued. James was determined to regain New Jersey and Delaware and so in July 1685 writs went out against those colonies. Writs were also issued against the Carolinas and the Bahamas in April 1686, followed in May 1686 by another against Pennsylvania.[10] Penn saw the warning signal earlier when the decision over the boundary dispute with Baltimore stressed James's ownership of the area that Penn was claiming. The separate moves against Pennsylvania and Delaware were significant in a couple of respects. First, they meant that the king never considered the counties of the Delaware Bay area as part of the grant in the Pennsylvania charter. Consequently, while James and Penn may have agreed over religious toleration, the relationship was not so special, at this point anyway, as to exempt Penn from the attack on his charter. Secondly, Penn realized what the commercial implications would be if the Delaware region was taken away. Penn argued this point when he petitioned the council claiming that the question was over the title of land or territory and not over power or dominion; consequently a *quo warranto* was inappropriate. Nevertheless, complaints about the colonies' contentiousness, not least because of their refusal to send a congratulatory address on James's accession, and the boundary dispute with Maryland, provided the excuse James and the lords of trade and plantation needed to resume Penn's charter.

In defence of his proprietorship, Penn drew an eloquent distinction between the terms 'territory' and 'dominion' or 'government'. By stressing that the question was over the title of land and not about ownership, he was at once acknowledging the king's supremacy over its government and that he himself was only proprietor of its territory who claimed its rents. Therefore, acting on the *quo warranto* was not necessary. To do so would mean the government was issuing a *quo warranto* against the king. Thus, he argued, it would be an absurd action to take. Penn was aware that the title to the lower counties was in question from the beginning and he therefore used it to his advantage. However, it was to be a different matter for Pennsylvania.[11]

The order against Pennsylvania was issued on 30 May 1686, but was revoked on 6 June. There is no doubt that the sudden stop was due to Penn's connections in high places as well as his own superb political astuteness and timing. Sunderland was back in power as secretary of state and thus he issued the order to stop the *quo warranto*. Although Sunderland was Penn's close friend, it would not have been enough to persuade the king to cease the attack on his proprietary. To ensure a favourable outcome, Penn ably influenced the decision by playing the commercial card with the erection of a new company composed of influential backers who had interests in the colonial fur trade in the north-western part of Pennsylvania, bordering New York. The move worked, because the day after the *quo warranto* was stopped, a charter was issued by Penn for the New Mediterranean Sea Company.[12] Penn's motive was twofold. He had to stop action against his charter and he needed to make money.

Many of the names in the list of company members were those of Whigs or of dissenters, who were not likely to have favoured the move against Pennsylvania in view of James's political behaviour towards his own colony of New York when he got rid of its elected assembly. Yet they belonged to a group which the king was increasingly anxious to cultivate at a time when his relationship with Anglicans and Tories was rapidly deteriorating. Therefore, James was not going to ignore the possibility of currying favour with potential supporters.

The names of the subscribers to the New Mediterranean Company indicated a connection between politics and trade. The president, Lord Montagu of Boughton, had spent time as ambassador in France. After he returned to England, he led the attack on Tory ministers during the Exclusion Crisis. He also espoused the cause of the duke of Monmouth, the illegitimate son of Charles II, during that time. He was in and out of favour, first as master of the robes and then dismissed, ending up back in James's good graces because he was once again received favourably by the king. As president of the new company, Montagu created an important link between Penn and the court. Others associated with it had also played a political role in the previous reign. Lord Vaughan had been governor of Jamaica from 1675 to 1678, after which he served in the

Exclusion Parliaments as member for Carmarthenshire. Sir John Hotham had represented Beverley, in the East Riding of Yorkshire and, like Montagu, sided with the opposition.

Penn realized that he needed a company made up of influential men who could circumvent the pressure of New York's interest at court and the Pennsylvania assembly. This was something the Free Society of Traders signally failed to do, mainly because it was an operation which functioned from the colonies and lacked enough vital influence in London. For a while, the incorporation of the new company seemed to have deterred any further attempts on Penn's charter. There is no clear evidence as to when or why the company ended, but there is no mention of it after 1688. Yet James had not given up his claim to the Delaware counties, and although a draft of release of the property to Penn was drawn up in 1688, it was never completed. This must surely have left Penn with an uneasy feeling, and one which would linger behind his political decisions in the future.

For the moment though, thanks to Sunderland, he had found a foothold at court. He consolidated this when, in May 1686, he went as envoy to The Hague. Ostensibly travelling through parts of Europe to visit Quakers and to proselytize, Penn was delegated by the king to travel to The Hague in order to find out how William and Mary viewed James's strategy for toleration. Although he did not go in the formal capacity of envoy, his visit was regarded as official. 'It is certain he was much with father Petre and was particularly trusted by the earl of Sunderland,' observed Bishop Burnet. 'So, though he did not pretend any commission for what he promised, yet we looked on him as a man employed.'[13] Penn had on a prior occasion in 1680 gone to Holland to address the prince of Orange on behalf of fellow Quakers in the Netherlands who were being persecuted. This time, however, Penn's hope that he could convince the pair on James's behalf was, alas, based upon sand.

Prince William assured Penn of his support for toleration, but he could not agree to abandoning the Test Act, because it was the only security for Protestantism, especially when the king was of a different religion. He agreed with Penn that conscience was a private matter, but it was no good promising toleration without enacting it first in law. Otherwise it could be revoked on the king's whim just as the Edict of Nantes had been by Louis XIV in 1685. Anyway, the number of dissenters in England was clearly a minority, and therefore to ignore the primary base of support for the monarchy, the Anglican Tories, was political suicide.

While William's view was more cynical, his wife's opposition came from her firm religious beliefs. Mary was a staunch Anglican and believed wholeheartedly, as future protector of the established Church, that she was responsible for the souls of her people. To open the door to what she considered nothing more than schismatic sects would weaken the pillar of religious belief and cause social instability. Only by James having a son would William and Mary's claims be superseded. Paradoxically, the birth of a son in 1688 sealed James's fate and ensured their claim.

Penn also tried to persuade Gilbert Burnet, who was attending the court at The Hague, to return to England and support James in his policies. In return, Burnet would be rewarded by preferential treatment from the king. James appreciated Burnet's role as an exiled Whig confidant of Mary and must have realized that if he could persuade Burnet, he would be able to sway her. Burnet's description of Penn's visit was laced with venom. An egotistical man himself, Burnet recognized a fellow in Penn. He depicted Penn's performance before William and Mary as one brimming with over-confidence, with an address which was given in a 'tedious and luscious way', all of which would only succeed in boring the listener.[14] Nonetheless, Burnet declined Penn's invitation on the same grounds as that of the prince and princess and probably because he had information that James had a contract out for his assassination. According to Burnet, Penn left him with a prediction that had been passed on to him by a man 'that pretended a commerce with angels'. According to this 'friend', in two years' time, 1688 to be exact, there would be momentous changes that would amaze all the world.[15] It was logical for Penn to think on the issue of toleration, given his and the king's vision of the whole thing in terms of a new Magna Carta. The reality, when it came, was the unthinkable.

On his return from The Hague, Penn apparently satisfied Sunderland with the accomplishment of his mission. Although he was not entirely successful, since the prince and princess baulked at repealing the Test Act, they had expressed their toleration for all, including Catholics. One sign of Penn's acceptance at court was his appointment as a deputy lieutenant in Buckinghamshire. This commission in the county militia, while perhaps curious for a Quaker, was quite fitting for a country gentleman.

A more significant sign of his arrival in power was his involvement with the Declaration of Indulgence in the spring of 1687. The Declaration was seen as more than just a repeat of the attempt in 1672 by James's brother, Charles, to carry through his promise at Breda to ensure the liberty of tender consciences. It was an edict of toleration, granting immunity from prosecution for breaches of the penal laws against religious dissent. In theory, it included not only Catholics and Protestant non-Anglicans, but even non-Christians. Significantly, the author behind the declaration probably was Penn. He certainly shared the motives behind it. He wanted religious and political liberties for his brethren, even if it meant taking a softer line than before on the Roman Catholics.

Penn's next step was to secure acceptance of the Declaration and promote the repeal of the penal laws and Test Act by writing tracts in favor of the repeal and indulgence, organizing addresses thanking James, and travelling up and down the country preaching in favour of repeal.[16] In one embarrassing instance, Penn was shouted down by the rabble and was forced to stop and get on his way with 'the mob knocking the bulks as he passed'.[17]

His tracts reflect several important points about him, all of which indicate a man who was a monarchist. However, Penn's view of monarchy did not extend to arbitrary rule. He hoped to persuade James's councillors as well as those in the houses of parliament to be flexible in their move towards toleration. Several of his tracts in the early part of the year 1685 had already turned the corner from previous statements of opposition to Catholic doctrine to statements of support for the inclusion of Catholics in the programme for toleration. *A Persuasive to Moderation* reflected his change of position, that toleration should be based on morality rather than on a specific religious doctrine. Thus his argument, as with earlier tracts that year, refuted attacks upon his apparent change of mind towards Catholics. It was not mere opportunism that explains Penn's change of mind. His earlier opposition to toleration for papists occurred during the crisis of the 1670s and early 1680s when the country was gripped with fear of a Catholic conspiracy. Now, under a Catholic king, there was no need to fear another Popish Plot. Penn's *Persuasive to Moderation* was followed in the spring and summer of 1686 by a number of pieces in which he stated unequivocally where he believed toleration rested. *Good Advice to the Church of England, Roman Catholick, and Protestant Dissenter* laid toleration squarely in the realm of English liberty and Christian principles. This theme was followed through in a series of letters, in 1687, starting with *A Letter From a Gentleman in the Country*, in which Penn argued that only by the repeal of the penal laws and the current Test Act could such liberty be secured. Thus his apparent switch from excluding Catholics in his fight for religious forbearance to their inclusion was as visionary as it was controversial. Penn's view was of a great charter, and he likened the idea to the Magna Carta. However, Penn was not without criticism, and rebuttals to his tracts flowed in from friends as well as enemies. In *Reflections on Penal Laws and Tests*, the writer argued for keeping the Tests, which would preserve the nation from the papist grasp. The most notable riposte to Penn's activity, however, was a piece attributed to the marquis of Halifax.

A Letter to a Dissenter urged the dissenters to consider the consequences of James's policies. It also warned them to be cynical about the king's motives for wooing them, arguing that they were being used as pawns in a game to convert the country to Catholicism. A further plea, *Three Considerations proposed to William Penn*, was a direct reference to Penn's involvement in the composing of the 1687 *Declaration of Indulgence* which was reissued in April 1688. Dean Tillotson expressed a growing belief that Penn was, if not a papist, then a sympathizer. Penn's friend William Popple made explicit this concern that so great an involvement in the king's policies led people to think of Penn as a papist.[18]

* * *

In 1687 Penn was appointed as one of the commissioners of enquiry to look into the abuses of the penal laws. The commissions, which had a total of 365 members during the period from December 1687 to July 1688, were set up to investigate irregular practices committed when levying fines on dissenters for breaches of the penal laws.[19] Along with his fellow Friend, George Whitehead, another conspicuous member of the London commission, Penn successfully brought charges of perjury against informers and prosecutors. However, his position at once signified Penn's important role in government and heightened his political visibility, something which would come back to haunt him in the days following the Revolution.

Penn was also given the post of superintendent of the hearth and excise taxes. In September 1688 a newsletter reported that he was 'made chief commissioner of thee excise of tea and coffee and pretends to advance the revenue'.[20] He was later to claim that nobody had a better set of proposals for augmenting the revenue than he had in James's reign. Indeed, he was hoping to see the king 'well established' with a parliamentary revenue. Until then he did not wish to be rewarded with office in case 'the world should think I used his [James's] favor that way'.[21] That was just as well, because Penn was viewed by his fellow Friends as becoming increasingly worldly. He was being compared to the great courtier in the book of Esther who was a greater favourite with his king than with his God. That courtier was more desirous of satisfying his pride and malice than his master's good and service.[22]

Penn's collaboration was part of James's strategy of making new alliances after he discarded the support of the Anglican Tories. Penn's name lent some credibility to the king's strategy, which otherwise was suspect to all Protestant shades of the religious spectrum. Nor was his name used in vain, because he travelled around the country holding hearings on alleged unlawful distraints of dissenters' goods.[23]

In the summer of 1687 the king finally dissolved parliament and set out to spearhead in person the campaign to convince people, either through reason or by browbeating them, to select amenable candidates for a new parliament. He had extended wholesale toleration to Catholics and dissenters alike, thus completely severing the Anglican Tories from his base of support. Penn was helping in the effort to fashion a pliable parliament by involving himself at the local level of politics. He was given the power to act as an intermediary regulating the corporations in Buckinghamshire and in Huntingdonshire. Writing from Kensington Palace to a friend and former Quaker, Robert Bridgeman of Huntingdon, Penn directed him to send a distinct account of all the representatives of that corporation and their political attitudes on the matter of the repeal of the penal laws and Test Acts. Penn was thus at the very heart of government in these months, collaborating with the king over the packing of parliament. He later justified his involvement by saying that it was the only way to achieve his goal of toleration by an Act of parliament even if it meant stacking the odds. 'I allwaies endeavoured an impartiall liberty of conscience to be established by law, that the Papists might never be able to null it, and this is all that can be charged upon me, and I count it no crime.'[24] In other words, the end sometimes justified the means, and Penn's language of denial was carefully chosen.

Penn was also on the road drumming up support for the king by organizing addresses of thanks, starting with his own brethren. However, the number of addresses, of which there were only 197 over a period of a year, and the kind of religious groups involved, qualified the success of the campaign.[25] Indeed, the prospects for a compliant parliament were not auspicious. On the contrary, responses to a crude public opinion poll undertaken by the king were ominous. James had the leading peers and gentry respond to three questions to ascertain their views on toleration. First, if elected to parliament, would they support the repeal of the penal laws and the Test Acts? Secondly, would they vote for candidates who supported the repeal? Finally, would they live peaceably with their neighbours no matter what their religious beliefs? By December 1687 the responses were largely negative. Penn, who had advised the king not to conduct the survey, concluded that an election must be postponed until March at the earliest.[26] He was being much more realistic than the king, showing as much awareness of gentry as of dissenting opinion. Early in the new year he told James Johnstone that

there would be a parliament at the end of May. I said I would wager twenty to one against. He began to laugh, and said I imagined Sunderland had more credit than he actually possessed – he hadn't the power to prevent it, and he would be ruined if he did not allow it. I replied that he had no need of power, he would use trickery instead. That is what I fear myself, he said.[27]

Sunderland in fact managed to put off the election until September, persuading James that his soundings in the constituencies did not augur well. By September, however, Sunderland and Penn were convinced that 'the Parliament will do what the king will have them'.[28] Unfortunately, the election had to be called off when news arrived that William of Orange was preparing to invade.

*　*　*

Meanwhile Penn had extended his role from adviser to an intermediary in another sphere of James's strategy for toleration. The circumstances surrounding the election of a president for Magdalen College, Oxford illustrate the heights to which Penn had flown and they give a rare glimpse into Penn's personality. To further James's aims, there needed to be places or seminaries for training future priests. One way he could achieve this was to use existing colleges for the purpose of educating novices. Several of the colleges had already succumbed to the king's wishes, with the conversion of college presidents and deans to the Roman Catholic faith or through the appointment of a papist as head of the college. The Oxford colleges of Christ Church and University College fell under the king's sway, as did Sidney Sussex in Cambridge. Magdalen College, Oxford was next, and it proved a turning point in the established Church's struggle to defend itself against the erosion of its privileges. Upon the death of the college's president, Henry Clerke, in March 1687, the way was clear for James to nominate someone who would be in line with his religious aims and, although the college had its own nominee, John Hough, the Catholic Anthony Farmer was put forward. A convert to Catholicism, Farmer had, according to Macaulay, lived a life filled with shameful acts, among which the Whig historian included his membership of the University of Cambridge. From there he slid into the life of a dissolute rake. Because of that and his religious persuasion, the Magdalen Fellows rejected his nomination and elected John Hough. This resulted in the dons being summoned to Whitehall, where Lord Chancellor Jefferys, not known for his patience, presided over the commission to look into the matter and concluded that the election of Hough was void. Realizing that the royal choice was a bit too heavy-handed, another more amenable candidate was suggested. Samuel Parker, bishop of Oxford, was an Anglican but a man of

Catholic sympathies. He therefore seemed a good compromise. The Fellows, however, could not go back on their oath to the elected Hough and so refused to accept the nullification pronounced by the commission. So, from March until September, when James arrived in Oxford, the college and the Crown were at stalemate. The refusal of the Magdalen Fellows to place a papist at their head, and then to reject a compromise overture, enraged the king. When James arrived at Christ Church, the Fellows were ordered to attend him, and when they appeared ready with supplications and explanations the king accused them of disloyalty and bade them go. In the end Parker was installed as president and the Fellows were ejected from their living.

The king thought that Penn, as intermediary, would be a credible person whom the Fellows could trust. He was a Quaker, but he was renowned for his virtue, even though there had been attempts at blackening his character. Penn's attempt to convey the king's proposal in order to find a way around the Fellows reneging on their oaths met with rejection not because he was being anything less than honest.[29] In fact, most of the Fellows got around the problem by simply not assisting in the admission of the new president. Penn suggested that in the short term Parker would be a president sympathetic to the king's policies, but he was also an ailing man, not long for this world. In the long term, therefore, Hough would inherit the bishop of Oxford's presidency of the college if only the Fellows would accept Parker. But in the eyes of the Magdalen men Penn's involvement was beyond the bounds of mere politics, and he showed a certain arrogance in his approach to their problems. He flippantly assured them that with three colleges in the hands of the papists, they would have nothing more to fear. He went so far as to lecture them on their selfishness for wanting to dominate the religious education of all children.[30]

There was a more serious issue at stake. By depriving Hough of his office or freehold, he was being deprived of his property and therefore his liberty. When the other Fellows were turned out of their livings, they too were being deprived of their liberties. Meanwhile, in Holland, Mary heard about the dons' plight and sent £200 to be distributed among them.[31] It was no less than a legal and constitutional matter and one that marked a crucial turning point in the already fragile relationship between the established Church and the monarch. Penn was no less culpable. Hough was appalled at Penn's lack of appreciation of what was at stake, especially after Penn himself preached on the crucial importance of liberty and property.

By the summer of 1688 James had a more pressing reason for parliament to meet. The queen was pregnant. The king's pilgrimages and supplications for a male heir to the throne had paid off, and when in June a son was delivered James was convinced that Providence had prevailed.

In September, James was at the height of his powers. The birth of the Prince of Wales conveyed a permanency about the present monarchy. But it also created a desperation among the Tories and Whigs. Dissenters were uneasy about James's appointment of Catholics to offices. For Penn, a shift was occurring in high places which saw the erosion of his backers. Rochester had been dismissed from the privy council the previous summer. Sunderland, while still in a position of influence, was being edged out by James's Catholic cabal. One of the cabal, Father Petre, a brash Catholic, was derisively labelled the first minister of state. With the pressure from the investors and the erosion of support from the Crown, Penn was warned by William Sewel that 'by one and the greatest faction you are held in hatred'. Penn could do nothing but continue to support the king and hope to be looked upon favourably by the incoming ministers, who included dissenters.

There were rumours earlier in the year that William of Orange would invade England in order to restore the liberties of Englishmen and to preserve the throne for his wife, James's daughter. Whatever the reason was, nobody in office thought that there was any credence to the rumour. Lady Sunderland did not think so in the first week of September when she wrote to Henry Sidney that the plan to pack parliament was still going ahead because: 'Mr Penn assures us that all will go as the king would have it and they are the knowing men in our world.'[32] However, the threat of invasion was becoming all too real, because later that month word came through that William had, indeed, set sail. Immediately James switched his allegiance back to the Anglicans and began the electoral process for a new parliament. Upon hearing that William's fleet was blown back by a gale to Dutch harbours, James took it as a sign from above that Providence had once again intervened, so the king ordered the writs for elections to be recalled. However, when he learned of William's landing at Torbay on 5 November, the king began backtracking by removing Catholic officials from their posts, and again issued writs for an election.

During this period, deep-seated doubts about the king must have come surging forth. Penn must have felt very insecure in the first instance when James stopped the issuance of writs, but his fears must have been heightened on the second occasion when the king undid everything that he and Penn had accomplished in the past year. The only thing that Penn could do was clumsily to issue a tract, *Advice in the Choice of Parliament Men*, in which he once again attacked the Catholic element. He also tried to cobble a draft of confirmation of his authority over the three lower counties, something which was never clarified, but it was too late. Only a partial draft was completed, dated 10 December 1688, the day before James made his first attempt to escape to France and the very day the little Prince of Wales and his mother were shipped off. James was caught at Faversham and brought back to London, but 13 days later he succeeded in escaping from London and then to France.[33] For the rest of Penn's life, he was plagued with doubts over his hold on Delaware, doubts that people in the new regime seized upon. He had more immediate problems in the panic that ensued right after the king's departure.

In the vacuum between James's departure and before the accession of William and Mary, uncertainty and fear pervaded the country. Anybody suspected of having been part of James's inner circle was rounded up. There was no doubt that Penn was looked upon with suspicion. His first encounter with hostility came during December 1688. The council of peers of the realm, acting somewhat like the colonial committee of safety during the early phase of the American Revolution, ordered the safeguarding of the ports and seizure of anyone deemed to be a threat to the government at such a time. Penn had been walking past Scotland Yard in Whitehall when some officers of the guard seized him on suspicion and brought him before the peers at Whitehall. In fact, Penn had come from Lord Godolphin, who had just spoken to Prince William. Clearly, there was a lack of communication within the government brought about by the chaos, because Penn's abrupt arrival before the peers, many of whom were his personal friends, was somewhat embarrassing for both sides. Ultimately, Penn was released on bail amounting to £5,000, which two of his supporters, Lord Philip Wharton and Charles Gerard, Lord Brandon, offered to pay.[34] Both were Whigs and no lovers of papists. Yet Penn was seen as a collaborator of James. In the Whig view of the Revolution, Penn and other dissenters who collaborated with the Catholic king were regarded as at best turncoats and at worst traitors. While many contemporary Whigs and dissenters undoubtedly shared this view, there was a significant number who did not feel that cooperating with the king was a betrayal of their principles. They argued that the end of universal toleration justified the means whereby they sought to attain it through working with the monarch. Penn was one of these people, and his defence of his position was clearly accepted by most of the peers before whom he was brought. In the event, though several other lords offered to give bail for Penn, 'two gentlemen of great estates in his neighborhood were his bayle'.[35]

Evidently the council was split over what to do in the interim between the flight of James and the acceptance of the government by

William. At this point nobody had decided that William was to be king. The greater fear was for the safety of the realm against a Catholic insurrection or invasion. For that, Penn was looked upon as a Jesuit in Anglican quarters, to the extent that he was referred to as 'Father Penn' by his enemies. His opponents in the council were led by Sir Robert Sawyer, former attorney-general to James and virulent opponent of Catholic toleration who resigned from office in 1687 over the issue. Thus he saw Penn as one of the key collaborators with James and his policies. Therefore, he accused the Quaker as a dangerous invader of English laws and liberties. It was true that Penn took part in the strategy to pack parliament and could therefore be accused of subverting the liberties of Englishmen. He tried to justify his involvement by explaining his desire to secure toleration by means of a statute in law. That could only be accomplished through parliament. The process of selection of parliament men was, perhaps, questionable, but Penn defended himself, saying that he had always endeavoured to secure liberty of conscience by law so that no papist could ever take it away. The explanation must have been particularly galling to the likes of Sawyer and incredible to the peers before whom Penn stood. One of the greatest political minds of the period was part of that group, George Savile, marquis of Halifax, who had chastised Penn in print for his methods. At this point, there was no hard evidence that Penn had ever subverted the freedoms of the people, so he was set free on bail. Penn had friends in high places, including the council. Nevertheless, he found himself arrested time and again and in greater danger than he had ever been.

· · ·

NOTES AND REFERENCES

1. *PWP*, III, Calendar of documents not filmed, p. 756, no. 6, Lord Sunderland on the approval of WP and others as deputy lieutenants of Buckinghamshire, 30 Nov. 1686.
2. Thus, when Increase Mather arrived in England in May 1688 to solicit the reissue of the Massachusetts charter he met with James and Penn in the king's closet with nobody else present. 'The Autobiography of Increase Mather', ed. M.G. Hall, *Proceedings of the American Philosophical Society*, 71/326, cited in *PWP*, III, p. 235 n.
3. Verney Papers, Claydon House microfilm 636, reel 41, Sir J. Verney to R. Verney, London, 11 May 1687; Sir R. Verney to John Verney, Middle Claydon, 15 May 1687. I am grateful to Professor Kent Clark for supplying this reference.
4. F.C. Turner, *James II* (London, 1950), p. 309.

5. Vincent Buranelli, *The King and the Quaker: A Study of William Penn and James II* (Philadelphia, 1962), pp. 104–15.
6. *A Seasonable Caveat Against Popery* (1670).
7. Philip S. Haffenden, 'The Crown and the Colonial Charters, 1675–1688', *WMQ*, 15 (1958), pp. 271–311.
8. Viola Barnes, *The Dominion of New England: A Study in British Colonial History* (London, 1923); David S. Lovejoy, *The Glorious Revolution in America* (London, 1972).
9. Andros to the Five Nations, 19 Sept. 1688, J.R. Brodhead (ed.), *Documents Relative to the Colonial History of the State of New York* (New York, 1853), III, p. 559.
10. PRO, PCR, 2/71, fo. 144v.
11. *CSP Colonial 1585–1688*, nos. 319, 320.
12. Bedford Record Office, DD.WY.736; *PWP*, microfilm 5:460.
13. Gilbert Burnet, *A History of His Own Time*, 6 vols (Oxford, 1833), IV, p. 140.
14. Ibid., pp. 139–41.
15. Ibid., p. 141.
16. *HMC*, 8th Report, I, p. 219, Penn's speech when he delivered the address on behalf of the Quakers, 1687.
17. *HMC*, 10th Report, App., pt IV, MSS of earl of Westmorland, p. 376, Sept. 1686.
18. *PWP*, III, microfilm 6:116.
19. Mark Goldie, 'James II and the Dissenters' Revenge: The Commission of Enquiry of 1688', *Historical Research*, 66 (1993), pp. 62, 66, 69; Friends Library, London, MS Book of Cases, I, p. 177; Narcissus Luttrell, *A Brief Historical Relation* (Oxford, 1857), I, p. 453; *HMC*, Downshire MSS, I, pp. 294, 301.
20. *HMC*, Downshire MSS, I, p. 301.
21. *PWP*, IV, p. 708, Penn to Harley, 22 June 1711.
22. Clarendon State Papers, 89, fos 175–6, Dublin, Sept. 1688.
23. Goldie, 'James II and the Dissenters' Revenge', p. 66.
24. Dr Williams Library, London, MS Morrice Q, pp. 353–4.
25. W.A. Speck, *Reluctant Revolutionaries* (Oxford, 1988), p. 183.
26. J.P. Kenyon, *Robert Spencer, Earl of Sunderland, 1641–1702* (London, 1958), p. 174.
27. Ibid., p. 187.
28. Ibid., p. 214.
29. *PWP*, III, microfilm 5:823, Letter to Dr Bayly, 26 Sept. 1687; Bodleian Rawlinson MS c. 938, fo. 117, Answer to WP by Magdalen Fellow over appointment, 3 Oct. 1687.
30. Thomas Babington Macaulay, *The History of England from the Accession of James the Second*, ed. Charles Firth, 6 vols (London, 1914), II, p. 250 n. 1. Hough accused Penn of being 'droll', meaning to jest or at best caught off his guard when he suggested alternatives.

31. Bodleian Library, Oxford, MS Smith 141, fo. 28.
32. R.W. Blencowe (ed.), *Diary of the Times of Charles II by the Honourable Henry Sidney*, 2 vols (London, 1843), II, p. 275, Lady Sunderland to Sidney, 3 Sept. 1688.
33. *PWP*, III, microfilms 5:900; 6:132, 161.
34. Robert Beddard (ed.), *A Kingdom Without a King* (Oxford, 1988), pp. 76–8, 174–5.
35. Ibid., p. 175.

Chapter 5

JACOBITE

The Revolution was anything but glorious for William Penn. His dream of gaining full toleration for his fellow dissenters was dashed. His chance to fulfil his father's wishes was snatched from him, all because James had alienated his subjects to the point where he was forced to flee the country. But Penn had been an integral part of that process. Now, under the new regime of William and Mary, Penn was suspect for aiding in subverting English liberties. Consequently, he was arrested a number of times. His proprietorship was taken from him and his English and Irish estates were in jeopardy, as was his life, but once the dust had settled Penn began to rebuild his career. This required gathering the tattered remains of the interest he had at court. Even then he had to prove to his friends that he was an ally and not an adversary of the new government. It was particularly hard to do since, by 1690, the mixed ministry King William had formed was dominated by Tories. The king hoped that by having both Whigs and Tories in government a check would be provided on extreme political behaviour by either party. Thus the Tory, Daniel Finch, earl of Nottingham, who was secretary of state for the southern department, was balanced by the Whig secretary of state for the northern department, the earl of Shrewsbury. But the controlling influence fell into the hands of a Tory. This was none other than Thomas Osborne, formerly earl of Danby, now marquis of Carmarthen. His emergence was probably due to the influence of Queen Mary upon her husband. For Penn, this meant a loss of support at court and the loss of his charter. It was not until 1694, when the Whigs began to acquire power again, that Penn regained his charter. Also, Mary's death that year removed another obstacle to Penn's rehabilitation. His involvement in bringing about the Affirmation Act, which enabled Quakers and others who refused to swear oaths to hold public office, finally convinced the Crown of his loyalty.

Although Penn was in custody four times between 1688 and 1691, no formal charges were brought.[1] There was disagreement in court circles over his involvement in plots to restore James. Some, like Sir Robert Sawyer, thought Penn to be a 'very dangerous fellow', while others, such as Charlwood Lawton, thought otherwise: 'had he been as busy as he has been represented . . . they would perhaps by this time have thought it their interest to have given him guards'.[2] But after 1690 Penn was viewed with increasing suspicion by friends and foes alike.

His situation was exacerbated by the threat of invasion by James in Ireland and his own disappearance at crucial periods. Penn definitely felt his life to be in jeopardy after the execution of a friend for conspiring against William and Mary, as he disappeared shortly afterward, from June 1691 to November 1692. For over sixteen months, hardly anybody knew where he had gone.[3] Some thought that he was in France. According to Robert Harley, Penn had indeed sailed across the channel. And there is one letter to the earl of Rochester which indicates that he was more elusive than in hiding. Why was he so elusive? Penn was charged with high treason in England and Ireland.[4] Whether or not he was a Jacobite will be dealt with shortly, but the immediate consequence of a conviction meant forfeiture of all his estates. Penn did the sensible thing and disappeared until he could clear his name. He was advised by Rochester, who was now a devout Anglican, that in return for his freedom he should go to his colony, but he refused to be treated like an exile, away from the centre of power where decisions could be made where he would lose everything anyway.

Penn's dilemma was made worse by the government's concern for the current state of affairs in the colonies. Pennsylvania had an absentee proprietor who was less than effective in keeping the colony to the terms of the charter, in particular the navigation laws. Nottingham, no friend to Penn, was first among the ministers to advocate a clamp-down. Nottingham's concern with the necessities of war reinforced his inclination to follow Crown policy, which was to install military governors in the North American colonies. Thus he backed the move to appoint Benjamin Fletcher as governor of New York, and ultimately Pennsylvania, and it was through Nottingham that the order was given for Penn's arrest.

Somehow Penn had to show his loyalty to the new regime and get support from within the privy council. There was very little evidence of that until 1694, when William remodelled the council and relied on the Whigs to guide him through the morass of English politics. Until then, Penn could only plead his innocence in vain and search around for a way to clear himself. For the moment, his hopes lay in the efforts of

Henry Sidney, Viscount Romney and Richard Jones, earl of Ranelagh. Romney was lord lieutenant of Ireland in 1690 and again in 1692. In between those years he served as secretary of state. Ranelagh was paymaster general and a privy councillor. Penn later referred to these men as the ones responsible for obtaining his freedom when, in 1693, he wrote about his dilemma. Also, in July of that year, Secretary of State Sir John Trenchard was lobbied to speak on behalf of Penn. Trenchard was reminded by Penn's agent Charlwood Lawton that he had a past obligation to Penn. 'I am confident I need not call to yr remembrance that you have obligations to Mr. Penn.'[5] Lawton was alluding to Penn's intercession on behalf of Trenchard in 1685 when the secretary was implicated in the Monmouth Rebellion. Trenchard was subsequently pardoned. At any rate, Penn knew that he was indebted to these men when he later wrote to his colonists, 'that it hath pleas[ed] God to worke my Enlargemt – by 3 Lords repre[sen]ting my case as not only hard but oppressiv[e]'.[6]

But it was not a matter of mere connections that afforded Penn his release. In fact, the evidence suggests that help was forthcoming only after Penn actively showed the king his loyalty. Until that moment, the king considered Penn as one of his greatest enemies. Sidney made this clear in a letter to Penn and added that 'he (the king) does not know why he should do you any good till he sees you have changed your mind, which can not be done, but by your doing him some service'. Sidney warned Penn that if he did not come to some terms then there was nothing that he could do for his friend any more. Penn would therefore have to suffer the consequences.[7] One of the reasons why William considered Penn an enemy was that he was allegedly aiding the French war effort by shipping wheat to France from his estates in Ireland, thus breaking the wartime embargo on trade with France.

In 1691 Penn was also charged by William Fuller, a Jacobite agent who presented perjured evidence, accusing him of supporting Jacobite efforts during James II's stay in Ireland during 1690, prior to the Battle of the Boyne. Perjured evidence was and is unacceptable in a court of law. On the other hand, Penn's estates extended to the area around the port of Kinsale where James landed and proceeded to issue the town with a new charter.[8]

So, was Penn a collaborator or was he the unfortunate victim of the power struggle? The notion that Penn was a Jacobite is as intriguing today as it was then. Those who regard him more as an icon than as a historical figure deny it categorically, refusing to accept that there could be any slur on his character. Those keen on promoting the idea that Jacobitism was a serious political movement enlist his case as evidence of its significance.[9] In between are historians who accept that Penn was embroiled in the strongly partisan politics of the age, but are sceptical about claims that Jacobitism was a widespread phenomenon. They regard the evidence for Jacobite activity in general, and his involvement in particular, as suspect. Short of a sworn confession signed by Penn it is hard to see what documentary evidence would satisfy the first group – and even then one suspects they would try to explain it. The second group are prepared to accept any contemporary source which seems to implicate Penn in Jacobite intrigue. One of the more solid sources is a series of six letters addressed to Jacobites and attributed to him.[10] Those who remain sceptical, however, while being prepared to accept that Penn might have corresponded with the exiled court in St Germains, dismiss this as no more than an insurance policy taken out by many politicians after the Revolution.[11]

Solving the mystery would answer many questions about Penn's activities during the period between the Revolution and the aftermath of the Battle of the Boyne. His eagerness to prove his worth to the new king in 1692 suggests that if indeed he was involved with James's invasion of Ireland, William's victory dashed any hopes for Penn on that score for the foreseeable future. There is also the language of Jacobitism to be considered. Certainly, on the eve of William III's arrival in England, there were few people in on the conspiracy to invite William, and, for that matter, most avowed that his arrival was only to safeguard the Protestant religion and a free parliament. There was no mention of him and his wife usurping James. Only when James fled England (with the acquiescence of William) was there any serious consideration of switching monarchs. Even when William and Mary were given the crown, there was a suspicion that the throne had been usurped. So the years following the Revolution were a time of psychological readjustment for England. As long as James was alive, there was a feeling of collective guilt by many who had sworn or declared their allegiance to him.

Psychologically, it would be extremely difficult for Penn to do an about-face. Like so many people at the time of William and Mary's accession, he was loath to commit himself to a new regime that sat so uneasily in London. More to the point, if a belief in the divine right of monarchs was a basic tenet of allegiance, as it was for Penn, then the psychological leap was almost impossible. Certainly, Penn's associates, Preston, Clarendon, and Francis Turner, bishop of Ely, refused to take the oath of allegiance to the new regime. Clarendon remained a nonjuror for the rest of his life. Moreover, there was no guarantee under the new regime of an extended toleration for Quakers. The Toleration Act of 1689 had excluded the Friends.

Until 1694, and for some time after he regained his charter, Penn remained under suspicion as one of the leading advocates of James's restoration. The evidence against Penn's involvement has been dismissed as inconclusive, but it has never been completely explained away. His whereabouts at crucial periods cannot be concretely determined and his connections with other confessed conspirators, among whom Richard Graham, Lord Preston, was one of the leaders, cannot be overlooked. The facts are these: on 27 February 1689, following the overthrow of James II, Penn was arrested after he let it be known that James was mounting an invasion. During the later part of February Clarendon commented on the rumour, saying that Penn had told him that James was, in fact, in Ireland.[12] Shortly after Clarendon's encounter with Penn, Lord Arran was arrested and questioned on whether Penn and another associate, Mr Graham, had dined with him the previous evening. The answer was in the affirmative.[13] Meanwhile Penn was allowed to remain free on bail, most probably due to the intercession of Secretary of State Shrewsbury.[14] After a court hearing, he was acquitted for lack of conclusive evidence. In March 1689 James II entered the port of Kinsale in Ireland. Kinsale and the area surrounding Cork were part of Penn's Irish lands. His second arrest was in June of the same year for high treason or treasonable practices following the arrest of his friend, Richard Graham, Lord Preston.[15] This time, he wrote to the marquis of Halifax, the lord privy seal, for help.[16] Although it is not known if Halifax did effect Penn's release, it appears that Penn was freed by August. Another arrest was made in September for which Penn had to endure a month's imprisonment. The fourth occasion of incarceration was in July 1690 when King William was in Ireland. However, prior to his arrest, Penn's whereabouts were uncertain. From June onward, nobody seemed to know where he was. His claim that he was ill and therefore not able to come to London any sooner has not been proven.[17] There were rumours that he might have been in Scotland getting support for James's invasion from Ireland. There is no substantive evidence in that direction either. What is known is that Penn could not be located. Meanwhile, William's army had decisively defeated James on 1 July at the Battle of the Boyne. Penn was released from prison in August, but he was due to appear before the King's Bench in the autumn. On 28 November he was cleared of the charge of treason.

Penn's final arrest occurred in February 1691, after Preston and some others involved in the conspiracy were caught with incriminating letters while attempting to sail to France the previous December. They were subsequently imprisoned. Among those letters were ones from Penn to James II. Over the next few weeks, Preston and his cohorts were brought

to trial and convicted of treason. When one of the convicted conspirators, John Ashton, was hanged, Preston agreed to talk in exchange for
his life. It was thought by the men around the king that Preston was the
only direct source who could concretely implicate Penn as well as Lord
Clarendon and the bishop of Ely.[18] Again, Penn went into hiding. Of
course, it can be argued that, by their very nature, confessions taken
under duress are unacceptable without further corroboration. Nevertheless, Penn's long relationship with Preston, Clarendon, and the bishop
cannot be dismissed out of hand. Corroboration came in the form of a
deposition by one Thomas White, owner of a boat which was to carry
Jacobite conspirators, including Preston and Penn, to France in October 1690. This puts Penn's correspondence in perspective, documenting
his role in the conspiracy and confirming the evidence against him.[19]
The plan was to go to Dover or Arundel, where Preston, Penn, and
'severall other persons of quality' would be disguised in 'seamen's apparell,
ready to be listed as his souldiers, till an opportunity offered, that they
might be landed any where on the coast of France'. The reward was
twenty guineas and other gratuities, not to mention some preferment
'as soon as times altered, which they confidently affirmed will be next
sum[m]er'.[20] The plan did not succeed because the secret sailing was
'publisht all over town that there was not a boy but knew it'. By the time
Preston was caught in transit with Penn's letters, Penn had been cleared
of the charge of treason. Quite possibly, his plan to sail to France was a
safeguard against a possible conviction, in which case he would make his
escape. When he was reprieved, he backed out of the plan and, instead,
gave Preston letters to be delivered to the king over the water.

Through an intermediary, Henry Sidney, who was now secretary of
state, Penn denied knowing of Preston's voyage and, furthermore, of
any plans for invasion by the deposed king and his French supporters.
On the face of it, the denial appears emphatic and unequivocal. But he
was referring directly to that particular event in December when Preston was apprehended. Penn had, in fact, equivocated in his language
when denying ownership of the letters found on Preston. Moreover,
he had previously told Sidney that he would tell the king everything he
knew that was of interest concerning the intrigues from France.[21]

Penn's position was made even more precarious because Sidney, a
good friend, saw the correspondence and would have recognized Penn's
writing. He was quite convinced that Penn was 'as much in this business
as anybody; and two of the letters are certainly of his writing'.[22]

In order to clear his name, Penn told Rochester that he had to go to
Ireland, where he was charged with treason.[23] In February 1692, Penn
was able to defend himself successfully from the charge because Fuller's

testimony was discredited. Now he could get on with the business of proving his loyalty to the new regime. He was also helped by the changing political scene, not least by the return of his political allies, the earls of Rochester and Sunderland, to the centre of power. Rochester was admitted to the privy council on 1 March 1692. While Sunderland did not hold any official capacity, he was what John Kenyon called 'the minister behind the curtain'. He was in contact with William as early as 1692, and by the spring of 1693 Sunderland was advising the king that the hitherto mixed ministry was not working and should be replaced with a Whig one. One of the casualties in that spring was Nottingham. Blamed for the capture of the English fleet at Smyrna, his sojourn as sole secretary, after Sidney left, was ended when Trenchard was appointed to the northern department. By November, however, the Whig ascendancy was complete with the dismissal of Nottingham, leaving Trenchard as sole secretary for the moment. The Whig Junto was installed, led by Charles Montagu, John Somers, Edward Russell, and Thomas Wharton, each committed to funding the war effort and to putting the nation on a sound financial footing. Rochester was back in a position of influence. Edward Ward, who became attorney-general, and Thomas Trevor, who became solicitor-general, both gave their opinions in favour of returning Penn's charter to him. By the time Penn was completely exonerated, the political scene had just about completed its metamorphosis.

For Penn, the political transformation meant that he could now proceed to clear himself of any charges of treason. In doing so, he would be able to safeguard his English and Irish estates and get his colonial charter back. In order for that to happen, he had to gain William's confidence. He did two things to show his support for the king. Despite the fact that he was a Quaker, he took steps to help the war effort. Thus he supplied victuals to the English forces and naval stores to the Navy from his Irish estates. To further this end, he also created a company to supply more materials. England was experiencing a shortage of staple flour, which was desperately needed in the making of food supplies for the troops. Ireland's harvest, however, was plentiful. And whereas in 1689 Penn had remarked to his colony that shipment of such supplies was in danger of succumbing to French privateers and thus the prices were trebling, now in 1693 his rationale was that war and poverty were 'looking men in the face' and the reason for supplying the English was not the war effort *per se* but to fight starvation.[24]

Following the recapture of Kinsale after the Battle of the Boyne in July, there were efforts to build up the port as an advance base for ships to sail out to meet French privateers. By June 1692, Kinsale was being used as a victualling port, and by the end of 1694 it had become a fully constituted naval yard. Supplies were needed at such a naval yard to build the ships. Hemp was being grown, albeit in small quantities, in England and Ireland, while pitch, tar, planks, and bolts could be shipped to the site. The shipment of timber was another matter. There was some timber to be had in Ireland, but not enough to supply a fleet. Therefore, it was bought largely from countries outside the English colonial system. Scandinavia provided timber, but it was expensive and the war made shipping dangerous. Resolving the problem was an opportunity for Penn to ingratiate himself with the government. There were other indications of Penn's moves to demonstrate that, despite being a Quaker, he was actively committed to the king's service and to support of the war effort. He did this by agreeing to the organization of a new company which was made up entirely of English merchants. In the middle of 1692 London investors petitioned for a charter to form a company in order to make masts for the king's ships.[25] Some of the members belonged to the New Mediterranean Sea Company. The formal petition for incorporation as the New Pennsylvania Company was read in council in May the following year. Essentially the new company was created out of the death throes of the Free Society of Traders and Penn's most recent attempt, in 1690, to form another company in the Susquehanna region. One of the reasons that the Free Society did not take off was the meddling of the Pennsylvania assembly. However, this time the new company was being run from London without hindrance from the colonial government. In fact, the charter was granted not by Penn but by the Crown because Penn did not at the moment have the right of government. Thus, when Penn agreed to go along with the company by granting them land, he was assenting in order to regain his full authority over his colony. Until Penn would commit himself to the Crown, his own charter remained in the hands of Governor Fletcher. Although Penn repudiated the legality of that fact, a compromise had to be effected if he was to get his charter back and the investors were to strengthen their hold over the colony.

Penn's involvement in the setting up of the new company can be deduced from linking his activities in organizing an address by the Pennsylvanians against Fletcher's commission with the petition for the new Pennsylvania Company. While he attacked the appointment of Fletcher as something that had no basis, especially since no *quo warranto* was issued against his government, he acted to convince the king of his loyalty. When Penn urged his colonists to send their protests to 'others in London + Bristol', he named Francis Plumstead as one of those others. Plumstead was also on the subscription list of the new company.

Other subscribers were close friends of Penn. Henry Gouldney, William Withers, Daniel Wharley, to name a few, were either confidants or relatives.[26] There was, at the same time, a similar company being formed in New Jersey by some of the same men who were in the Pennsylvania company. Be that as it may, Penn's role as accessory rather than instigator of the company's formation is indicated in a letter he sent to Lord Keeper Somers in April 1694. It was a reply from the proposed company to the objections he gave against their request. There is no evidence as to what the request was. However, it could not have been a request for a charter since they had already petitioned the Crown for it. The implication is that it was about one of the clauses in the draft of the company's constitution which was being negotiated.[27]

The company was intended to benefit investors on the English side and its business aims were directed towards furthering the war effort by supplying the materials farmed from the colonies. Thus they undertook to 'to apply themselves to the making of pitch tarr . . . and to send for men of knowledge therein from abroad to furnish the king with ten tunns . . . to plant hemp and flax for sail cloth to apply themselves to the building of ships . . . to deliver what quantities of plank shall be thought fit . . .'.[28] There was one other stipulation and that was that the members were restricted from trading privately or stock jobbing, something that was practised to the detriment of former companies. By December 1693, the charter was recommended for approval subject to a five-year limit and, in effect, its formation paved the way for returning the government of Pennsylvania to Penn a year later.[29]

Another show of coming to terms with King William and Queen Mary was made by contributing a scholarly treatise on peace and the future of Europe. Penn wrote a proposal suggesting a solution to the troubles of Europe, which continually ended in conflict. *An Essay Toward the Present and Future Peace of Europe*, published in 1693, revealed two things about Penn. The piece was one way of showing his commitment to peace rather than war, thereby offsetting the impression that he was supporting the war against France, but it also exhibited another aspect of Penn. Penn envisioned a political union of European countries, regardless of religious affiliation, whereby member countries would resort to negotiations before aggression. The essay also illustrates Penn's political astuteness by recognizing that such a union, which included Turkey, would go a significant way towards offsetting French influence. Although Penn's theory did not become reality, his proposal gave him credibility in the eyes of the English government so that, by 1696, he was on the road to political rehabilitation.

* * *

A drastic turn of events gave Penn another opportunity to come to terms with the new regime. The attempted assassination of William III in 1696 set in motion a chain of legislative action which resulted in the passing of the Affirmation Act which effectively extinguished any further hope of Jacobite support from the Quakers. The Act, which made it legal to affirm rather than swear an oath, enabled them to transfer their allegiance to William in good conscience. Once they could affirm, the Quakers could participate politically. Penn knew at first hand the restrictive power of the oath requirement when, during the Exclusion elections, and to his embarrassing dismay, he was blocked from voting at the polls because the returning officer demanded that he first swear an oath.

Penn had been instrumental in massaging the passage of the Act. For years, he had argued in public and in print, citing historical example after example of objections against oath taking. He pointed out to the king that, in 1577, one of his Dutch predecessors, another prince of Orange, had allowed the Mennonites to affirm in place of an oath.[30] Penn knew, as well as the government, that there was a steady growth of Quaker mercantile interests and with that growth came the cross-connection between the business and political communities. The urban Quaker tradesmen and merchants increasingly demanded action to facilitate their entry into city guilds and councils, which was being denied them because of the oath requirement.[31] Without some political remedy, a whole host of freedoms were not open to them, such as not being able to carry out any transactions for customs and the excise, give evidence, or be admitted to copyholds. Nor could they answer prosecutions in ecclesiastical courts for tithes and church-rates.[32] Voting rights and taking up the freedom of the corporations were particularly important to businessmen. Quakers sometimes overcame these obstacles by using proxy oath-takers, but it meant troubled consciences. This hindrance was particularly significant at the centre of economic and political power, London, where by 1677 there were at least fourteen substantial Quaker merchants.[33] These, together with merchants and tradesmen throughout England and Ireland, represented a notable contribution to the government's economy. Lord Shannon realized this when he observed of the Quakers of Cork, 'most . . . are the greatest traders in the town'.[34] The push for a remedy was also coming from the non-Quaker section of society because, just as the Friends bore the brunt of the disadvantages incurred from refusal to swear, the non-Quakers also felt its effect. Just as the Quaker suffered imprisonment, loss of property, or fines, the non-Quaker could suffer the wrath of justice if his only witness was a Quaker who could not give evidence without submitting to an oath.[35]

As proprietor of Pennsylvania and as a political force Penn was a focal point for investors, no matter what their religious inclination, because his companies did not require oaths. Hence his New Mediterranean Sea Company embraced a cross-section of society which included men of political stature who would later give impetus to the eventual success of the Affirmation bill.

It was not until parliament convened under William and Mary in 1689 that the Quakers saw a reasonable chance of beginning the process of petitioning for a bill to relieve them from taking the oath.[36] The reasons for this were twofold. The Toleration Act allowed for freedom of worship by dissenting groups, but it did not extend to the elimination of swearing oaths by religious authorities and laymen alike. Only by dispensation, or for certain exceptions, was an oath not required. For example, the nobility and officers presiding over a court martial did not have to take an oath. There was, however, still some confusion, which persisted throughout William's reign, over the eligibility of Quakers for official positions. The attempt by John Archdale, Quaker and elected MP for Chipping Wycombe, to take his seat in parliament was thwarted by his refusal to take the oaths, since he believed that 'my declarations of fidelity might in this case, as in others where the law requires an oath be accepted'.[37] It is true that the Toleration Act gave relief to dissenters in the form of freedom of worship, and qualified Quakers for exemption from the penalties of the penal laws by making a declaration in place of swearing an oath. Nevertheless, the Act still upheld the Corporation Act of 1661 and the Test Acts of 1673 and 1678, the first two requiring oaths to be sworn by office holders in borough corporations or under the Crown, while the third required members of parliament also to swear an oath of allegiance.

William's support for the Affirmation bill was a reflection of his own view on toleration.[38] His faith might have emanated from a religion based upon the tenet of predestination, but it did not extend to persecution. Prior to the Revolution, William made his position clear to Penn. He favoured general toleration, even for papists, but he refused to follow James's attempt to repeal the Test Act, which he felt was the only 'real security' in maintaining the Protestant religion.[39] Macaulay described William's stand eloquently: 'For all persecution he felt a fixed aversion, which he avowed, not only where the avowal was obviously politic, but on occasions where it seemed that his interest would have been promoted by dissimulation or by silence.'[40] Also, William saw the Act as a political expedient towards the securing of the throne. Certainly at the accession of William and Mary the oath of allegiance was used as a weapon to root out Jacobites. However, given William's attitude towards toleration, it is clear that the clause including the oath was also a bid by the Tories and the Anglican Church to prevent dissenters from holding office. There was also the 'fear of division among the clergy over the question of allegiance'. William's priorities were clear. By replacing the oath with an affirmation, he could clinch the support of the Quakers for the new regime. Without the support in both houses backed by the king's encouragement through his placemen, moreover, the bill would not have succeeded.[41] But the bill's success was dependent upon a sympathetic House, for which Penn appeared to campaign. He was not devoid of friends in high places in the new government to ease his efforts. Writing to Charles Talbot, duke of Shrewsbury, at the time of the 1695 general election, Penn asked for what amounted to a protection pass so that he could travel through the country.[42] The election proved to be what Penn was hoping for, because it returned a Whig majority. This underpinned a ministry dominated by the Whig Junto, all of whom were sympathetic to dissent and friends of Penn. Lord Somers, Charles Montagu, Thomas Wharton, and Edward Russell, earl of Orford made up the circle of managers on whom Penn relied to ease his path back to preferment by way of supporting Affirmation. Backed by a Whig-dominated House of Commons, the bill was virtually guaranteed passage, but not without a crucial delay, one which proved to be an opportunity for the king and the Quakers.

The attempt on the king's life resulted in members of parliament and the peers initiating an Address abhorring the bid to kill his majesty. Included in the wording of the Address was a call for revenge upon any who tried to kill the monarch. The Friends could not see their way clear to sign such a document until the offensive wording was eliminated, and they needed a means whereby they could attest to the final document without swearing. The final product proved suitable for most Quakers.

Initially the Affirmation Act was enacted for five years. Consequently, it became necessary for the Friends to put pressure on parliament to renew it. Penn continued that push for complete liberty of conscience while exhorting his brethren to be 'charitable' towards fellow Quakers who scrupled against the present wording of the bill.[43] He also warned them to be careful not to abuse the present Act for fear that its survival would be jeopardized.[44] It reached its final form in 1722, and by then the Quakers were regarded as being among the most loyal supporters of the Protestant succession of the House of Hanover. The passing of the Affirmation Act and Quaker subscriptions to the Association abhorring the plot to assassinate William II marked a crucial transformation in the process by which they were reconciled to the regime established by the Glorious Revolution.

· · ·

NOTES AND REFERENCES

1. PRO, PCR, 2/73, 24; *HMC Fleming*, 280, 285, 314.
2. BL Add. MS 70017, fo. 128, Charlwood Lawton to Trenchard, 26 July1693.
3. One who did claim to know was the bishop of Norwich, who wrote to the archbishop of Canterbury on 22 April 1691 to inform him that 'an honest Quaker assures me that Wm Penn is not laden up, nay he adds he is with friends here in towne'. Bodleian Tanner MS 32, fo. 83.
4. BL Add. MS 70015, fo. 79.
5. BL Add. MS 70017, fo. 128, Lawton to Trenchard, 26 July 1693.
6. *PWP*, III, p. 382, Penn to Friends in Pennsylvania, 11 Dec. 1693.
7. *PWP*, III, p. 332, Sidney to WP, 7 Nov. 1691.
8. The charter in Kinsale museum carries the Great Seal of Charles II! This was presumably because James had dropped his own seal in the Thames when he fled Whitehall.
9. E.g. Eveline Cruickshanks, 'Attempts to Restore the Stuarts, 1689–96', in Eveline Cruickshanks and Edward Corp (eds), *The Stuart Court in Exile and the Jacobites* (Edinburgh, 1995), p. 2, where Penn is placed in 'the most active group working for a restoration after 1689'.
10. These are in the Browne Manuscripts in Westminster Cathedral Archive. They were discovered by Dr Paul Hopkins, who used them for his Ph.D. thesis, 'Aspects of Jacobite Conspiracy in England in the Reign of William III' (Cambridge University, 1981), to claim that Penn was actively involved in Jacobite plots.
11. Thus the editors of Penn's papers, while expressing doubts about the authenticity of the letters in the Browne Manuscripts, concede that one might have been written by him, which they publish in *PWP*, III, pp. 664–6. 'Ironically', they claim, it is not Jacobite in tone, but on the contrary expresses concern about the threats from France and James II. The irony is on them, however, for the writer clearly adopted a pro-Williamite stance as a cover to communicate the weakness of William's regime as perceived by a Jacobite.
12. Clarendon Diary, 25 Feb. 1689: 'as I was walking over the Park I met William Penn, who confirmed the same to me, and told me, he believed it.'
13. Clarendon Diary, 28 Feb. 1689.
14. *PWP*, III, pp. 235–6, Penn to Shrewsbury, 7 Mar. 1689.
15. *PWP*, III, p. 251.
16. *PWP*, III, p. 65.
17. *PWP*, Penn to the earl of Nottingham, 31 July 1691, pp. 283–4.
18. *CSP Domestic 1690–91*, pp. 228, 244, Sidney to King; Carmarthen to King. Preston's evidence was apparently corroborated by Matthew

Crone. See his deposition in Wiltshire Record Office, Savernake Forest MSS, large vellum bundle of 'loose papers', unfoliated and undated. However, Preston refused to confirm Crone's story. *HMC Finch*, III, pp. 149, 308–45.

19. Huntington Library, San Marino, Calif., Ellesmere MS EL8584. For Penn's involvement in Jacobite activities and for a discussion of this document, see my forthcoming article in *Historical Research*.

20. Ellesmere MS EL8584.

21. *CSP Domestic 1690–91*, p. 282.

22. *CSP Domestic 1690–91*, p. 228.

23. *PWP*, III, pp. 351–2. Rochester had advised Penn to go to Pennsylvania.

24. *PWP*, III, pp. 263, 383.

25. PRO, CO, 391/7, fo. 97, 12 June 1692.

26. J.R. Woodhead, *The Rulers of London 1660–1689* (London, 1965), p. 179.

27. *PWP*, III, microfilm 6:828, Penn to Somers, 17 Apr. 1694.

28. PRO, CO, 389/13, fo. 48, Abstract of the Pensilvania Merchants Proposalls.

29. PRO, CO, 389/13, fos 47, 50–1, 60120v; *PWP*, III, pp. 397–8.

30. William Penn, *A Treatise of Oaths Containing Several Weighty Reasons Why the People Call'd Quakers Refuse to Swear* (1675), pp. 30, 161–2; Penn, *The Case of the Oaths Stated* (23 May 1689).

31. David Scott, 'Politics, Dissent and Quakerism in York, 1640–1670' (D.Phil. thesis, York University, 1990).

32. Evan Davies, 'The Enforcement of Religious Uniformity in England 1668–1700 with Special Reference to the Dioceses of Chichester and Worcester' (D.Phil. thesis, Oxford University, 1982); G.V. Bennet, *The Tory Crisis in Church and State 1688–1730* (Oxford, 1974); M.E.W. Jones, 'Ecclesiastical Courts in Oxford and Peterborough', *Transactions of the Royal Historical Society*, 5th ser. (1955), V.

33. *The Little London Directory of 1677: The Oldest Printed List of the Merchants and Bankers of London* (1863).

34. *HMC Ormonde*, VII, p. 121, 30 Aug. 1683.

35. FLL, *Book of Cases*, I, p. 228.

36. *Commons Journal*, X, 22–3, 6 Feb. 1688/89.

37. Durham Record Office (Pease Collection), 4/71(i), 3 Jan. 1698/99; Cheshire City Record Office (Assembly Records), A B/2, fo. 174, 10 Oct. 1672. The confusion over office holding can be traced back to the Declaration of Indulgence and the attempts to hold local offices, as in the case of the Chester City council elections when several Quakers were elected but were forced to decline when required to take the oath for the well governing and regulating of corporations.

38. Jonathan I. Israel, 'William III and Toleration', in Ole Peter Grell, Jonathan I. Israel, and Nicholas Tyacke (eds), *From Persecution to Toleration: The Glorious Revolution and Religion in England* (Oxford, 1991), pp. 129–70.

39. As quoted in the *Anthology of Poems on Affairs of State*, ed. George de F. Lord (New Haven, 1975), p. 443; Gilbert Burnet, *A History of His Own Time*, 6 vols (Oxford, 1833), IV, pp. 693–4.
40. Thomas Babington Macaulay, *The History of England from the Accession of James the Second*, ed. Charles Firth, 6 vols (London, 1914), II, p. 814.
41. Henry Horwitz, *Parliament Policy and Politics in the Reign of William III* (Manchester, 1977), pp. 21–3; Horwitz, *Revolution Politicks: The Career of Daniel Finch, Second Earl of Nottingham, 1647–1730* (Cambridge, 1968), pp. 87–8.
42. *PWP*, III, pp. 414–15.
43. Clements Library, University of Michigan, Ann Arbor (Quaker Collection), 1710; *PWP*, microfilm 6:519.
44. FLL, *Book of Cases*, II, pp. 238–42, 234–5; in 1715 the Act was made perpetual in England, then in Scotland, then in the plantations for five years.

Chapter 6

PROPRIETOR

Hardly had Penn got the proprietorship of his colony back than it was faced with a new threat. In 1696 colonial policy in England was given a significant new emphasis by the passing of yet another Navigation Act and the creation of a Board of Trade and Plantations. Both were inspired by reports from Edward Randolph that the Crown was losing revenue due to it by massive evasion of the Navigation Acts in America, especially by the charter and proprietary colonies. Randolph had been an indefatigable agent of the Crown since his appointment to the colonial customs service under Charles II. It seemed as if scarcely a creek or cove from New England to the Chesapeake was not subject to his scrutiny. His recommendations led directly to the 1696 Navigation Act.[1]

Randolph dwelt on the ineffectual collection of colonial duties. His memorial was taken seriously, because warnings were sent to the proprietor of Pennsylvania, as well as the chartered and proprietary colonies of Rhode Island and Carolina, not to trade with the Scots. This prohibition arose out of the Darien affair. In 1695 the Scottish parliament passed an Act incorporating the Company of Scotland trading to Africa and the Indies. The object of this company was to found a colony on the isthmus of Panama, then known as Darien. This colony, called New Caledonia, was intended to give Scots the opportunity to catch up with other European nations in the colonization of the New World. Darien was so strategically placed that a settlement there could effectively combine eastern and western commerce in the way that the Panama canal was to do two hundred years later. The scheme was so attractive to investors that most Scots with any liquid capital subscribed to it. Unfortunately English merchants objected, since the scheme antagonized other European powers, not least Spain, which claimed sovereignty over Darien. These objections led to restrictions on the activities of Scots in the English empire.

In 1696, a new and improved Navigation Act 'for preventing frauds and regulating abuses in the plantation trade' was passed. The Act attempted to close loopholes left by the previous one by specifically aiming at stopping the Scots trade with the proprietary and chartered colonies. Additionally, it required goods to be shipped only on ships built in England, Ireland, or America. It increased the penalty for fraudulent security certificates to forfeiture of ships and goods. Parliament also recognized the threat of the growing independence of the proprietary colonies and curbed them by making them more accountable to the Crown. This began from the top down. Governors were required to take an oath to uphold the navigation laws and, if found negligent, they were to be fined a hefty £1,000. If proprietors of colonies appointed governors to act for them their appointments had to be approved by the Crown. Colonial customs officers were to be appointed by the governors and the governors were held accountable to the English customs commissioners for the officers' behaviour. Vice-admiralty courts were to be introduced into the colonies to try offences against the Navigation Acts. The clause which, although not naming Penn specifically, had the greatest impact upon him and his colony was that prohibiting the selling of land by proprietors to other than 'natural-born subjects of England, Ireland, Wales, or Berwick without prior consent of the crown by order in council'.[2] Not only did this clause stop Scottish traders buying land in the king's colonies, something which Randolph accused Penn of allowing in the lower counties, it was also a death blow to the revived Susquehanna Company, some of whose subscribers were Scottish.[3]

Where the Navigation Act stemmed directly from alleged depredations in the colonies, the Board of Trade and Plantations was created out of the dissatisfaction felt by English merchants over the government's handling of the country's trade, the increasingly precarious trade balance, and the loss of ships due to war and the piracy that accompanied it. William's priority in building up the naval forces was at the expense of the protection of merchant shipping. There was an attempt to stem this problem with the fitting out of Kinsale as an advance base for ships to sail out to meet the French cruising on the western side of Britain, but the port was not completed until 1695. By then, the tide of the war had turned in favour of the English. Nevertheless, the mercantile community viewed this as an insidious plot to undermine English trade by the Dutch king. Pennsylvania's government was implicated in these concerns. The businessmen's perception of the current trade committee of the privy council was that they had little influence over its decisions. This feeling of inadequacy was emphasized by the royal approval of the formation of the Scottish East India Company. English investors in the colonies feared that the Scottish trade would hinder their own. Whether the fear was justified or not is irrelevant. The perception that it was real was cause enough to consider alternatives to the current way of dealing with colonial policy.

Pamphlets and tracts expressed concern over how the lack of credit and the war were adversely affecting trade. The mercantile magnate Josiah Child wrote an analysis of the war's effect on the economy, while offering solutions to the cash-flow problem that the trade was experiencing.[4] But peppered throughout the first half of the 1690s were tracts which attested to the growing importance of England's trade with her Atlantic colonies and the necessity of getting a firmer grip on them.[5]

Losses of ships costing thousands of pounds due to privateering and piracy were alarming incidents. Toward the end of 1695 an investigation was launched in the House of Lords into losses experienced by merchants trading with the colonies. While the Pennsylvania merchants' loss was less than the Barbados merchants' loss of £387,100 or the Leeward Island merchants' loss of £138,000, for instance, their losses, amounting to £11,800, were not insignificant. The problem of piracy was exacerbated by disorganization over sending convoys to protect merchant shipping. Sometimes the convoy was not put together in time and the merchant ships, already laden, would sail alone. Sometimes, too, the convoy was operated by inexperienced seamen and consisted of old ships which got separated from the group and became vulnerable to privateering. There was also the problem of English crews turning to piracy because it was more profitable. The case of Captain Kidd is the most notorious example, but it illustrated the increasing problem on the high seas. Compounding this dilemma was the collusion with smuggling and piracy of some colonies, including Pennsylvania and its lower counties.

Towards the end of the war, there were moves by the mercantile community and parliament to rectify these problems. A Board of Trade was created out of the necessity to get a grip on colonial affairs and as an attempt to curb the Crown. The king had agreed to its formation, but he was reluctant to sign the patent, as a result of which the Country opposition in the House of Commons, led by Robert Harley, proposed to set up a Board appointed by, and answerable to, parliament. In the event the ministers managed to stave off the opposition and create a Board appointed by the Crown, but not without a struggle. They carried one resolution by only one vote. Nevertheless, the Board of Trade and Plantations was successfully established in May 1696.[6]

Penn's reaction was mixed. On the one hand the Navigation Act and the Board could be of assistance to his own attempts to exert proprietorial control over anti-proprietorial elements in the colony. But the Act would adversely affect his own plans to develop Pennsylvania's economy through the extension of the fur trade by way of the Susquehanna Company. More ominously, the Board was used by his old antagonist Randolph as a means of exercising Crown control over his proprietorship. In his Memorial, which led directly to the Navigation Act and indirectly to the setting up of the Board of Trade, Randolph proposed a scheme which would effectively strike at the heart of Penn's authority. It provided for the proprietaries and chartered colonies to be brought under more direct control of the Crown by the introduction of vice-admiralty courts into them. For this purpose Pennsylvania and the three lower counties were to be split. Vice-admiralty courts in Pennsylvania were to be placed under the governor of New York, while those in Delaware would be assigned to Maryland, which would prevent illegal trafficking in tobacco by the merchants of the lower counties. In this Randolph was backed by the governor of Maryland, Francis Nicholson, who accused Penn's colonists of colluding with Scots in the smuggling of tobacco to destinations in Scotland or Europe without paying duty, in cases with flour or bread at each end to delude the customs officials.

The introduction of the vice-admiralty courts into the colonies was also a direct attack upon the powers of the colonial governments and one which would provoke a reaction from the Pennsylvania assembly. Until the creation of the vice-admiralty courts, there was no direct authority from the Crown to effectively prosecute colonial offenders against the navigation laws. Too often colonial courts were limited in their duties or failed to convict offenders who, for instance, evaded the payment of duties to the customs officers. The Board's aim was to get a grip on the proprietary colonies and this was given direction by Blathwayt and Randolph. The two men left little hope for the Pennsylvania government to continue in its semi-autonomous behaviour. Blathwayt was associated with Lord Baltimore in the days of the boundary dispute between Pennsylvania and Maryland. Randolph was an ardent centralist. However, the Board's policies were not necessarily in conflict with the proprietor. Penn was just as anxious as the Board, albeit for different reasons, to gain a firm hand over his colony. He actually planned to sell his interest as proprietor. However, his intentions would be thwarted if the colony was left in its present chaotic state. Writing years later, Penn's secretary, James Logan, confirmed that Penn intended from the beginning to use the colony as an investment and eventually sell its government while retaining its territory. But the problems over collection of rents from his tenants throughout his proprietorship created an obstacle to selling off the colony.[7] Penn's investment in the colony was not realizing a profit. His attempts were continually thwarted, either through his failure to successfully charter companies or through the inability to collect rents. With the exception of the period of his visit to the colony just after its founding, there was flagrant disobedience of his wishes and blatant ignoring of the charter terms and English laws. Nevertheless, he could not allow the Board to impose its authority over the proprietorship to the extent where he could be threatened with a takeover. Consequently, Penn used his interests with other proprietors to head off Randolph and Blathwayt's two-pronged attack, namely to establish Crown-appointed officials, such as attorney-generals, in the colonies and to redirect proprietorial powers to the Crown. With the help of colonial cronies such as Craven, Daniel Coxe, Colleton, Berkeley, and John Winthrop, two petitions were presented to the king protesting against the actions of the Board. Randolph charged Penn with overstating his powers by accusing him of saying that his proprietorial power outstripped the authority of the Board when it came to extending its authority via the admiralty court in the colony.

That the colonial governments did not erect admiralty courts, even though there was provision in their charters, was both a legal technicality and a matter of budget. Technically, breaches of the navigation laws had thus far been prosecuted in common law courts. The only need for the admiralty courts was for the 'condemnation of prises', which were few, and the expense of that could not be afforded. This much was said by Penn and other proprietors in their petition to the Board in December 1696. In January, this petition was followed by another to the king requesting that the proprietors might, according to their charters, commission their governors as vice-admirals in the colonies with 'such powers relating to the Admiralty jurisdiction, as the governors of yo[u]r Ma[jes]tys other plantations have'.[8] A month later, the problem was taken out of their hands when Attorney-General Thomas Trevor addressed the legality of it all, saying that the king had every right to erect courts of admiralty. With that decision, a vice-admiralty judge in the person of Robert Quary was appointed for Pennsylvania, West Jersey, and Maryland. Quary seemed suited for the job because of his past experiences, first as deputy secretary and acting governor of Carolina, then as a resident of Pennsylvania.

Meanwhile, Penn requested a copy of Randolph's charges. When this was not forthcoming, he used his connections with Charles Mordaunt, earl of Monmouth and later of Peterborough, to obtain one. While Randolph may have had the ear of Blathwayt, Penn used his relationships with powerful political figures to evade Randolph's charges. With connections on both sides of the Atlantic, pressure could be brought to bear on the Board over its centralization policy.

The Board of Trade became fully operational after the formal ending of the war with France, and with it Randolph was able formally to bring the charges of fraud against Pennsylvania. In the charge, Penn's infirm governor, William Markham, was accused of taking bribes from privateers, not least his son-in-law.[9] Furthermore, Randolph asserted that Penn never really had the right of government of the lower counties. Although Penn was able to slap down Randolph's assertion on this count with proof in his favour, he now had to put up an argument against sending men for New York's defence. He claimed that New York was not necessarily the frontier for the colonies. In fact, he asserted Pennsylvania's immediate problems on its western boundaries. This was a complete reversal of the argument by the provincial government, and Penn's earlier stand, that the colony was well insulated from attack.[10] Notwithstanding his ingenuous defence, implementation of the Navigation Act was straightforward, with an order issued in April 1697 to proprietors to observe the laws. This was followed in May by an order specifically for proprietors, whose governors were not nominated by the king, to sign a bond. Penn tried avoiding this requirement as long as possible, for, in December, William Popple was writing to him reminding him that he still had not signed the bond. Penn's dilemma was further compounded by more charges that the Pennsylvania government was still protecting pirates. The first target of the newly constituted Board was 'the war on piracy'.[11]

The second aim of the Board was to turn the proprietary colonies into Crown colonies.[12] This was very ominous for Penn. Already Maryland had been taken from Lord Baltimore and placed under the government of the Crown as a forfeit for the proprietor's dubious role in the Revolution. Penn himself had temporarily lost Pennsylvania for similar reasons. The drive against the other proprietary colonies was to achieve success in 1702 when New Jersey was taken over by the Crown. Although Pennsylvania and the Carolinas successfully resisted the Board's efforts under William and Anne to transform their status, this was not a foregone conclusion. On the contrary, for the rest of his life Penn felt threatened by the drive against his proprietorship. His strategy was to stave it off until he could do a deal with the Crown on his own rather than the Board's terms. In this struggle he was to exploit every ounce of his political influence and use all his contacts among prominent politicians. He succeeded so well that Pennsylvania was to survive as a proprietary colony down to the American Revolution.

* * *

The first salvo in the assault on the proprietary colonies after the establishment of the Board of Trade was fired in the House of Lords in February 1697. The House set up a committee chaired by the earl of Rochester to consider them. Randolph produced for it a list of proprietors which concluded 'that a clause be brought in to invest the government of all the proprieties in his majesty'.[13] Pennsylvania was singled out as being most notoriously in need of resumption, and Penn was hauled before the committee. There he was warned by the chairman, Rochester, that 'if there be further complaint against the Proprietors . . . the Parliament may possibly take another course in this matter which will be less pleasing to them'.[14]

Penn got the message that he was in serious trouble and needed all the help he could muster to get out of it. Ominously, one of his earlier allies, Rochester, who had helped him get the charter for Pennsylvania, was now backing Randolph and leading the attack against him. He therefore pulled out all the stops to counter this assault.

An early ally who proved pivotal in Penn's fight against the initial attack on his colony was Richard Coote, first earl of Bellomont. Bellomont was a Whig, and had considerable influence with Lords Shrewsbury and Somers, as well as with John Locke, one of the first commissioners on the Board of Trade. Letters to and from Shrewsbury and Somers show the effect of this influence. Shrewsbury, writing to Penn, was 'persuaded' by Bellomont that Penn was sincere in his protestations. More significant was Bellomont's friendship with Locke.[15] In the final analysis, it was Locke's influence that directed the Board's policy, which resulted in Bellomont's appointment to the governorship of New York in place of Fletcher in 1698. In return for his help in contesting Randolph's accusations, Bellomont wanted Penn's assistance in his bid for the governorship of New York. To do this, Fletcher had to be removed. Here Penn was able to help by organizing colonial protests against Fletcher. Penn was not above a dirty tricks campaign when he presented a letter from a former deputy collector for New York, Peter Delanoy, complaining of Fletcher's abuse of authority as governor. The fact that the letter was already eight months old and exaggerated Fletcher's behaviour out of proportion to the situation did not bother Penn. Fletcher was accused of prancing around town in a carriage drawn by six horses. In fact, this was part of the negotiating process between the governor and the five Indian nations. He was trying to impress them by driving the chiefs of the nations around town in his buggy. The smear was followed by a petition against New York by the New Jersey proprietors complaining that Fletcher was trying to extort duties from them. The same complaint was being made by Connecticut's Governor

Winthrop. Added to these were other charges ranging from bribery, aiding pirates, corrupt appointments, to generally being insulting to the colonists. Penn clearly did not consider these attacks personal, just business. Fletcher was simply in the way, because when Bellomont took over the governorship in 1698, Penn advised Fletcher to 'linger about' for a while and he would obtain for him the government of Maryland. Maryland's governor, Francis Nicholson, certainly knew of this presumption. For Fletcher's part, he abhorred such a comment and resolved to depart for England.[16] The magnitude of Penn's 'great interest' at court was taken seriously enough for prayers to be offered up that Nicholson would survive the Quaker's onslaught. Penn's hints to Fletcher that he could influence the Board to remove Nicholson from Maryland took on significance when Nicholson actually was shifted to the governorship of Virginia through the influence of another member of the Board, John Locke. As Robert Quary, no friend of Penn, wrote to the Board of Trade from Philadelphia in 1699, 'it is the general discourse of this place that Mr Penn hath greater interest at Court now than ever he had in King James's reign'.[17]

Penn was not just indulging in a smear campaign to save his own position. He recognized the problem of defence in the colonies and he was well aware of the lack of cooperation among the individual governments on this issue. He was concerned with the illegal trade that was operating in the colonies. Both these issues, he knew, would have a detrimental effect on his powers as proprietor. He was also anxious to neutralize Randolph's influence. He therefore produced two proposals. One was to shore up the defence of the colonies and the other was to resolve the problem of fraud. *A Briefe and Plaine Scheame how the English colonies in the North parts of America may be made more useful to the Crown and one another's peace and safety with an universal concurrence* was the result of Penn's consultation with fellow proprietors and colonial agents over how to safeguard their rights, while addressing the problem of the colonial governments. It appeared to have the backing of Blathwayt, according to Bellomont. The draft which Penn presented to the Board in February the following year had been in the making since the previous autumn. It stressed the coming together of the colonies' representatives in North America at least once a year. This 'congress to consist of twenty persons' would be to 'hear and adjust all matters of complaint or difference betweene province and province' over problems such as debts, frauds, and supplying quotas of men during wartime. All this would take place, of course, under the supervision of the king's commissioners.

Further proposals were made in 1697 for the advancement of trade which were clearly a compromise to meet the aims of the Board while circumventing Randolph's attack on the proprietaries. Here Penn used his long relationship with Secretary of State Trumbull to influence the privy council and particularly Sunderland to 'speak, as he promest me he would to the K[in]g', adding that he hoped Sunderland would also speak with other members of the council to look with favour on the proprietors and not 'at the most fals[e] insinuation of a little officer'. Clearly, the little officer was Randolph.[18] The first proposal outlined the major concerns of the colonies and possible solutions, emphasizing the material advantages of and ways to capitalize on colonial produce. In order to accomplish this end, three things were necessary: more people, time, and discipline. This could be achieved by his proposal for a colonial congress set out in his *Briefe and Plaine Scheame*.

Another proposal sent to the Board a week later suggested that masters and commanders of ships post £2,000 security. Copies of the contents of the ship were to be kept by the collector of the plantation, and the master, and a third copy was to be sent to the custom house in London so that the ship would be forced to land first in England. Further provision was made for a numbering system for certificates so as to prevent false ones being produced. There would also be more encouragement for cruisers in the seas to detect ships coming from places other than directly from English ports.

To encourage commerce and reduce the temptation of illegal trade, Penn advocated free access between colonies, much as there was in England between counties. This proposal was partly an attempt to heal a long-standing problem between Maryland and Pennsylvania over excess charging of duties between the two colonies. However, this is where Penn's three principles – people, time, and discipline – had to be implemented. There had to be enough people to produce the needed commodities. Time had to be allocated for the paying of customs duties, and there had to be discipline of the work-force. The present Act of Parliament made it difficult to encourage foreigners to settle in the plantations. Further, to encourage investors in the colonies, no imposition of duties should be made within a seven-year period during which the price of the commodity was set, while, at the same time, more duty should be imposed on foreign goods. Lastly, some kind of discipline should be enforced so that industry would flourish. Wages, for instance, would be high enough so that the common people no longer had to live hand to mouth, but moderate enough to encourage them to live in sobriety and industry. In the end, the proposals were rejected, no doubt because they smacked of increasing colonial autonomy. The Crown was not in the business of decentralizing. Quite the contrary, it sought to bring the colonies, including Pennsylvania, more directly under its control.

The year 1698 found Penn better placed than at any time since the Revolution to exploit his political clout to stave off the drive against Pennsylvania. For the general election held that summer was the first at which Quakers were allowed to poll by affirming rather than swearing an oath to the returning officers, thanks to the Affirmation Act of 1696. As he was widely regarded as their leader, Penn was thought to be able to deliver the votes of the Quakers to aspiring candidates. Thus the marquis of Normanby wrote to him 'desiring your help toward an Election of a Knight of the shire for Worcestershire, since Mr William Walsh is put upon standing for it by all those of his own principle there. I mean such as are of a larger mind & more indulgent to all mankind than to exclude any sect from an equality of libertyes & advantages.'[19] By this he presumably meant those who supported the Affirmation Act. The fact that Normanby was a Tory while Walsh was a Whig showed that support for the Quakers came from across the political spectrum. This is further revealed by the range of contacts which Penn was able to make as a result of his assumed electoral influence. Lord Poulet, another Tory, wrote to request his support in a by-election the following year because of 'the great interest . . . you have thro out this Kingdom'.[20]

Penn's influence in the elections of 1698 also appears to have been instrumental in cementing a relationship with Robert Harley, the leader of the Country opponents of the Whig ministry at the time. The first surviving letter of Penn's to Harley refers to elections in Buckinghamshire, where his own influence was greatest. Penn recognized that Harley appealed to backbench Tories as well as Whigs when he asked him to resist any 'persecuting temper' that might arise in the Commons, observing that 'I know thy double Influence in the House, to moderate one sort [Tories] and to Excite tother [Whigs] to help us'. He asked him to remind MPs that 'Liberty of Conscience is one of the Articles of the Originall Contract of this Revolution'. He also requested a favour of Harley 'in case anything should be started that should concern the Plantations & especially those in Propriety. Pray be a friend to the Absent.'[21] Penn was about to absent himself from the country, having been virtually ordered by the Board of Trade to go to Pennsylvania and put its affairs in order. He was to be away from England from September 1699 to December 1701.

While he was away something did indeed come up which concerned the proprietary colonies – a serious bid to resume them by the Crown. The first shot across the bows came in March 1700 when the Board presented to parliament a report on its activities since its creation in 1696. William Blathwayt, the commissioner with the most authority on the Board, and a determined opponent of charter and proprietary colonies, drew attention to the 'great irregularities' in their government. The report recommended their reduction 'to a more regular conduct and complyance with their duty in reference to the Trade of England'. As the historian of the Board's activities in these years observes, 'this was not a brazen call for resumption . . . but it was not surprising that William Penn feared some trouble from the Commons in the next Parliament'.[22]

In fact the main threat to his position came from the Lords, where a bill to resume the chartered and proprietary colonies received its first reading on 24 April 1701. It maintained 'that the severing of such power and authority from the Crown and placing the same in the hands of subjects hath by experience been found prejudicial and repugnant to the Trade of this Kingdom and to the welfare of his Majesty's other plantations in America and to his Majesty's revenue arising from the customs by reason of the many irregularities committed by the Governors of those plantations and by those in authority there under them by incouraging and countenancing pirates and unlawful traders'.[23] On 3 and 17 May two lawyers, John Dodd and Constantine Phipps, who had been retained by proprietors and others affected by the bill, appeared in the Lords to make Penn's case against it.[24] Penn's son William was called in to give evidence on 12 May. Penn himself, absent three thousand miles away, anticipated this onslaught. He made sure that a broadsheet was published in England early in 1701 reflecting the essence of his argument in favor of proprietary colonies: *The Case of William Penn, Esq. As to the Proprietary Government of Pensilvania*. Penn argued that divesting him of dominion over his colony would deprive him of his property just as much as removing his right to the territory: 'Powers are as much property as soil; and this is plain to all who have Lordships or Mannours in England.' He also pleaded the advantage of a proprietary government over that of a royal official who has no other interest than to serve his time and collect his salary.[25]

Penn apparently briefed the counsel who appeared for him when the bill was before the Lords. They read letters he had written in 1697 and 1698 and a proclamation he had issued against pirates. But Quary, amply briefed by the Board of Trade, produced a formidable array of evidence against him.[26] One of the claims Quary made was that two ships condemned by the court of admiralty in Pennsylvania had nevertheless sailed to England, 'relying on his great interest at Court to have them cleared'.[27]

Penn also instructed his son, William junior, in a letter of 2 January 1701 how to defend his interests against the threat to his proprietorship.[28] He furnished William with a list of points to make in favour of proprietary colonies, repeating some of the points made in the tract and adding others. He then asked him to enlist thirteen politicians in his cause. Their names reveal the wide range of his contacts. The first three to be mentioned by Penn were Lords Sunderland, Godolphin, and Rochester. These had been the 'Chits' of Charles II's reign who had helped to get him his charter in the first place. They were also now in power, having ousted the Junto at the turn of the century. Sunderland was not in office, but the *eminence grise* behind ministerial appointments. Godolphin was head of the Treasury and Rochester lord lieutenant of Ireland. Next to occur to him were two peers whose acquaintance he had made in William's reign. The earl of Monmouth had helped him with his dispute with the Board of Trade in 1697. As we have seen, the marquis of Normanby had drawn on his electoral influence in 1698. The next peer he named was the earl of Carbery, whom he probably knew through his first wife, who had been courted by Carbery, a man known to Pepys as 'one of the lewdest fellows of the age'.[29] Penn then listed three prominent Whig peers, Cholmondley, Devonshire, and Macclesfield. Immediately after these he named four Tory members of the House of Commons, Sir Christopher Musgrave, Sir Edward Seymour, Robert Harley, and Colonel James Graham.[30]

Penn also got the Society of Friends in London to campaign against the bill. On 9 May the Meeting for Sufferings formed a committee to lobby against it. Quaker brethren such as George Whitehead, Henry Gouldney, Edward Haistwell, and Daniel Quare had honed the technique of lobbying in the early days when fighting for toleration. They now saw the Board's attack as an assault on religious freedom, particularly at a time when a dispute within the Quaker ranks led by George Keith resulted in what became known as the Keithian schism. Keith led the attack upon Quakers, and the Friends were convinced that this filtered into the attack upon the colonial charter. Hence their stand against it in 1701.[31]

Whether William Penn junior received help from any of these when he appeared before the Lords on 12 May is not known. The bill received its second reading on the 23rd and was committed to a third reading. But the committee never met, its meetings being put off until parliament was prorogued and then dissolved. This was probably because the houses were distracted with the impeachment proceedings against the Junto, which took up much of their time this session. As a result the bill to resume proprietary governments was lost.

The Crown's attempt at taking over the proprietaries was defeated but was sure to be brought up in the next session of parliament. As soon as Penn heard the news in September, he made plans to return to

England. Other changes were occurring over the summer of 1701. Parliament was prorogued in June and a struggle for power was again in the offing in the corridors of Whitehall. The Whigs were trying to get William III to dissolve parliament and change the composition of the ministry in their favour, but for the moment the king did little to appease them. He was otherwise engaged in Holland, trying to get an alliance together against Louis XIV. Penn was kept abreast of the situation and made sure of that through his contacts with both Tory and Whig friends. It was through them that he gleaned the possibility that, though the resumption bill had been defeated, the new session in the autumn might turn out differently. Penn contemptuously called the likes of Quary, Randolph, and Jeremiah Basse of New Jersey 'little tools' of the anti-proprietary groups operating at Whitehall. As Randolph's biographer observes, 'very few men could bring [Penn] to the edge of profanity, but Randolph was one of them. "He is the Scandal of the Government . . . as arbitrary a villain as lives . . . The Fellow is crafty and industrious but as false and villainous as possible . . . His name and a lye goes for the same thing 1000 Miles upon the Continent of America".'[32]

If the policy of resumption came to pass, then Penn wanted compensation for the loss of the government of his colony. He hoped that he would be reimbursed for his property at not less than £20,000.[33] This last point is the vital clue to Penn's motives.[34] Penn was used to threats of colonial takeover by the Crown, and he had experienced the loss of his charter once before. This time, however, the situation was different because he finally decided that if he could not keep his government he would sell it.

Once Penn returned to England, he followed up his attack by meeting with fellow colonial proprietors and political allies. He continued to fight full reunification by suggesting a watered-down version whereby the civil government would remain in the proprietors' name while the military government would be reunited to the Crown.[35] But the Board saw the proposal leading to headaches of the kind the Crown had to endure with a similar set-up in Massachusetts, and declined to take up the offer.

In November 1701 the king dissolved parliament and called for an election. This snap dissolution caused the Tory ministry he had formed earlier in the year to collapse. Godolphin resigned from the Treasury in protest at it. Advised by Sunderland, William turned again to the Junto and began to reconstruct the ministry during the general election held in December. The new parliament which met in January 1702, however, still had a Tory majority and elected Harley again as Speaker, defeating a Whig candidate. Meanwhile Penn had arrived back in London to lead the campaign against the reunification bill. He threw in his lot with Harley, who had been forward among the politicians who opposed the resumption bill and had looked after the interests of the absent proprietor. Penn had written to his 'Honored Friend' the Speaker before he left Pennsylvania: 'I cannot for bear thinking my selfe safe where I have such a friend in the Chaire.'[36]

The two men had much in common. Both came from dissenting backgrounds. Their Presbyterian fathers had played prominent roles in the civil wars and Interregnum and had made their peace with the Restoration regime. Harley and Penn, however, had refused to conform. Harley remained a Presbyterian and attended meetings until 1704. Penn had become a Quaker. They had been on opposite sides during the reign of James II, when Penn was a Courtier while Harley captured Worcester for the Prince of Orange during the Revolution. During the 1690s, however, their paths converged when Harley led the Country opposition to the Court and sought to set up a Board of Trade appointed by parliament rather than by the Crown. When this move failed and a Board nominated by the king was established in 1696, it pursued policies which Penn perceived as opposed to his interests, and he sought allies to protect himself against them, prominent amongst whom was Harley. He had been prepared to protect Penn's interests if the resumption bill had ever been introduced into the Commons, where as Speaker he would have had formidable influence over the debates. That had been unnecessary in 1701, when the bill had not passed all its stages in the House of Lords. In 1702, however, with a new bill threatened, Harley's help could again prove invaluable. Fortunately for Penn, although there were further enquiries into the colonial governments in the House of Lords in February, they failed to result in another bill, since the session was brought to an early end with the sudden death of William III on 8 March.[37]

The accession of Queen Anne transformed the political scene in Penn's favour. His old friend Godolphin was appointed to the post of lord treasurer and, when parliament met later in 1702, his new friend Harley again became Speaker, this time as the ministerial rather than the opposition candidate. Together with the earl of Marlborough, who became commander-in-chief of the forces abroad, these three formed a formidable trio, known at the time as the triumvirate. Penn's relationship with these men gave him direct access to the very heart of power in England. It was to enable him to retain power over Pennsylvania.

Anne's other ministerial appointments were initially not good news for Penn. She kept her uncle, Lord Rochester, in his post of lord lieutenant of Ireland and she promoted the earl of Nottingham, leader of the High Church Tories and Penn's nemesis, to the senior secretaryship of state. Nottingham was credited with the appointment to the Board of Trade of two fellow Tories, Lords Dartmouth and Weymouth. These strengthened the position of the Tory Blathwayt, who had been the most zealous promoter of the bid to resume the proprietary colonies for the Crown.

Although no new bill for that purpose was to be presented to parliament under Anne, the Board did not drop its aim and continued to harass Penn. In April 1702 they summoned him to attend a meeting of the commissioners to answer charges brought against Pennsylvania by Robert Quary, judge of the vice-admiralty court in the colony. Quary's most serious charge upheld the jurisdiction of the court, claiming that Penn had invaded it by appointing water bailiffs on his own authority. His other charges included accusations that Penn had permitted illegal trade, left the colonists undefended, and had falsely claimed the right to the government of the three lower counties. Penn vigorously rebutted them all.[38] The Board referred the first charge to the attorney-general, who delivered his opinion in July 1702 that Penn had not infringed the authority of the vice-admiralty court by appointing water bailiffs.[39] This was a political as well as a judicial victory for Penn. As he wrote to his secretary James Logan on 21 June, 'The scene is much changed since the death of the king, the Church party advances upon the Whig, and yet I find good friends, sorely against some people's will.'[40]

Among his good friends were the 'triumvirs', Godolphin, Harley, and Marlborough. They helped him win the next round with the Board, which occurred over the summer of 1702 when it refused to ratify his appointment of Andrew Hamilton as his governor in Pennsylvania and Delaware. Penn informed Logan on 28 July that the lord treasurer, Godolphin, and the lord privy seal, Normanby, 'promess to recommend him [Hamilton] to the Queen the next Cabinet or have her reasons'.[41] In September Anne went to Bath with her husband Prince George of Denmark to try to cure his asthma. Godolphin accompanied her there, as did Sarah Churchill, the formidable wife of the earl of Marlborough, who was then on the Continent preparing for the campaign. They took advantage of the six weeks' access to the queen without any High Church Tory being present to impress upon Anne the necessity of relying upon moderate Tories and Whigs to pursue the war effort. They also gained an entrée for Penn, who went personally to wait on the queen at Bath to obtain her consent to Hamilton's appointment. After a two hours' audience she agreed to endorse it for one year, though only on condition that her approval of it did not imply that she had set aside her right to the lower counties on the Delaware. The Board seized on her reservations about Penn's title to the lower counties to challenge it, a challenge he responded to by claiming that it rested on 'deeds of feofment from the Duke of York, and his letter of Attourney . . . to give me possession, and submission, wch they readily did by Turf and Twig and Water'.[42] This did not satisfy the Board, which insisted that Penn acknowledge that the queen's approval of Hamilton's appointment 'shall not be construed in any manner to diminish or set aside her Majesties Claim of Right to the said three lower Counties'. Penn grudgingly signed a document to this effect on 10 December 1702.[43]

By the beginning of 1703 Penn felt that he had got the better of the Board. He was able to inform Logan that no resumption bill would be brought forward that year, and that he had persuaded the Board to adopt procedures from the court of chancery when dealing with complaints against colonial governors, so that the parties would have clear notification in writing of any charges. As a result, 'nobody may be murdered in the dark, a great reformation and relief, & for wch american Govermts owe me their good will'.[44] When the Board continued to pester him with what he considered to be petty questions he complained to Godolphin, and sought an interview with the lord treasurer to stop its harassment.[45] 'It is the General discourse of the Quakers that the Lords of Trade and Plantations are Mr. Penn's Enemies,' observed Quary in July, 'but that he vallues them not, having a greater Interest then all of them, and shall be able to Carry on all his designs in spite of them.'[46]

The most important of Penn's designs was an offer he made to the Board in May to sell the government of Pennsylvania to the Crown.[47] This seems to have been an odd moment to choose, when he had clearly got the upper hand in his dealings with the commissioners.[48] Yet that he felt he had the advantage is implied in an observation he made on the proposal in a letter to Logan. 'I am actually in Treaty with the Ministers for my Govermt,' he wrote. 'I believe it repents some they began it; for now tis I that press it, upon pretty good terms, as well for the people as selfe.'[49] It is significant that he referred to ministers and not commissioners. Penn was not just dealing with the Board of Trade but with the ministry. Presumably those who regretted pressing the resumption of proprietaries were the earl of Nottingham, secretary of state, and Lord Weymouth, president of the Board of Trade, who had backed William Blathwayt's campaign against them. He went on to say that he hoped to settle on good terms 'in the judgemt of the wisest & best of my Frds'. He did not name those friends, but he was currently seeking the advice of Lord Treasurer Godolphin over his dealings with the Board. Just how close to Godolphin Penn was in 1703 is confirmed by the outcome of a remarkable deal which Blathwayt, clearly trying to keep on good terms with the triumvirs, offered to the duke of Marlborough. Edward Randolph, then in Philadelphia, informed Blathwayt in June about a tract of 150,000 acres of land in the disputed area on the border of Maryland and Pennsylvania, which he claimed had not been granted either to Baltimore or to Penn. Randolph also claimed that Penn was aware of this tract and was endeavouring to get the queen to grant it to him. He advised Blathwayt to approach Anne to get her to grant the land to him, possibly in conjunction with Lord Cornbury. On receipt of Randolph's letter, however, Blathwayt passed it on to Marlborough, suggesting that the duke should ask her for it. 'The only one I foresee may give any obstruction in this matter is Mr Pen,' Blathwayt observed. 'And because I know he has the favor of my L[or]d Treasurer it may not be amiss that your Grace do pre-engage his Lo[rdshi]p in this concern which cannot otherwise admitt of any difficulty.'[50] Nothing more appears to have come of this deal. Presumably Penn, with Godolphin's help, managed to scotch it. Certainly he kept in close touch with Godolphin and Speaker Robert Harley about the progress of the negotiations over the sale of the government of his colony.[51] It seems pretty clear, then, that the 'wisest and best' of Penn's friends who were advising him about the sale were the lord treasurer and the Speaker.

Penn apparently received an encouraging response to his offer, for on 18 June he sent the Board detailed proposals.[52] He would surrender the government of Pennsylvania for £30,000 on certain other conditions. Of these one of the most crucial was that he would receive a patent for the three lower counties 'according to a Grant begun by the Late King James, & had been finished had he stay'd one week longer at Whitehall'.[53] Penn had always been uneasy about his title to Delaware, as his pained reaction to the conditions attached to the queen's approval of Hamilton as governor had shown. He now wanted this to be confirmed. He also wished to keep some of his proprietary powers such as the right to nominate governors and vice-admirals. The Board's reaction to these proposals came in a report to the House of Lords on 16 December 1703. The commissioners essentially rejected Penn's terms as being 'very un-reasonable'. He was 'demanding not only a great sum of money, but in effect much larger powers from her Majesty than what he offers to yield, and likewise a new and positive grant of the three lower counties'.[54]

Penn cannot have helped his case with High Church Tories such as Nottingham and Weymouth by his support at this juncture of Daniel Defoe, who was in prison for publishing his controversial tract *The Shortest Way with the Dissenters* in December 1702. The immediate occasion of the pamphlet had been the progress through parliament of a bill backed by High Church Tories to outlaw the practice of occasional conformity, whereby dissenters qualified for public office by taking communion in the Church of England, in compliance with the letter of the Corporation Act of 1661, but thereafter broke its spirit by attending their own conventicles. *The Shortest Way* had been but one of many publications critical of the bill. Penn himself had published *Considerations on the Bill now depending for preventing occasional conformity*. He had taken up the cudgels of dissenters in general when he attacked the bill on no less than seven fronts, all of which contributed to the infringement of religious liberties gained from the Toleration Act of 1689. Thus he had homed in on the bill's wording of what constituted a 'truly scrupulous' conscience. Penn argued that such a term, as well as the word 'conventicle', could be 'misconstrued', producing the opposite effect from the intent of the bill. The object then could be an attempt to restrict the liberties of the person. What if, he asked, a person had to attend the funeral of a dissenter? Would that be considered a conventicle and therefore outside the law? There was not much in the bill which affected Quakers since they did not take communion, even occasionally, in the established Church. Penn, however, never operated solely from a Quaker platform but in the wider world of dissent. Hence his support for Defoe.

The Shortest Way with the Dissenters had gone much further than a mere critique of the contents of the occasional conformity bill. Adopting the guise of a high churchman, Defoe had called for the rooting out of dissenters, who were less than humane in the eyes of the Church and should be dealt with as such, by deportation if not by extermination. The earl of Nottingham took this seriously, and placed a notice in the official *London Gazette* offering a reward of £50 for the arrest of those responsible. Defoe's hoax had backfired, and he was arrested in the summer of 1703. Penn offered to intercede on Defoe's behalf and on 18 July 1703 wrote, apparently to Nottingham, requesting a reprieve for his fellow dissenter.[55] His intervention was unavailing, for Defoe was pilloried three times, fined, and imprisoned. But while it would add further weight to the dislike and suspicion in which Penn was held by High Church ministers, it could only have helped to cement his relationship with Harley, who respected Defoe's stance and arranged for his release from prison.

In the spring of 1704 changes were made in the ministry which reduced the influence of High Church Tories and strengthened that of Penn's friends, the 'triumvirs'. Nottingham resigned as secretary of state, and was replaced by Harley. There were also changes in the Board of Trade, from which Weymouth resigned as president. Although Blathwayt remained as a commissioner, he was removed from the post of secretary at war by the duke of Marlborough, signalling that his credit at court had been considerably weakened.

Penn's response to the Board's rejection of his proposals for Pennsylvania was to drop the request to continue exercising some of the powers he enjoyed as proprietor, and to reduce the amount of compensation for the loss of the government to £20,000. He had initially stipulated that amount in his draft proposal, and then increased it to £30,000, though he had since let Godolphin know that he would settle for £20,000.[56] But he never relinquished his claim to Delaware. Nor did the Crown concede it. This was the main sticking point which prevented a deal being struck with Penn, although negotiations continued to the eve of his death.[57]

Although the proposals eventually came to naught, they did help Penn in his disputes with the Board of Trade. For while the Board never ceased to complain about proprietary colonies, they dropped their campaign against them in general and against Pennsylvania in particular. As Penn wrote to James Logan in March 1704, 'I am more likely to keep my government than ever, or to have some equivalent for it; and take this from me: *that if you do but the Queen justice in her revenue, and discountenance illegal trade* . . . you will not be molested hence, but protected. This the *ministry* assures me here.'[58] Penn's friends in the ministry got the Board off his back. Thus, when news reached him that Hamilton had died in April 1703 he had to nominate another governor for Pennsylvania. This time his nomination, of the Anglican John Evans, went through smoothly. The queen passed it on to Nottingham with her approval, and the secretary forwarded it to the Board, which accepted it without condition. When Penn had to appoint a governor to replace Evans, whom he dismissed in June 1708, the Board was barely consulted. This was because by then the duke of Marlborough had arrogated to himself the appointment of colonial governors. Marlborough insisted on military men and recommended Captain Charles Gookin, an army officer, to the post. The only role played by the Board was to endorse the queen's approbation and to receive a £2,000 bond from Penn as surety for Gookin's good behaviour.[59] At a time when Penn was so strapped for cash that he was actually in a debtors' prison this was a prodigious sum to raise. It almost certainly came not out of his own pocket but from those of his ministerial friends.[60]

By then these were primarily Godolphin and Marlborough. Harley had resigned in February 1708 in protest at the appointment of Whigs in the administration. He would have regarded Marlborough's choice of a governor for Pennsylvania as another sign of this trend. For Gookin was an officer in the regiment of Thomas Erle, a colleague of Marlborough's, and a Whig member of parliament so close to Godolphin that he acted with a group in the Commons known as the 'Lord Treasurer's Whigs'.[61] Godolphin introduced Gookin to the queen at Windsor prior to the new governor's departure for Pennsylvania, and she wished him a good journey. As Penn observed with obvious satisfaction, Anne had approved of Gookin 'at first offer'.[62] The days when his nomination of a deputy to govern his colony would have been challenged by the Board of Trade were over.

· · ·

NOTES AND REFERENCES

1. See Michael Garibaldi Hall, *Edward Randolph and the American Colonies, 1676–1703* (Chapel Hill, 1960). Randolph was relentless to the end. The very boat which took him on his last voyage to America in 1702, where he was to die shortly afterwards, he impounded when it reached Virginia (ibid., p. 222).
2. Merrill Jensen (ed.), *English Historical Documents: Documents of the American Colonies to 1776*, 2nd edn (1969), IX, p. 359.
3. See Mary Geiter, 'The Incorporation of Pennsylvania and Late Stuart Politics', Ph.D. thesis (Cambridge University, 1993), p. 228.
4. Ibid., pp. 219–20.
5. Ibid., p. 220.
6. For the circumstances surrounding the creation of the Board see I.K. Steele, *Politics of Colonial Policy: The Board of Trade in Colonial Administration 1696–1720* (Oxford, 1968), pp. 3–18.
7. Deborah Logan (ed.), *Penn–Logan Correspondence* (1819), III, 317; Richard S. Dunn and Mary Maples Dunn (eds), *The World of William Penn* (University of Pennsylvania, 1986), pp. 37–52.
8. *PWP*, microfilm 7:293.
9. See Ellesmere MSS 9577–9581.
10. See Geiter, 'Incorporation of Pennsylvania', p. 244.
11. Steele, *Politics of Colonial Policy*, ch. 3. For a discussion of piracy in Pennsylvania see pp. 47, 55, 70, 144.
12. Steele, *Politics of Colonial Policy*, ch. 4.
13. Hall, *Edward Randolph*, p. 172.
14. Ibid., p. 174.
15. Peter Laslett, 'John Locke, the Great Recoinage, and the Origins of the Board of Trade: 1697–1698', *WMQ*, 3rd ser., 14 (1957), n. 82.
16. Ellesmere MS EL 9594, Nicholas Byard to Francis Nicholson, 30 Dec. 1697.
17. Huntington Library, Blathwayt MSS, Box 4, BL 2.
18. *PWP*, III, pp. 475–6; *HMC*, Downshire MS 75, I, pt. 2, p. 272.

19. *PWP*, III, p. 555.
20. HSP Acc. no. 637, Poulet to WP, 22 Apr. 1699; microfilmed in *PWP*.
21. *PWP*, III, p. 568, WP to Harley, 30 Jan. 1699.
22. Steele, *Politics of Colonial Policy*, p. 68.
23. *HMC House of Lords MSS*, IV, p. 315. Cf. the draft of the bill in Blathwayt's papers: Huntington Library, Blathwayt MSS, Box 5, BL 289.
24. *HMC Lords*, IV, pp. 315–16.
25. *The Case of William Penn Esq., as to the proprietary government of Pensilvania; which together with Carolina, New-Jersey, &c. is intended to be taken away by a bill in Parliament.* An anonymous reply, *Reflections on the Printed Case of William Penn, Esq.*, was clearly a religious attack.
26. *HMC Lords*, IV, pp. 317–55.
27. Ibid., p. 318.
28. *PWP*, IV, pp. 27–9.
29. *PWP*, I, p. 68 n.
30. Penn was writing so hastily that his handwriting deteriorated. He himself made corrections to his spelling of these names. This makes them hard to read. But what the editors of the Penn papers read as 'Sqr' Harley is probably 'Spr', an abbreviation for Speaker, Harley being Speaker of the House of Commons. Col Grimmill Penn originally wrote as 'Grime'. James Graham, formerly privy purse to James II and Tory MP for Westmorland, was known as Colonel Grimes. After Graham Penn added '&c', perhaps referring to other Harleyites. He also drew his son's attention to three Carolina proprietors who would be expected to support his case: Lords Shaftesbury and Bath, and Thomas Amy. He concluded his list with Lord Berkeley, who had family connections with the earl of Portland. Later he thanked the dukes of Devonshire and Somerset, Lords Dorset, Jefferies, Normanby, and Poulet, and Sir Heneage Finch, Robert Harley, John Howe, Sir Christopher Musgrave, and Sir Edward Seymour for their help. Whereas the peers comprised Whigs as well as Tories, the MPs were all Tories. *PWP*, IV, p. 73.
31. Steele, *Politics of Colonial Policy*, p. 73. Penn himself detected a religious motive behind the attack on proprietary colonies. 'For except Carolina,' he wrote to Charlwood Lawton on 27 August 1701, 'they were all granted to Non Conformists and then the meaning is that no Dissenters even in a wilderness at 3000 miles distance & at the other end of the world shall enjoy the powers first granted them for their Incouragement & Security in their Hasardous & most Expensive Enterprises.' *PWP*, IV, p. 73. There seems to have been little substance to confirm these suspicions. Steele, *Politics of Colonial Policy*, p. 80.
32. Hall, *Edward Randolph*, pp. 214–15.
33. In letters of 26 August 1701 to his 'noble friends in the House of Lords' he claimed Pennsilvania had cost him £30,000: 'if the king must have our Governments let us have satisfaction.' HSP Acc. nos. 391, 392, 393. *PWP* microfilm.

34. *PWP*, IV, pp. 66–74, WP to C. Lawton, 18 Aug. 1701.
35. *PWP*, IV, p. 153, Heads for a Bill for reuniting to the Crown severall Colonies under proprietary Governments particularly that of Pensilvania.
36. *HMC Portland*, IV, p. 19.
37. *HMC Lords*, V, pp. 77–93.
38. *PWP*, IV, pp. 160–5.
39. *PWP*, IV, pp. 176–7.
40. E. Armstrong (ed.), *Correspondence between William Penn and James Logan*, 2 vols (Philadelphia, 1872), I, p. 112.
41. *PWP*, IV, p. 179. Penn was also being assisted by the dukes of Queensberry and Somerset. Both were members of the cabinet, Queensberry as commissioner for Scotland, Somerset as master of the horse.
42. *PWP*, IV, p. 197.
43. *PWP*, IV, p. 200. Penn's reluctance to concede this point is indicated by his attempt to describe Anne's claim as her 'pretentions', a wording which the Board disallowed.
44. *PWP*, IV, pp. 206, 210, Penn to Logan, 24 Jan. 1703.
45. *PWP*, IV, p. 218, Penn to Godolphin, 12 Feb. 1703.
46. Quary to the Board of Trade, 25 July 1703, quoted in Steele, *Politics of Colonial Policy*, p. 79.
47. *PWP*, IV, p. 221.
48. The editors of *PWP* also clearly find Penn's sudden decision surprising, and speculate that he resolved to offer to sell his colony because he despaired of developments there, and because of his own deteriorating financial position (IV, p. 221). But there was no immediate crisis which could have prompted Penn to make the gesture out of despair, and in the political situation in which he found himself in England he had every reason to feel buoyant.
49. *PWP*, IV, p. 222, Penn to Logan, 6 June 1703.
50. BL Add. MS 61133, fos 81–3, Randolph to Blathwayt, 30 June 1703; Blathwayt to Marlborough, 12 Oct. 1703. I owe this reference to Professor Stephen Saunders Webb. Blathwayt ended his letter by requesting that if the proposal met with Marlborough's approval he would like to be 'your Grace's steward'.
51. *PWP*, IV, pp. 258–60, WP to Harley, 9 Feb. 1704. Penn refers to a letter he had written 'to our great Frd the Ld H Treasr'.
52. *PWP*, IV, pp. 224–6.
53. See below, pp. 61–2.
54. *PWP*, IV, p. 221.
55. *PWP*, IV, p. 228. Defoe wrote to Penn thanking him for his intercession on 12 July 1703 (ibid., pp. 228–9).
56. *PWP*, IV, pp. 225, 260.
57. See *PWP*, IV, pp. 318–21, 345, 353–60, 392–3, 571–3, 583–4, 681–6, 689–91, 725–6.

58. Deborah Logan (ed.), *Penn–Logan Correspondence*, I, pp. 271–2.
59. *PWP*, IV, pp. 607–8. There was no time limit on Gookin's governorship of Pennsylvania, as there had been when Hamilton was approved, though Penn had still to acknowledge that the queen was not waiving any claim to Delaware by approving of Gookin's appointment as governor of the three lower counties, which was at her pleasure.
60. It is significant that Penn did not appear to know the exact amount of the bond paid for Gookin's abiding by his duties as governor when he wrote to Logan on 3 March 1709 saying it was '2 or 3,000l' (*PWP*, IV, p. 638). He would surely have known it was £2,000 if he had paid it himself. There were rumours that the duke and duchess of Marlborough had paid it.
61. For a discussion of the 'Lord Treasurer's Whigs' see W.A. Speck, 'The House of Commons 1702–1714: A Study in Political Organisation' (D.Phil. thesis, Oxford University, 1966), pp. 186–94.
62. *PWP*, IV, p. 617, WP to Samuel Carpenter and others, 28 Sept. 1708.

Chapter 7

COLONIZER

At what point Penn was introduced to the potential of colonial development cannot be ascertained, but it almost certainly pre-dated his religious conversion. His knowledge of colonization most certainly stemmed from England's early colonial activities and he would have been aware of the kinds of development taking place across the Atlantic. English colonies in North America were of three types: chartered, Crown, and proprietary. Each of these could, and did, develop different kinds of governments according to the political outlook of their developers.

The first attempt at expanding the English empire in the direction of North America was through the formation of chartered companies such as the Virginia Company and the Massachusetts Bay Company. In the case of the Virginia Company, subscribers in the form of shareholders had a stake in the transatlantic ventures. The Massachusetts Bay Company subscribers comprised only those who also migrated to the New World. As a result, the Chesapeake area was established as a commercial endeavour while the Massachusetts Bay area was settled out of religious as well as commercial considerations. In both cases, chartered companies were seen by the Crown as a way to expand the English empire at relatively little expense. Only when the Virginia Company was in danger of going bankrupt, and Massachusetts exhibited rebellious behaviour, did the Crown assume complete control. Thus, where previously the companies had nominated the governors of the two colonies, the king now appointed them. Crown colonies therefore fell under the direct control of the monarchy. This only came about when there were problems in the colony which threatened England's empire or, as in the case of New York, through inheritance. In 1674, as part of the peace treaty with the Dutch, the Crown gained the area of New Amsterdam. Renamed New York, after the king's brother, James, duke of York, it became a Crown colony on James's accession to the throne. Proprietorships were the third way in which colonies were developed. There could be a number of proprietors involved in colonial ownership or only one. New Jersey and Carolina were run by more than one proprietor. New Jersey had as many as twenty-four at one time and Carolina had eight. Maryland, New York (until James became king), and Pennsylvania were sole proprietorships.

Another factor influencing Penn's interest in the colonies which invites speculation was the transatlantic activity of his father, Sir William. As a captain in the English navy in the 1650s, the elder Penn sailed across the Atlantic in an attempt to capture Hispaniola from the Spaniards. Although the expedition failed in its immediate objective it did succeed in capturing Jamaica, and the voyage may have been an eye-opener to future colonial ventures for the Penn family. However, the first direct evidence of the younger Penn's interest in a colonial matter is a letter of 1673 in which he recommended somebody, possibly a relative, to the duke of York for a post in either the Carolinas or Virginia.[1] He probably heard about the position in the colonies through friends of his father, amongst whom was one of the Carolina proprietors, George Monck, duke of Albemarle. Sir William Penn and Monck were contemporaries, who travelled in the same circles. Both had played crucial roles in the restoration of Charles II.

The next time we hear of Penn's colonial aspirations is in the mid 1670s as a trustee of New Jersey. Initially, the proprietorship of New Jersey was granted to Sir George Carteret and Sir John Berkeley for their loyalty to the Crown during the troubled years before the restoration of the Stuarts. As a gesture of gratitude for such loyalty, James granted a section of his New York proprietorship to Carteret and Berkeley. In 1674, Berkeley sold his half to a friend, Edward Byllynge, a Quaker. Because of lack of ready cash, Byllynge persuaded another friend, John Fenwick, to buy Berkeley out and hold the deed in trust until Byllynge could afford to reimburse Fenwick. Fenwick demanded a share of the property, whereupon Byllynge refused and a quarrel ensued. Rather than bring discredit to the Quaker community and lose the venture, the dispute was referred to a mediator, William Penn. The upshot was that three trustees, including Penn, were appointed to solve Byllynge's financial difficulties. Shares were sold and West New Jersey became a haven for the Quakers. To ensure complete political and religious freedom, which was not possible in England for dissenters at that time, a constitution was fashioned that would guarantee the right to vote and to hold office, and to worship according to one's belief without persecution. The West New Jersey Concessions and Agreements of 1676 provided a model for Penn's future involvement in the colonies.[2]

Before New Jersey could be marketed as a liberal domicile, however, there was a question over jurisdiction. By the time Byllynge had bought New Jersey, it had been taken by the Dutch and retaken by the English during the Anglo-Dutch wars. When England had regained the territory in 1674 by way of the Treaty of Westminster, Charles II's reconfirmation of the area from New York to New Jersey to his brother meant that James, in turn, had to reconfirm what he had initially given to Berkeley. When James learned that Berkeley had sold his portion to the Quakers, he seized the opportunity to claim jurisdiction over the New Jersey government. Consequently the concessions were hindered by the duke's claim, and this proved to be a problem for some time. As long as there was a question over the rights of New Jersey, attracting settlers would be very difficult. Because of New York's claim, it meant that its governor could demand authority to tax New Jersey. Penn's role in the affair was to be legal advocate. He had already made a name for himself in the courts from the Penn–Meade trial, so his reputation and his relationship with the Court would be effective in sorting out the legal quagmire. Penn set forth his argument against the duke's claim in *The Case of New Jersey Stated*, where he convincingly argued that the powers Berkeley acquired from the duke when he bought the land were passed on to the new owner. Furthermore he maintained that 'the conveyance he made us, Powrs & governmt are expresly granted, for that only could have induced us to buy it'. Penn used Lockean language and echoed the sentiment of the Magna Carta to press New Jersey's case by arguing in terms of natural rights and the consent of the people, phrases which reverberated down to the American War for Independence. Obtaining the right of government was essential to safeguarding the settlers' rights. Moreover, their rights as Englishmen, under English law, were being abused. They were part of a nation that conquered the wilderness, therefore to be treated as one of the conquered was against 'natural right' and to be taxed without a say in the matter was the equivalent of having their goods taken from them without their consent.[3] The decision was given in favour of New Jersey. In essence Penn had trumped the duke, secured the boundaries and rights of New Jersey, and extended his own holdings across the Delaware to Pennsylvania.

Even after he became proprietor of Pennsylvania, Penn remained involved in Jersey politics, up to 1702 when its charter was taken over by the Crown. Although Byllynge was the author of the Concessions, the West New Jersey constitution, who influenced him is up for speculation. Penn's influence in the development of this document cannot be positively ascertained, but it was in many ways more innovative than the constitutional arrangements for Pennsylvania.[4] Still, the concept of a more effective or actual representation formed the basis of the Penn-sylvania constitution and influenced later colonial political thought.

Reports from the other side of the Delaware River were as favour-able, if not more so, for expansion. By 1680, furs, which were the main item of trade, were already becoming scarce along the eastern coast of the colonies. Although New Jersey boasted an abundance of beaver, otter, black fox, and other furs further north of the colony, its territory was limited by its boundary with New York in the north while the Delaware River bordered the colony on its west side. Moreover, the position of the channel in the Delaware River made it difficult to get near the ever-receding source of pelt because it swung closer to the opposite shore.[5] This geographical fact may have further enticed Penn in the direction of setting up his own colonial venture.[6]

The founding of Pennsylvania, therefore, must be looked at in a broader context of the religious environment and in political terms. The colony was to be the political solution, born out of a political crisis at home, to the problem of dissent. If we look at the colony's development from that perspective, then the holy experiment, as Penn termed it, was indeed a success. The free practice of different faiths, except for Roman Catholicism, was necessary to a successful economy. Political participation by various religious groups was also a condition for a productive society. Penn was later to remark on that fact when he visited New York in 1683. While there he attended a meeting, presumably a Quaker gathering, which the governor, though a Catholic, also attended.[7] Consequently, a secular culture emerged where religious affiliations were not so import-ant as was the freedom to participate in government without hindrance.

Penn had achieved a charter for his new colony in 1681, but it re-mained on paper until he could persuade settlers to migrate to it. By the time the charter was given to Penn, he was well versed in colonization. He gained the practical experience needed by managing his father's Irish estates. His time as a trustee and as one of the proprietors of New Jersey gave him some insight into the problems of running a colonial venture. However, both plantations had already been established. Now, with the prospect of a virtually unsettled territory before him, Penn had the task of creating a colony that would reflect his own outlook, and at the same time prove profitable. The framework within which these aims could be achieved was provided by the charter from the Crown and the various frames of government which were formulated between 1681 and 1701. While the charter was written within a relatively short time, the constitutions for the colony evolved over a period of twenty years.[8] First, though, Penn had to present to the privy council a draft of the charter for Pennsylvania, which, after substantial revisions, was finally approved. Penn had to negotiate with interested parties outside his grant – the Crown, the duke of York as proprietor of New York, and Lord Baltimore, proprietor of Maryland – when establishing his powers as proprietor under the charter. After that, he had to create a constitution for the new settlement. He also had to attract the right sort of settlers in order to make a successful colony. Thus the promotional literature had to be written with the utmost care. There was also the present condition of the plantation itself. Far from being a wilderness, there were settlers who had been living in the Delaware valley for some time. Swedes, Finns, and some Dutch inhabitants were scattered across the area. This chapter explains how Penn dealt with these challenges.

* * *

Penn did not succeed in retaining all the proprietorial powers set out in his charter. This was because the full weight of the privy council committee was behind the centralization policy towards the American colonies which had been going on since 1676. Hence the Bishop of Durham clause, which would have given the proprietor the quasi-palatinate authority granted to Maryland's proprietor, Baltimore, was removed. But there were distinctions between the members of the committee for all that, for although they shared a common vision of the Crown's role in the development of Pennsylvania, there were divisions over just how strong a role the Anglican Church should play.

Except for Lord North, the members of the committee who met to discuss this aspect of the charter had been associated either with Penn in his youth or with his father when he was alive. Arthur, earl of Annesley, was involved in Ireland as a commissioner during the Act of Settlement. He was sympathetic to Presbyterianism. He, no doubt, would have known Admiral Penn in both capacities. Laurence Hyde, earl of Rochester, knew Penn well, as did his brother, the earl of Clarendon. They were both sympathetic to religious toleration. Their appreciation of the necessity of religious liberty as a concomitant of free trade determined their position on the colony's religious provisions. Thus, although they acquiesced in the bishop of London's request to obligate the proprietor to provide an Anglican chaplain, any more demands on religious conformity were rejected. Consequently, even though Penn was not allowed the power to have patronage of presentation to churches, thereby having control over religion himself, neither was there any attempt by the council to impose any strict regulation on worship. In the end, it was left to North and the secretary to the committee, William Blathwayt, to carve out the legal jurisdictions of the proprietor. North, clearly a Court man, guarded the royal prerogative against any encroachments and ensured that the navigation laws were enforced. There is no evidence that suggests the king's intervention in reviewing the charter. That the king reposed his complete trust in North was shown in 1683 when North was given the title of Baron Guildford. Blathwayt represented a new kind of bureaucrat, an administrator rather than a politician. Upon replacing Penn's old family friend, Robert Southwell, Blathwayt reflected the new approach to dealing with the expanding English empire by actively advocating centralization and systematization of every aspect of colonization. The penultimate draft, setting out the boundaries and terms of the proprietor of Pennsylvania, restricted Penn in one sense, but gave him the latitude he needed to form his own political structure within the colony. The final draft, then, formed the basis upon which the constitution of the colony was written.[9]

Notwithstanding the creation and adaptation of the frames of government, Penn had to get the word out about his new venture, otherwise his investment would be lost. Publicizing the enterprise and attracting the right sort of people to invest in and to migrate to the new colony was crucial to its success. He already had experience in publicizing the attractions of a colony, having been involved with promoting West New Jersey. Within the first year of the granting of his charter, Penn published four promotional tracts in English and two translations, one German and one Dutch, for Pennsylvania.[10] His first tract was entitled *Some Account of the Province of Pennsilvania in America lately granted under the Great Seal of England to William Penn Etc. Together with Priviledges and Powers necessary to the well-governing thereof. Made public for the enformation of such as are or may be disposed to transport themselves or servants into those parts.* In it he gave 'publick notice . . . to the world . . . that if they should happen to like the Place, Conditions, and Constitutions (so far as the present Infancy of things will allow us any prospect) they may if they please, fix with me in the Province hereafter described'.[11] An abbreviated version of *Some Account* was published as a broadsheet with the title *A Brief Account of the Province of Pennsilvania in America.* In it Penn sang the praises of his colony for prospective settlers. The first point he made was that 'the place lies 600 miles nearer the sun than England', an attractive proposition for potential colonists from that rain-sodden island. 'I shall say little in its praise to excite desires in any,' he continued disingenuously; 'whatever I could truly write as to the soil air and water, this shall satisfie me, that by the blessing of God and the honesty and industry of man it may be a good and fruitful land.'[12]

Attracting settlers was only part of the aim of making the colony prosper. There were also the investors who had no intentions of emigrating. In *Some Account* and its shorter version, *Brief Account*, Penn appealed to the vanity of the English mercantile group by describing the colonies as the seeds of nations which should be promoted as places for the increase of mankind and beneficial for commerce. Penn's description of the location of the colony and its potential commodities is also an indication that he was aiming his promotional literature at mercantile investors as well as at immigrants. Items such as silk, flax, hemp, wine, cider, furs, and tobacco were commodities that found markets worldwide. Penn hoped to seduce merchants who were involved in the transatlantic trade to and from Europe. Thus a detailed description of how the trade of the middle colonies operated across the Atlantic was included in the advertisement. 'They send to the southern plantations corn, beef, pork, fish and pipestaves and take their growth and bring for England, and either sell them here or carry them out again to parts of Europe.'[13]

The second section of *Some Account* laid out the colony's constitution. At first glance, it appears to be concerned only with settlers. It stresses the rights and freedoms of Englishmen, 'so that no law can be made, nor money raised, but by the people's consent'. However, the fact that the first draft of the frame of government pre-dates the first purchase of land, while the list of readers to whom the tract was addressed is headed by traders, planters, and shipmasters, and finally eminent Quakers, indicates Penn's immediate priority for investment. The remaining sections of *Some Account*, while concentrating on suitable people to be involved in the settlement of the colony, also puts in the forefront investors who would not necessarily emigrate. The type of people who would be most suitable to the venture were laid out in order. First, there were those who would buy shares, whom Penn advised to send overseers to the colony to protect their interests. The rest of the people Penn aimed at were renters, traders, and servants.

What is intriguing about these promotions is the underplaying of religious reasons for migrating other than a mention that an eye to the providence of God should direct prospective settlers. Even that is tempered with a practical approach. 'So soon as any are ingaged with me,' promised Penn, 'we shall begin a scheam of draught together, such as shall give ample testimony of sincere inclinations to encourage planters, and settle a free, just and industrious colony there.'[14] In this respect, the colony's advertisements were quite different from those of New Jersey where overwhelmingly Quaker emigrant hopefuls were solicited. Penn knew that the scope of the venture was too big for people of a single persuasion. It was to be a practical experiment where anyone could improve their lot regardless of their religious or political bent. Penn offered practical advice on the arrangements to be made for the 'journey and its appurtinances and what is to be done there at first coming'. The voyage would cost £5. 10s. for masters and mistresses and £5 for servants. The fare for children under seven would be 50s., though babies not weaned could travel free. Emigrants should take with them 'all sorts of apparel and utensils for husbandry and building and household stuff'. They should be willing to spend two or three years 'without some of the conveniences they enjoy at home'.[15]

The kind of settlers Penn hoped to attract to the colony was also spelled out in his tracts. First he appealed to 'industrious husbandmen and day labourers'. But he specifically aimed his appeal at 'laborious handicrafts especially carpenters, masons, smiths, weavers, taylors, tanners, shoemakers, shipwrights, etc.'.[16] Soliciting for the huddled masses was left to nineteenth-century propaganda. Penn needed people who could build a colony from scratch. There was very little room for the unskilled poor or the destitute. The skilled were given preference.

The kind of people who were actually attracted to the colony can be established from an analysis of six lists of immigrants who arrived in Pennsylvania in the first century of its foundation. Although the proprietor cast his net wide, and obtained colonists from Ireland and Scotland in the British Isles, and from France, Germany, and the Netherlands in continental Europe, they mostly came from England and Wales. It has been claimed by David Hackett Fischer that they were drawn from a distinct English province which he dubs 'the North Midlands'.[17] Five of the six maps he published to illustrate his analysis of the lists do indeed reveal a bias towards Lancashire and Yorkshire, or what contemporaries called 'the north country'.[18] The exception is, however, significant. This is the map which plots the places of origin of 589 people who purchased property from Penn in Pennsylvania between July 1681 and March 1685.[19] Fischer dismisses it as a list of investors rather than of immigrants.[20] Some undoubtedly were. John Poyer, a tanner of Robeston, Pembrokeshire, for example, purchased 750 acres of land in Pennsylvania in October 1681. He consequently appears among those first purchasers listed. But Poyer never left Wales. In July 1682 he entrusted Jenkin Griffith to take up 250 acres on his behalf, paying his passage and providing sustenance for four years. Subsequently, in 1686, he sold all his estate and inheritance in Pennsylvania to William Jenkins of Tenby, and wrote to Griffith to inform him of this transaction, asking him to deliver half the stock of his holding to Jenkins on his arrival in the colony.[21] But without such corroborative evidence it would be hazardous to assume that a majority of those listed were investors rather than migrants. It has been calculated that two-thirds of the early purchasers migrated to the colony.[22] Moreover, the 589 first purchasers are a much more representative sample of those whom Penn recruited than the 92 Quaker autobiographers, or the 111 Quaker ministers engaged by the Philadelphia Yearly Meeting from 1684 to 1750. So far from being drawn from the north of England, however, they came from counties scattered throughout England and Wales. Cheshire was the county with the most first purchasers, some 55 all told, but Wiltshire came a close second with 53. However, London scored higher than any county, accounting for 107 of the 589. Some Londoners, indeed, were investors rather than immigrants. These included John Aubrey, the celebrated biographer. Penn had tempted him with a personal promotional letter in 1683, claiming that

> The Aier, heat and Cold Resemble the heart of France: the soyle good, the springs many & delightfull. the fruits roots corne and flesh as good as I have comonly eaten in Europe. I may say of most of them better. Strawberry's ripe in the woods in Aprill, and in the Last Month, Peas, beans, cherrys & mulberry are here. Much black walnutt, Chesnutt, Cyprus, or white Cedar and mulberry are here. The sorts of fish in these parts are excellent and numerous. Sturgeon leap day and night that we can hear them a bow shot from the Rivers in our beds . . .[23]

Although Aubrey resisted the temptation to migrate to a colony where the fish could be heard leaping out of the rivers, he accepted a grant from the proprietor in 1686 of six hundred acres 'without my seeking or dreaming of it. He asked me to plant it with French Protestants for seaven yeares gratis and afterwards make them to pay such a rent.'[24] Other London purchasers, such as the gentlemen, lawyers, physicians and merchants, doubtless like Aubrey obtained Pennsylvania real estate as an investment and did not cross the Atlantic themselves, sending tenants to occupy their claims or even selling them to others.[25] But the carpenters, shoemakers, and tailors along with all the other tradesmen and craftsmen, who made up the overwhelming majority of first purchasers from London, almost certainly went to America. They were indistinguishable from the Bristol and other urban purchasers who bought land from Penn in the 1680s, exactly the types whom he hoped would settle in Pennsylvania. By moving to take up their purchases they were among the first in a migration across the Atlantic which stimulated the growth of the population of the colony from an estimated 700 in 1680 to 30,000 by 1718, the year of Penn's death.

Most of these were rural dwellers. Pennsylvania became one of the most fertile agricultural regions in the colonial era, giving it the reputation of being 'the best poor man's country'.[26] Penn was determined 'that the province might not lie like a wilderness as some others yet doe by vast vacant tracts of land but be regularly improved for the benefit of society'.[27] His land policy was designed to realize this ideal.[28] For administrative purposes he also carved his colony into three counties, Bucks, Chester, and Philadelphia. These were sometimes referred to as the three upper counties, to distinguish them from the three lower counties of Delaware. This rural hinterland of Philadelphia became the bread basket of the colonies and exported a surplus of agricultural produce. Penn was anxious to develop the commercial potential of Pennsylvania.

Later, in 1685, Penn published another piece of promotional literature as an exercise in damage control. Factions which had emerged almost from the colony's inception had reached boiling point and their notoriety was spilling over to London. In economic terms the colony was booming, but politically it was becoming infamous. Attempting to offset the bad publicity, Penn wrote *A Further Account of Pennsylvania*, which brought out the positive aspects of the society. The tract followed a similar pattern to his previous advertisements by playing down the religious element and playing up the property component. In it he claimed that in the upper three counties of Pennsylvania and the lower three of Delaware there were 8,500 people, half of whom were English while the others were Irish, Scots, Finns, Swedes, Danes, Dutch, German, and French.[29] The emphasis is clearly on the dominance by the English population. Penn, though equitable in his dealings with the initial peoples there, nevertheless knew the importance of portraying a familiar and increasingly civilized environment. A couple of years later, a more forceful tract, *Excellent Privilege*, was published to answer negative reports. It was clearly an attempt to allay the worries of the London merchants involved in the colony's trade. Penn wrote personal letters to clients reassuring them, and published some that defended the colony from the 'idle and unjust stories that the malice of some invent, and the credulity of others prepare them to receive against it'.[30] Meanwhile the proprietor scolded his colonists, warning them that 'the world was watching them' and 'faith without works' would not remove the bad impression that was being formed.[31]

Before Penn threw in his lot with the new regime of William and Mary with the formation of the New Pennsylvania Company, he had been promoting another settlement further west of Philadelphia. This was proposed in *Some Proposals for a Second Settlement* in 1690, complete with a planned city. The city would be built at a convenient location some fifty miles west of the Delaware River. The new settlement would become the new trading centre on the continent, thus capitalizing on Daniel Coxe's grant for all the land west of the Susquehanna River to the Pacific Ocean. The river and its environs would then be the meeting point for trade between east and west. Penn's attempt to generate interest was aborted because of his other problems that year and because of the war between England and France, known as the war of the League of Augsburg or King William's war, depending on which side of the Atlantic one stood. But towards the end of the war, which was concluded with the Treaty of Ryswick in 1697, Penn raised the possibility of the venture again. This time a subscription list was drawn up, and there was an overwhelming response, in the form of 450 signatures put down on the agreement. Again the settlement was aborted, possibly because Penn failed to live up to his promise to return to the colony within two years of the agreement. However, the war was probably the main reason, because, although it was nearing conclusion, sporadic fighting was still going on. It would have been impossible to develop the land west of the Susquehanna, due to continuing raids by the Indians from the Ohio valley into the region. Still, Penn continued to think big, and by 1709 he was once again drumming up support for an even grander scheme than before. Also by this time, there was another war over the Spanish succession, between England, who supported the Habsburg claimant, and France, who backed the Bourbon successor. In North America it was called Queen Anne's war. Previously, in 1703 Penn was reported to have been involved in plans with Charles Mordaunt, the earl of Peterborough, to launch a westward design similar to that which his father had undertaken in 1655. His motive was to secure Pennsylvania's trade with the West Indies. Pennsylvania had developed a substantial trade in the Caribbean, and control of the Caribbean by the French would destroy the colony's trade.[32] Pennsylvania merchants traded with the islands in grain, flour, meats, barrel hoops, staves, and shingles, but Jamaica and Barbados were the principal ports for Philadelphia's trade in timber. Penn realized the importance of getting a grip on the islands early on in the war and proposed a comprehensive plan to secure the West Indies by conquering the area of Mexico. The areas under scrutiny within the Mexican territory were Oaxaca, which was 'wide open and wealthy' – presumably a reference to the silver mines – and the Chiapa province, which held an abundance of cochineal used for dye. If the English could establish themselves in the Mexican territory, it would be a strategic coup, whence 'they will be able to control the whole of America'.[33] This would create a vast trading area in the Caribbean and the Gulf of Mexico of which Philadelphia would be the entrepôt.

* * *

The city of Philadelphia also grew rapidly. As early as 1690 Penn claimed that 'divers persons . . . by their industry and charge have advanced that city from a wood to a good forwardness of building (there being above one thousand houses finisht on it)'.[34] He greatly exaggerated the number of houses in 1690, for there were only about 400 in 1700.[35] By then there were about 2,500 inhabitants in Philadelphia. An observer in 1698 noted that although it contained an 'abundance of fine rich buildings', already 'in truth it's a monster the head bigger than the body'. He concluded that the town was 'overpopulated', a conclusion based on the fact that the hinterland consisted entirely of farms, so that there was no market for the city's produce.[36] In fact the exchange of goods and services was not restricted to the immediate vicinity, for Philadelphia, as we have seen, soon became an international port, trading principally with the West Indies.

Penn himself laid out the rectangular grid design between the Delaware and Schuylkill rivers when he visited his new grant in 1682. There has been much speculation as to why he called the city Philadelphia and where he derived the pattern that was to become the template for cities across North America in later years. At first Penn planned for a nameless 'large Towne or Citty', but soon decided to call it Philadelphia. The name was no doubt chosen for its Greek meaning, the 'City of Brotherly Love'. It was also the site of one of the seven churches in Asia Minor to which the Book of Revelation was dedicated by St John. At the same time it was a modern city with which merchants in the Levant Company, many of whom invested in Pennsylvania, currently traded. There were several European models for new towns in the seventeenth century. James I had established Londonderry in Ireland in its opening decades. Much of the City of London was rebuilt after the disastrous fire of 1666. But Londonderry, a garrison town surrounded by walls, bears no resemblance to early Philadelphia. While some of the new buildings of London might have inspired Penn, much closer to his grid pattern was the new capital of Piedmont at Turin laid out by the dukes of Savoy. Penn had visited Turin while on the Continent in the years 1662 to 1664 and could not have failed to be impressed with the wide streets leading from the river Po, and the rectangular blocks of the Piedmontese capital.

Penn kept control of the allocation of lots in Philadelphia. He planned to allocate prime sites to the leading first purchasers, clearly anticipating that they would need town houses as well as country houses like the gentry in England. He himself had a house fronting the Delaware in the city, and also built Pennsbury manor some miles upstream where he could escape the demands of proprietorial business and live the life of a country gentleman. By reserving the distribution of lots or 'plats' as they were called in Philadelphia he incurred some resentment, especially since he held some back for later disposal. In 1684 he was presented with a 'humble remonstrance and address of several the adventurers, free-holders and inhabitants and others therein concerned' protesting at his plans for the development of the city.[37] Penn partly drew the sting of their attack on his autocratic ways by promising to grant Philadelphia control of its own affairs with a city government. This promise he fulfilled on his last visit to his colony in 1701 when he issued a charter creating a corporation of a mayor, aldermen, and councilmen. Even so his autocratic attitude and suspicion of urban autonomy was evident from his failure to grant the corporation the right to raise taxes and from his insistence that the first mayor should not be elected but nominated by himself. Elitist attitudes to elections were also reflected in the restriction of the franchise to those who had been resident in the city for two years and were worth at least £50. Philadelphia was to be controlled, if not by an aristocracy, then by a mercantile oligarchy. For although the gentle-men whom Penn hoped to entice to the city failed to migrate there, a community of wealthy merchants settled on Society Hill, so called because the lots there were ceded to the Free Society of Traders. When the com-pany collapsed its place was taken over by such merchant princes as Samuel Carpenter, Isaac Norris, and Edward Shippen.

These leading merchants of Philadelphia were all Quakers. But the City of Brotherly Love was never a city exclusively of Friends. On the contrary, in 1702 James Logan, Penn's secretary, and a Quaker himself, wrote to the absentee proprietor that the city comprised over half the inhabitants of the county of Philadelphia, 'two thirds of these I believe are no Friends, which brings town and country upon a balance, the greater part of the country [county] being Friends'.[38] Besides Quakers there were Anglicans, Baptists, Presbyterians, and Swedish Lutherans in the city. Nearby Germantown, although Quakers accounted for two-thirds of the population in 1690, had Lutheran, Moravian, and Mennonite churches too. Pennsylvania was already ethnically as well as religiously diverse. As Isaac Norris observed in 1710, 'wee are a mixt people.'[39] Besides English and Welsh, and the Swedes and Dutch who preceded them, there were Scots, Irish, Germans, and other Europeans. Slaves of African origin had also been brought into the Delaware valley before the English claimed it. In 1684 a ship from Bristol landed 150 slaves in Philadelphia. The early Quakers were clearly not averse to slavery. Indeed, it has been estimated that one in ten of the families inhabiting the city in 1700 owned slaves.[40] The ethnic mix of peoples of European and African ancestry together with the native North Americans in Penn's colony meant that from the outset Pennsylvania rapidly became a model for the melting pot of later centuries.

. . .

NOTES AND REFERENCES

1. *HMC Dartmouth MSS*, pt 1, (1887), p. 23. The manuscript credits the Noble Person as Lord Dartmouth, but he was a contact for the correspondents with the duke of York. Thus the letter was most likely addressed to the duke of York. The person whom Penn was recommending was probably his relative, Culpepper.

2. *Concessions and Agreements of the Proprietors, Freeholders and Inhabitants of West New Jersey* (1676). Penn is also credited with drafting the *Epistle of Penn, Lawrie and Lucas respecting West New Jersey* (1676): Hope Francis Kane, 'Notes on Early Pennsylvania Promotion Literature', *PMHB*, 63 (1939), pp. 144–68.

3. William Penn, *The Case of New Jersey* (1679); *CSP Colonial*, no. 1123, p. 419, 19 Sept. 1679.

4. John E. Pomfret, *Colonial New Jersey: A History* (New York, 1973), p. 41. According to Pomfret, Edward Byllynge was the author of the *Concessions*.

5. There were, of course, native Americans who were involved in the fur trade with the settlers. See Francis Jennings, *The Invasion of America: Indians, Colonialism, and the Cant of Conquest* (London, 1976), pp. 97–104 for the effects European and British demand for fur had upon Indian society, as well as the supply of peltry.

6. *CSP Domestic May 1684–February 1685*, the earl of Perth, Sir George Drummond, and James Drummond to the earl of Sunderland, 22 Aug. 1684. In a curious turn of events, Penn was later accused of violating the rights of East New Jersey.

7. *PWP*, II, p. 504.

8. See below, Ch. 8.

9. See Ch. 8 for the discussion of the making of Pennsylvania's frame of government.

10. See Kane, 'Notes', pp. 145–7.

11. *Some Account of the Province of Pennsilvania in America; Lately Granted under the Great Seal of England to William Penn* (London, 1681). The introductory four points made by Penn are almost identical to the 1680 tract *The Benefit of Plantations or Colonies*, which Charles M. Andrews attributes to Penn in *The Colonial Period of American History*, 4 vols (Yale University Press, 1975), IV, p. 337 n.; Kane, 'Notes', p. 151 cites a reprint of *The Benefit* in *Select Tracts Relating to Colonies*, ed. Oglethorpe (London, 1732).

12. Edwin B. Bronner and David Fraser (eds), *William Penn's Published Writings 1660–1726: An Interpretive Bibliography*, in *PWP*, V, p. 270.

13. *Some Account*.

14. *Some Account*.

15. *A Brief Account*.

16. *A Brief Account.*
17. David Hackett Fischer, *Albion's Seed: Four British Folkways in America* (Oxford, 1989), pp. 438–41. The lists were of arrivals in Philadelphia 1682–87, residents in Bucks county, Quaker ministers engaged by the Philadelphia Yearly Meeting 1684–1773, Quaker autobiographers, Quaker arrivals in Philadelphia 1682–1750, and the first purchasers of land from William Penn. English readers express bemusement when they see the map of the 'North Midlands' on p. 447. In addition to the counties of Warwickshire, Staffordshire, Leicestershire, Derbyshire, Nottinghamshire, and Lincolnshire, which do indeed constitute what most people in England would recognize as the north Midlands, it also includes the whole of Wales, the border counties of Gloucestershire, Herefordshire, Worcestershire, Shropshire, and Cheshire, together with the six northern counties of Lancashire, Yorkshire, Cumberland, Westmorland, Durham, and Northumberland!
18. Ibid., pp. 440, 439.
19. See *PWP*, II, pp. 630–64. The editors emphasized that these lists do not include inhabitants of the Delaware valley before 1680, settlers in the three lower counties, or those who settled in Pennsylvania who purchased land from others and not from Penn. Nevertheless it is the most authoritative source for the type of people Penn attracted to his infant colony.
20. Fischer, *Albion's Seed*, p. 441.
21. William Clements Library, University of Michigan, Ann Arbor, Harmar MSS, Vol. I, fos 1–3: lease and release from Penn to Poyer, 25 Oct. 1681; indenture of Poyer and Griffith, 31 July 1682; Poyer to Griffith, 26 Aug. 1686. Cf. *PWP*, II, p. 651.
22. Gary B. Nash, *Quakers and Politics: Pennsylvania 1681–1726* (Princeton, 1968), p. 16.
23. *PWP*, II, p. 395.
24. Oliver Lawson Dick (ed.), *Aubrey's Brief Lives* (Bristol, 1962), p. 75.
25. In addition to Aubrey there were three London gentlemen among the first purchasers, one of whom, William Markham, certainly went to Pennsylvania. They also included a surgeon, four physicians, four lawyers, and fourteen merchants. The merchants were particularly prone to invest in the colony rather than migrate to it, though at least one of them, James Claypoole, moved to Philadelphia.
26. James Lemon, *The Best Poor Man's Country* (Johns Hopkins University Press, 1976).
27. *PWP*, III, microfilm 5:641.
28. See below, p. 141.
29. *PWP*, V, p. 320.
30. *PWP*, III, microfilm 5:634; FLL, Penn Papers, V, pp. 1660–1726.
31. FLL, *A General Epistle* (1686); *PWP*, III, pp. 93–4.
32. J.D. Alsop, 'William Penn's West Indian Peace Aims of 1709', *The Journal of Caribbean History*, 19 (May 1984), p. 70; Frederick B. Tolles,

Meeting House and Counting House: The Quaker Merchants of Colonial Philadelphia 1682–1763 (New York, 1948), pp. 86–7.

33. *Correspondence of Colonel Hooke*, ed. W.D. Macray, 2 vols (Roxburghe Club, 1870–71), I, pp. 6, 8, Memoirs of the marquis of Torcy, 18 Feb. 1703.
34. *Some Proposals for a Second Settlement in the Province of Pennsylvania* (1690).
35. Mary Maples Dunn and Richard S. Dunn, 'The Founding, 1681–1701', in Russell F. Weigley, (ed.), *Philadelphia: A Three Hundred Year History* (New York, 1982), p. 11.
36. Blathwayt papers, Colonial Williamsburg, Vol. VI, folder 2, John Usher to William Blathwayt, Sept. 1698.
37. Dunn and Dunn, 'The Founding, 1681–1701', pp. 16–17.
38. Edward Armstrong (ed.), *Correspondence between William Penn and James Logan*, 2 vols (Philadelphia, 1872), I, p. 102. The inhabitants of the other two counties in the colony, Bucks and Chester, were mainly Quakers.
39. Quoted in Sally Schwartz, *'A Mixed Multitude': The Struggle for Toleration in Colonial Pennsylvania* (London, 1988), p. 42.
40. Weigley (ed.), *Philadelphia*, p. 30.

Chapter 8

LAWGIVER

Montesquieu compared Penn in his capacity as proprietor of Pennsylvania with Lycurgus, the ancient Greek lawgiver who allegedly devised a constitution for Sparta.[1] While the achievement of Lycurgus might now be considered mythical, Penn certainly put his mark on the constitutional settlement of his colony.

In this respect he played a more powerful role in Pennsylvania than the governors of most other English colonies in North America. In the charter colonies of New England the governors were elected, while in the Crown colonies of New Hampshire and Virginia they were nominated by the king. There were other proprietary colonies. The duke of York was proprietor of New York until he became king in 1685, when it became a Crown colony. New Jersey and the Carolinas were subject to proprietors, though their powers were disputed and dispersed through several individuals. Only Maryland had a single proprietor like Pennsylvania, the proprietorship being held by the Calvert family headed by Lord Baltimore. The Calverts could be said to have enjoyed even more autonomy than Penn, since the Maryland charter contained a clause giving them the same privileges as the bishop of Durham in England. Penn tried to have a similar clause included in his charter, but, as we shall see, he failed. Lord Baltimore, however, forfeited his proprietorship to the Crown in 1689, and the Calverts did not recover Maryland until 1715. While Penn also lost his colony in 1692 he regained it in 1694 and for two decades was the only sole proprietor of an English colony in North America.

The charter itself, to which the king set his seal, evolved from several drafts. First submitted by Penn's attorney, John Darnell, each successive draft was altered by members of the committee of the Lords of Trade until the final version was completed. Crucial to the final outcome was the agreement by the duke of York and Lord Baltimore, whose lands were adjacent to the new province. Although the duke agreed to relinquish the three Delaware counties, Baltimore continued to claim territorial rights for the Maryland area.

The first part of the charter described such physical aspects of the land granted to Penn as the rivers, lakes, rivulets, ports, bays, and inlets leading to the said land. The grant also included the soil, mountains, woods, fens, islands, and whatever else made up the territory. In consideration of future industry, Penn was given the rights to mining of any natural resources. All of this was encompassed within an area which was bordered on the east by the Delaware River and north by the 43rd degree of latitude ending at the New York boundary. To the south, the charter stipulated the boundary position at twelve miles above New Castle, Delaware. From there, Penn's grant would run five degrees west along the 40th degree of latitude. This delimitation of his boundaries caused problems for Penn to the north and south. While the boundary conflict in the north with New York was muted, the dispute between Penn and Maryland's proprietor, Lord Baltimore, lasted until the middle of the eighteenth century.

The second and much longer part of the charter dealt with the powers that were vested in the proprietor. This section became the most problematic. The earliest known draft set forth proprietorial powers that were semi-regal. Although it was not written by Penn himself, it did not proceed to the committee without his approval. After all, he would be the direct recipient of the grant. Penn therefore initially was aiming at more power than might be expected from a Quaker. Penn was no democrat and he was no republican. He was, however, anxious that there should be a consensus within the new society. Penn's view was that the style of government was of less moment than that government rested on a firm basis of law. This was best expressed in the preface to his constitution, when he wrote that 'Any Government is free to the People under it (whatever be the Frame) where the Laws Rule, and the People are a Party to those Laws, and more than this is Tyranny, Oligarchy or Confusion.'[2]

Copied from the Maryland charter, which had modelled the proprietorship on the palatinate of Durham, the so-called bishop of Durham clause gave jurisdiction to the proprietor which effectively usurped the Crown's prerogative powers. For example, he could appoint at pleasure judges and justices of the peace. In all cases, including murder and treason, the proprietor was the ultimate source of appeal, not the king. The king could not impose taxes without the consent of the proprietor and assembly. Indictments and writs would also be issued in the name of the proprietor instead of the monarch. The ability to confer honorary titles was another element which essentially challenged royal authority. Although the clause was eliminated in the final draft, it revealed Penn's ambition. A further example of his aspirations was the inclusion of the clause enabling him to have jurisdiction over the admiralty courts as well as having the power to make war. Again this was later modified to exclude the power over the admiralty courts and to limit Penn's power to make war.

There was nothing in the first few drafts which included obedience to the Navigation Acts. Neither was there anything that would require the approval of laws made in the colony by the king in council.

The final draft paved the way for Penn to set out the structure of government in his constitution for Pennsylvania, but was much more restrictive in the rights of the proprietor than the previous proposals. This was mainly due to the comments by Chief Justice North and the secretary to the privy council, William Blathwayt. Between the two of them, Penn's initial powers were stripped. He could 'ordain, make, and enact . . . any laws whatsoever for the raising of money for the public uses of the said province'.[3] Other laws concerning the behaviour of society in general were for Penn's government to make as long as they did not clash with English law. Penn still could appoint judges and justices and officers for carrying out the law. Further to the making of laws for the new colony, these had to be sent to the privy council for perusal within six months of their passing in the colony. Penn's power to pardon was reduced to crimes other than murder and treason.

Trading rights were made explicit in the charter. Under the Navigation Act, goods shipped from the colonies first had to touch down in an English port before being exported to Europe. Moreover, duties were to be paid on goods that would be re-exported to other foreign ports. To guarantee that somebody, on behalf of the proprietor, would be contactable if any problems arose over the colony, the privy council required that an agent for the colony be within reach. Otherwise the consequence would be the resumption of the colony. This last stipulation was to prove too true when, in 1691, Penn lost his proprietorship.

One area that was left vague was the concern over religious toleration. There was an attempt to include a section acknowledging the practice of beliefs other than those of the Church of England. This section was cut out and replaced with a statement to the effect that if there were twenty or more inhabitants who requested an Anglican minister, they would receive one without any hindrance. There was no mention of provisions for other religious practices.

Once the charter was given final approval, Penn was able to begin fashioning a frame of government for his new colony. There are twenty known drafts of the Pennsylvania constitution, all of which not only illuminate William Penn's motivations but illustrate other influences outside his Quaker environment. Essentially, the constitution was a work in progress because it was never completely satisfactory to anyone. Penn definitely wanted to attract financial investment in his project and to keep the final say in decision-making in the executive. Although the assembly tried to wrest that control from the governor and the council, they did not succeed until 1701 with the final frame of government. Therefore, it is essential to discuss four phases in the development of the frame of government: the first from 1681, when Penn began to hammer it out, until he published it in May 1682; the second as it was altered in 1683 after he had held discussions in Pennsylvania; the third in 1696; and the final version of 1701.

The essential feature of Penn's frame of government was the structuring of the legislature. There were various proposals as to how the 'parliament' should be construed. The drafters of the document represented different interests with different motives. James Darnell, Penn's lawyer, composed some of the earliest drafts in which he tried to claw back some of the proprietorial powers lost in the charter. Those early drafts formed the basis of the final version. Through draft after draft, the constitution, changing names with new versions, metamorphosed from a liberal document, the Fundamental Constitutions of Pennsylvania, in which the government was made up of an upper and lower house and the lower house had legislative power, to the Frame of Government, in which power was firmly under the control of the proprietor's appointee, the governor, and a council chosen from the wealthier sort. Penn was accused by his Quaker friend, Benjamin Furly, and his one-time political associate, Algernon Sidney, of departing from the concept of natural rights bound up in proper representation.[4] Furly ascribed the changes to 'a few corrupt & guilty courtiers' while Sidney accused Penn and the ruling elite of having more power than the Turk.[5] The version which Penn took to Pennsylvania in 1682 became a major source of dissatisfaction felt by the settlers over issues of power. It was also the beginning of factional strife that was to plague the colony throughout its early history. Factional disputes developed, where the interests of the proprietor were increasingly challenged. Sides were taken, but though the anti-proprietary interests gained strength within the colony itself, the proprietary interest held the ultimate power in the corridors of London. Even when Penn lost his charter for a brief time after the Glorious Revolution, this was due less to the political instability of the colony than to the circumstances surrounding Penn's alleged Jacobite support of the exiled king.

In the preamble to the Frame of 1682 Penn ruminated on the origins of government, drawing on the Bible as well as more recent models.[6]

When dealing with Scripture he must have felt almost like God drawing up the ten commandments for the people of Israel. Such laws were necessary because of man's transgressions. He quoted Paul's Epistle to the Romans, chapter 13: 'Let every Soul be subject to the higher powers; for there is no Power but of God. The Powers that be are ordained of God', and concluded from it that 'this settles the Divine Right of Government beyond Exception'. As for contemporary political thinkers, though he had clearly considered Harrington, Hobbes, Locke, and Sidney, he found them too divided to offer a convincing model. For while they agreed on the end of government, which was happiness, they disagreed about the means. Ultimately the laws depended upon morality. For 'Governments, like Clocks, go from the motion Men give them'. He had tried to form a government to secure 'the great end of all government, viz. To support Power in Reverence with the People, and to secure the People from the Abuse of Power'.

Essentially the government was to be made up of a governor, council, and assembly. The governor would be appointed by the proprietor. The provincial council and general assembly would be chosen by the freemen of the colony. A freeman was defined as anyone who owned a minimum of 100 acres of land of which ten were cultivated; or anyone who was formerly a servant or bondsman and, upon gaining his freedom, took up fifty acres and cultivated twenty of them; or anyone else who paid scot and lot, that is, taxes. A third of the provincial council would rotate yearly. Penn clearly envisaged a rotation of offices to try to prevent the emergence of an entrenched oligarchy, implementing ideas from James Harrington's *Oceana*. The whole of the assembly would be up for yearly elections. Voting would be by secret ballot.

When Penn first visited his colony in 1682 he took with him this frame of government, which he presented to the assembly for ratification. At the first meeting, however, he encountered serious opposition. There was an immediate rejection of the terms of the constitution. Eventually in 1683 a compromise was reached in which Penn agreed to a number of changes to the frame.[7] Representation was reduced to more manageable numbers. Where, previously, there had been designated 72 council representatives 'most eminent for wisdom, virtue and ability', and 200 representatives for the assembly, the council would now have 18 members, three from each of the six counties, and the assembly would have 36 members, six from each county. These six counties comprised the three 'upper counties' of Bucks, Chester, and Philadelphia in Pennsylvania, and the three 'lower counties' of New Castle, Kent, and Sussex in Delaware.

Nevertheless, the core of power still rested in the governor and the provincial council. That is, the council retained the right to initiate all legislation for the colony. Although the assembly could accept or reject the proposed laws, the bone of contention was over the right to introduce bills for consideration. Penn envisaged a representative assembly which could merely accept or reject laws submitted by the council, perhaps an echo of Poyning's law, which kept the Irish parliament subservient to the English privy council. Consequently, influence by the assembly in the government was frustrated. Thus the council had the power to create courts of justices, including judges, treasurers, and masters of rolls. The assembly could elect sheriffs, justices, and coroners, but the governor had the final approval. Ultimately, however, the assembly sat in session only at the pleasure of the governor and provincial council. The proprietor, through his governor, would also have a negative vote and the governor commanded a treble vote in council.

Those who had objected to the frame of government continued to resent this concentration of power in the proprietor and the council. Their resentment fomented factions between representatives who supported the proprietor and those who did not. In the formation of these factions religious affiliation mattered little. The religious make-up of proprietary and anti-proprietary groups was varied. Although the majority of the representatives from the three upper counties were Quakers, Penn's main supporters, William Markham and Nicholas More, were not. Those from the three lower counties were largely Anglicans. Most of the power lay within the area of Philadelphia. The council, made up of men of means plus the section of the assembly that was closely tied to the transatlantic trade, formed an alliance in government which produced legislation which prejudiced the other representative elements of the colony. As Pennsylvania's population increased and new settlers spread westwards into the back country, tensions over representation in government increased. The reason for this was that although areas such as Chester expanded, the proportion of representation did not. Thus, while there was a desperate need to create a stable infrastructure in these areas, thereby necessitating a voice in government, the main area of political influence remained in and around Philadelphia. Only when the assembly could wrest the legislative initiative would the governor and council be forced to accept the need to expand representation. Until then, conflicts would occur. The problems in Pennsylvania resulted in destabilizing the government to the extent that Penn's charter was threatened. Because there continued, in the privy council, a strong push for centralization, from 1685, Penn's role as proprietor was under threat.

The third attempt at a settlement, in 1696, came about because of an imperial crisis in which Penn had lost his proprietorship of the colony. Governed by a royal appointee, Benjamin Fletcher, the colony was virtually under the auspices of New York. With that, the colony's constitution was voided. Upon the resumption of the charter by Penn, some of the general assembly sought to create a new settlement. They undermined the proprietor's authority by giving the assembly the right to initiate legislation. The number of representatives was reduced to two per county for the council, four for the assembly. The voting qualification was lowered in the counties to ownership of fifty acres, but raised in the city to those worth £50, where before all inhabitants paying taxes had been allowed to vote. The residential qualification for voters was extended to two years. This affected newcomers, many of whom were not Quakers. Although the assembly still reflected a Quaker majority, by 1696 the population did not. The determination to protect Quaker interests is seen in the provision that those who scrupled oaths should be allowed to affirm. But there was more to the motive behind the creation of the new frame than safeguarding the religious persuasion of the Society of Friends. The rural backlash was a reaction to the dominance of Philadelphia merchants, many of whom still had ties across the Atlantic. The proposed new frame reflected a desire to transfer influence from the mother country to the colony as well as from the city to the country.

In 1701 the final frame of government was effected as a result of Penn's refusal to acknowledge the 1696 frame and his intention to fashion a new one along the lines of Locke's proposals for Virginia. Penn never really recognized the 1696 frame and made this clear when he arrived in Pennsylvania in 1699. Elections were to be conducted according to the 1683 constitution. Meanwhile, he did allow a motion to go forward for yet another new frame. Penn was not acting inconsistently, but in keeping with the philosophy of members of the Board of Trade, such as Somers and Locke. He was devolving more independent authority upon the assembly. Penn's connection with Locke went back to his time as a student at Oxford, but there is no substantive evidence that he was in direct contact with him at that time. However, Penn was in contact with one of Locke's close associates, Lord Somers, who was lord chancellor and president of the Board of Trade. As a member of the Board also, Locke was heavily involved in colonial affairs. He wrote a brief on how Virginia's administration should operate. There is a similarity between his proposals for Virginia and the ones implemented in Pennsylvania's 1701 frame.

First and foremost in the new frame, or Charter of Privileges, was the protection of religious liberty. Nobody who professed belief in one

Almighty God would be molested. Anybody who believed in Christ could hold office. Penn accepted a provision of the 1696 frame when he limited the number of representatives to four from each county. The assembly now had the power to choose its own speaker and sit in its own adjournments. Above all, it held the right to initiate legislation. Moreover, the council was reduced to an advisory body, effectively making the legislature unicameral in make-up. Lockean influence can be seen in other aspects of the new constitution and its partner, the frame of land settlement. The choosing of sheriffs and coroners upon good behaviour was straight out of Locke's brief on Virginia.[8] The controversy over the surveying of land and its granting was more particularly Lockean.

There remained the matter of where power lay, whether it should reside in the assembly or the governor and council. For Penn, it was necessary to keep crucial aspects of power, such as judicial appointments and initiation of legislation, within his sphere. From his perspective, this was the most important aspect of colonial politics. The day-to-day running of the colony was left to the colonists. Only when their laws and their behaviour were seen to be contradictory to English interest, thereby threatening his proprietorship, did Penn intervene decisively. One example was his ongoing dispute over the lack of payment of land rents or quit-rents. In retaliation for failure to pay, Penn would threaten to veto any forthcoming legislation and repossess any indebted land. The reaction by the Pennsylvania assembly was to attempt to erode Penn's proprietorial powers.

There was the additional problem of ethnic and religious differences between Pennsylvania and Delaware. The three lower counties were settled before Penn took possession. The bulk of the settlers were Swedish, Finnish, Dutch, with some English Anglicans. They consequently differed from the upper Quaker counties over the management of the colony. Throughout the 1680s and into the 1690s, there was dissension over the administering of justice in the Delaware region. There were complaints that court justices refused to travel the Delaware circuit. Consequently, councillors from the lower counties met to commission their own judges. When it came to the defence of the colony, things got worse. Situated further down the river from Philadelphia, the three lower counties were more vulnerable to attacks from the sea, particularly in times of war. This occurred following the accession of William and Mary in 1689. King William's war, involving war between England and France, spread to the colonies. The dispute over supply for defence increased instability in the colony and became one of the reasons for Penn's loss of the charter from 1691 to 1694. Even then, under royal government, Penn's colony refused to vote war supplies. It was quite clear, from a religious and political point of view, that the two areas were incompatible. In 1691 Delaware effectively seceded from Pennsylvania, a secession which Penn reluctantly recognized. When the final charter of liberties was granted in 1701, a proviso was included which granted Delaware the right to form its own government.

In 1704 the lower counties took advantage of this concession and elected their own assemblymen. Thereafter there were two legislatures in Penn's colony. These to some extent took over his lawmaking powers. But ultimate control over the legislation of the two assemblies lay not in Philadelphia or in New Castle but in London. All laws passed in the colony had to be approved by the privy council, and Penn used this as a long stop to veto those he did not like. In some years more than half the acts passed by the Pennsylvania assembly were disallowed by the proprietor. Penn thus kept control over the lawmaking powers of his colony from across the Atlantic.

· · ·

NOTES AND REFERENCES

1. See below, p. 167.
2. The Frame of Government, 1682.
3. The Charter for Pennsylvania, 1681; Merrill Jensen (ed.), *English Historical Documents: American Colonial Documents to 1776* (1969), pp. 93–102.
4. Benjamin Furly to Penn, *PMHB*, 19 (1895), pp. 297–306; *PWP*, II, pp. 228–37.
5. *PWP*, II, pp. 228–9; William I. Hull, *William Penn: A Topical Biography* (London, 1937), p. 229.
6. *PWP*, II, pp. 212–27.
7. These were enacted in the Act of Settlement. *PWP*, II, pp. 362–6.
8. Peter Laslett, 'John Locke, the Great Recoinage, and the Origins of the Board of Trade: 1697–1698', *WMQ*, 3rd ser., 14 (1957), pp. 370–402; Lovelace MSS (Bodleian Library, Oxford), John Locke's papers on Virginia.

Chapter 9

DIPLOMAT

Penn's role in the colonies took on more substance when he became proprietor of Pennsylvania. His new position enabled and required him to become part of the wider colonial sphere. He had to deal with external affairs as well as internal ones. There were several issues arising from his proprietorship which required him to deal with people other than his own colonists. Those which are discussed below concern the boundary disputes with Maryland and New York; the handling of relations with native North Americans; and the problem of intercolonial defence.

* * *

Penn's dispute with his southern neighbour was not resolved finally until Mason and Dixon ran the line between Pennsylvania and Maryland in the 1760s. Before then there were many abortive attempts to settle the boundary, starting in Penn's lifetime. The dispute arose from the geographic areas delineated in the charters of the two colonies. In 1632 Charles I granted to Lord Baltimore the land between the Atlantic Ocean and the Chesapeake up to the Delaware Bay 'under the fortieth degree of north latitude'.[1] Charles II's grant to Penn in 1681 described the southern boundary of Pennsylvania as 'a circle drawn at twelve miles distance from New Castle northward and westward unto the beginning of the fortieth degree of northern latitude and then by a straight line westward'.[2] Unfortunately an arc described twelve miles from New Castle on the Delaware River at no point intersects the fortieth parallel. In fact it falls so far south of it that Baltimore complained it overlapped with his grant. Because the Maryland charter set out its northern boundary at 'under' the fortieth parallel, the question arose as to how far under did that mean? While it was in Baltimore's interests to have it as near to the line as possible, it was in Penn's to push it as far south as he could. This

129

created a disputed area of land between the Delaware and Susquehanna rivers. In the east this extended from Philadelphia, which was actually on or even just below the line, to the edge of New Castle county. As we shall see, Baltimore even disputed Penn's right to territory within Delaware, claiming that it fell within the grant by Charles I to Maryland. In the west the grey area covered the region between the Conestoga River and the mouth of the Susquehanna in the Chesapeake Bay.

Baltimore was kept informed by the lords of the committee for plantations of Penn's petition for a charter in 1680. He made representations to them about the implications for his own colony of the granting of Pennsylvania. His agents insisted that the northern boundary of Maryland stretched to the so-called Susquehanna fort, apparently an old Indian fort, which lay just north of the mouth of the Susquehanna River and below present-day Safe Harbor dam.[3] Penn at first seemed to accept this arrangement while his charter was being thrashed out. In September 1681, however, he wrote to the inhabitants in the northern part of Maryland, which he now saw as his territory, urging them to desist from paying taxes to Baltimore.[4] This was a follow-up to Penn's claim made in his first promotional tract, *Some Account of the Province of Pennsilvania*, that the new territory included access to the Chesapeake Bay. The competing claims were known to at least some of Penn's potential investors. James Claypoole, a mercantile investor with worldwide links, was very hesitant to become involved in the beginning because he was aware of possible objections from Baltimore over the boundaries of Pennsylvania.[5]

When Penn went to his colony in 1682 more direct negotiations could be held with Baltimore in Maryland. Measurements were taken which boded ill for Penn's assertions about the exact location of the fortieth parallel.[6] At one point he was desperate enough to hint to Baltimore that he had an offer which would be hard to refuse if only they could speak in private. When they did meet in December Penn urged his neighbour to yield the mouth of the Susquehanna to him, for otherwise his grant from the king of the river would 'prove but a dead lump of earth'.[7] Penn's methods were, at the very least, suspicious. His reading of the existing maps was questionable. He ignored some appropriate maps, and devised his own interpretation in order, as he put it, 'to correct the errors of those maps that have taken any part of this country'. Those 'erroneous' maps included one compiled by Augustin Hermann which the king acknowledged as the official survey for Virginia and Maryland. Although there was disagreement between previous cartographers over the position of the fortieth parallel, ranging from seven to eight minutes, the margin of error is slight compared with Penn's claim that Hermann's boundary was off by as much as forty minutes.[8] Although the issue is a confusing one, it is clear that at the outset Penn accepted the agreement to limit his southern border in the west to the fort in the Susquehanna. The issue became cloudy only after Penn realized his mistake and the necessity of having the boundaries lowered in order to reach the Chesapeake Bay.

The meeting between the two proprietors in December ended acrimoniously. Both Penn and Baltimore took their quarrel to London, sending conflicting accounts of their discussions to the committee of trade.[9] Penn also used his connections with prominent courtiers. Eminent amongst these was the earl of Rochester, who had backed Penn from the beginning. He now used Rochester to draw to the attention of the king the problem of the boundary. Writing to the earl in July 1683 he begged that his colony, 'so hopeful and flourishing (already the wonder and envy of her neighbours) . . . may not be bruised and spoiled by the encroachments of the Lord Baltimore'.[10] In September Penn sent William Markham as his agent extraordinary to present his case to the king and his ministers while he was absent in Pennsylvania. Markham delivered presents from Penn to courtiers, starting with the king, who had been sent snakeroot water, then used as a tranquillizer. The duke of York was presented with an otter skin, which he thought would make a fine muff. Others were given American timber, which Markham trundled round London in a cart, delivering planks to their town houses. Among the politicians he contacted were Lords Halifax, North, Radnor, and Rochester, who Markham assured Penn were all his 'fast friends'.[11] Both proprietors lobbied members of the privy council to their side. Baltimore was in favour with the duke of York because of their common religious beliefs, though this did not stop Penn from writing to James to point out 'the pretensions of that person'.[12] He also wrote to the duke in June 1684 to protest against Baltimore's ordering the construction of a fort in New Castle county, a provocation which had led to violence between men sent from Maryland and Penn's supporters. The commander of the fort refused to move when ordered to do so by the New Castle authorities, claiming he had a commission from Baltimore. He even threatened to order his soldiers to shoot and kill anybody who tried to demolish the fort. Having learned that Baltimore had gone to England, he was leaving Pennsylvania, 'following him as fast as I can'.[13]

Upon the death of Charles, James, now king, turned his attention to the dispute. He had not forgotten that he gave up his claims on the Delaware for political expediency. Now that Baltimore was claiming that part of the three lower counties was within his grant of Maryland the situation regarding Delaware could be clarified. When the Lords of Trade announced their decision it was a total defeat for Baltimore, a partial victory for Penn, and a vindication of the king's claims in that area. The Lords upheld Penn's claim that no part of Delaware could ever have been a part of Maryland, for when Baltimore received its charter it was already occupied by Europeans.[14] Since Penn claimed that the government of Delaware was not in question but only its territory, the committee confined itself to this matter. The minutes of the Lords of Trade from August 1685 to their final decision on the dispute on 17 October show that they settled the question of the disputed land, but did not address the issue of the government or dominion. Penn was aware of the vague way in which he had been granted the Delaware region in 1682, and astutely worded his petition to that effect by stressing that the dispute was over the title of land and not an issue of power. By acknowledging this fact, Penn was acknowledging the king's supremacy over the government of the lower counties, and that he himself was only proprietor of its territory, which limited him to claiming its rents. This argument later served Penn when a *quo warranto* against Delaware was threatened.

The decision of the Lords of Trade on 17 October that Delaware was not within Baltimore's patent was a triumph for Penn. He could scarcely conceal his delight when he wrote to the council of Pennsylvania to inform them of it. 'This I thought would please you and the country, to whom communicate it in wisdom, avoiding indecent joy.'[15] Although the border between Pennsylvania and Maryland still remained unresolved, Baltimore did not trouble Penn about it for the rest of James's reign. He lost the government of Maryland in 1689, when it became a Crown colony. The only disturbance he gave Penn again was to revive the question of the lower counties. He petitioned the queen in January 1709 to repeal the order of 1685 which said they were not part of his patent. Penn, however, was able to use his superior influence with the ministry to get Baltimore's petition dismissed almost out of hand. He complained about it to Lords Somers and Sunderland, both members of the cabinet. 'They agreed with me,' he informed Logan, and 'excused the Inadvertency of the reference [to the Board of Trade].'[16]

*   *   *

Another area of proprietorial interest was Indian affairs, which, to some extent, impinged upon imperial policy. This was a complicated process whereby, prior to the sectioning off of Pennsylvania and Delaware, the land was under the auspices of New York and its Iroquois Five Nations. In 1676, the governor of New York, Edmund Andros, made a number of loosely connected treaties, known as the Covenant Chain.[17] This Chain acted as a means of stabilizing relations with the Indians following the disastrous effects of the conflicts with the natives in Virginia known as Bacon's Rebellion and the Indian uprising in New England called King Philip's war. The granting of the Pennsylvania colony in 1681, thus cutting it off from New York, did not necessarily mean that the Chain was broken. What did threaten the Chain, however, was Penn's lack of appreciation of the delicate balance which Andros had struck when the new proprietor attempted to set up separate trading agreements in the form of a Covenant of Friendship. So, while his personal relationship with the local Indian tribes of the Susquehannocks, Conestogas, and Delaware was peaceful, the ramification of separate trade treaties was to destabilize Anglo-Indian relationships overall. The primary motive for Penn's treaties with the natives was trade. The need to extend the Pennsylvania boundaries as far north and south as possible would benefit Penn's commercial plans. At the moment, the New York–Pennsylvania boundary had not been surveyed and the Maryland–Pennsylvania line was in dispute. Both opened opportunities for expansion by the new proprietor.

William Penn is credited with being the most liberal and farsighted statesman when it came to his colony's relationship with the Indians. The wording in the final draft of his charter over the issue of the Indians reflects this concern. It was quite different from the initial draft of the charter, which posited a more aggressive attitude towards the natives. Taken from the Maryland charter, it would have given Penn *carte blanche* to make war or peace with the Indians. However, the final version stipulated that only in war did Penn, as captain-general, have the authority to attack. What is interesting is the first instruction in the charter to 'reduce the Savage Natives by Gentle and just manners to the Love of civil Society and Christian Religion'. The notion that they were savage did not necessarily imply that they were aggressive, but rather uncivilized or primitive. Certainly Penn did not regard them as savage in any pejorative sense. He took the trouble to learn the language of the Delaware, or Lenni Lenape, Indians he encountered in the vicinity of Philadelphia so that he did not need an interpreter. His own impression of them as 'natural sons of Providence' when he visited his colony for the first time was distinctly favourable.[18] Thus he described them as being

> proper and shapely, very swift, their language lofty. They speak little but fervently and with elegancy. I have never seen more natural sagacity considering them without the help, I was going to say the spoyle of Tradition. The worst is that they are the worse for the Christians who have propagated their views and yielded them tradition for the worse and not for the better things. They believe a Deity and Immortality without

the help of Metaphysics . . . They make their worship to consist of two parts. Sacrifices which they offer of their first fruits with marvellous fervency and labour of body, sweating as if in a bath. The other is their canticoes as they call them, which is performed by round dances sometimes words, then songs, then shouts, two being in the middle that begin a direct chorus. This they perform with equal fervency but great appearance of joy. In this I admire them . . . I have made two purchases and have two presents of land from them.[19]

Penn negotiated land from the native Americans based upon the presumption of fairness on both sides. There is no evidence to support claims that the Indians deceived Penn about their ownership of land, or that he did other than treat them fairly. Those he dealt with recognized this long afterwards, remembering him affectionately as 'Miquon'.[20] He did, in fact, adopt a conciliatory and peaceful approach to the natives. Moreover, this policy had been advocated by the English government since its involvement in the colonies, and did not just stem from Penn's integrity. The earliest advice on how to approach the natives was from the bishop of London, Henry Compton, who recognized that, while the English had conquered the territory from the Dutch, separate terms of ownership had to be made with the natives. What made Penn's approach different from that of other colonies was his success. Just before he went to Pennsylvania in 1682 he took the trouble to write to the Indians there to assure them of his love, and to desire them to love his friends. 'When the great God brings me among you, I intend to order all things in such manner, that we may all live in love and peace one with another.'[21] He made a treaty with the Delaware Indians shortly after his first arrival in the colony. The date and details of this treaty are not known, though Benjamin West's historic painting perpetuates the legend of its having been concluded under an elm tree at Schackamaxon. By 1685 Penn had spent £1,200 purchasing territory from the Delawares up the river that bears their name from New Castle to the falls above Burlington.[22] Penn's motive was also quite practical. He realized the necessity of gaining access for Pennsylvania traders to strategic areas occupied or controlled by Indians. By creating an atmosphere of trust and goodwill, trade could flourish. This approach was in keeping with Penn's advocacy of toleration as a prerequisite to profitable commerce.

However successful Penn was with the Indians within his own colony, his lack of appreciation of the native American network of communications, which ignored artificial boundaries set by Europeans, resulted in the disruption of the overall relationship between the English Crown and the native peoples. In keeping with Penn's desire to have two outlets to the sea and his future plans of expanding the fur trade northward, he not only had to negotiate with the Delaware Indians for land on the west bank of the Delaware River; he also needed the agreement of the Susquehannocks in the west and the Iroquois in the north in order to expand his boundary the full length of the Susquehanna River. Thus in October 1683 he purchased the mouth of the Susquehanna from the Susquehannocks despite Lord Baltimore's claim to the area.[23]

Penn hoped to expand the fur trade northward from Pennsylvania to New England mainly through the creation of companies, starting with the Free Society of Traders, the New Mediterranean Sea Company, and the Susquehanna Company. The Free Society's primary trade was in fur, and its members looked to Philadelphia as the new hub in the fur trade. The commodity would be brought into the town before being shipped down the Delaware and out to other ports. The failure of the Society was due mainly to cash flow problems, but its demise was also due to political conflict between Pennsylvania merchants and London subscribers. It owed something too to the company's coming into conflict with the duke of York's trading interests, because of its attempts to impinge on the Albany trade.[24] Penn's efforts in this direction were at the root of the conflict. In a letter of June 1682 to the Indian 'Emperor of Canada', Penn wrote saying that he set up a company to trade with the emperor's people.[25] By proposing this, he also planned to extend his trading rights further north above Albany, New York.

The intent was clear to the current governor of New York, Thomas Dongan. In September 1683 he ordered the Albany commissioners to put a stop to Penn's attempts until boundaries were sorted out. Less than two weeks after Dongan's order, two of the five Iroquois nations, the Cajugas and Onnondagas, reinforced their commitment to the government of New York.[26] Meanwhile Penn was in the process of soliciting the Crown for the islands in the Delaware River. The duke of York ordered Dongan to keep control of the waterways connecting Albany with the ocean. Furthermore, the governor was ordered to obstruct New Jersey's trade with the Indians so as to preserve that market for New York. There were also instructions to buy Staten Island before the proprietors of the Jerseys could acquire it. The duke's province had long been trading with the Indians along the northern part of the Susquehanna River, but Penn now claimed everything below the 43rd parallel. This would have placed the Mohawk River within his northern boundary. The Onnondagas obviously did not accept this, because they sold the Susquehanna River to Dongan, clinching the deal with a belt of wampum. Notice was given that Penn's people could not settle there.[27] The dispute over the northern boundary remained a problem for Penn for over a decade until he was able to purchase the area from Dongan.[28]

Even then, it raised questions of ownership, since at the time of Dongan's deal with the natives, he was acting as governor for the Crown. Obviously, he was also acting on his own behalf. Thus the purchase by Penn could be construed as illegal because the area was not Dongan's to sell. There was enough doubt in that regard for Penn's heirs to purchase the area again in 1736, putting it firmly within their jurisdiction.[29]

Although this purchase secured the upper reaches of the north-eastern branch of the river for Penn, his claim to the rest, and in particular the stretch from the forks to the Chesapeake, had to be confirmed by the Susquehannocks. On Penn's second visit to his colony he made a point of getting their agreement in September 1700. He followed this up by inviting them and other Indians involved in the Susquehanna valley to Philadelphia, where a treaty was concluded in April 1701.[30] The treaty was signed by Penn and nine colonists and ten 'Kings and chiefs'. In it they agreed to a firm and lasting peace between them for ever thereafter. The signatories on both sides pledged themselves to keep the peace between their peoples. The Indians agreed to be bound by the laws of Pennsylvania 'while they live near or amongst the Christian Inhabitants thereof'. Though they were to enjoy the benefit of those laws too, as Francis Jennings notes, 'One may take that with a grain of salt; whatever Penn may have intended, Indians did not sit on Pennsylvania juries.'[31] Trade was to be conducted only with people approved by Penn, effectively giving Pennsylvanians a monopoly. This was a real triumph for Penn in his dispute with New York. The Indians who accepted the treaty were brought firmly within his Chain of Friendship. The Indians who agreed to Penn's treaty also undertook not to assist any other nation 'whether of Indians or others' that was not friendly towards the English government. Although England and France were technically at peace when the treaty was signed, the agreement was aimed at the French.

* * *

There was another dimension to Penn's imperial role and that was the complication of war. Throughout his career, he sought military solutions to his colonial problems in one form or another, whether it was supplying the English navy with timber and tar or appointing military men to the post of colonial governor. This was especially true after the Glorious Revolution of 1688. England fought France in two major wars from 1689 to 1697 and from 1702 to 1713. The gap between the treaty of Ryswick of 1697 and the outbreak of the War of the Spanish Succession in 1702 was generally accepted as a mere breathing space. For nearly twenty-five years Penn had to contend with the stipulation in his colonial charter that made him responsible for the defence of the colony.

For England's conflicts in Europe impacted on the stability of English possessions in the New World. It was partly because he was not in a position to act as commander-in-chief in his colony that he was deprived of his government of it in 1691. As we have seen, it was only when he showed a willingness to contribute to imperial defence that he regained his proprietorship in 1694.

Realizing that he was very much on his good behaviour to take care of Pennsylvania's defence, Penn thought of ways in which he could satisfy his critics that the Quaker colony could be trusted to play its part in the empire. Thus in 1697 he drafted 'a Briefe and Plaine Scheame' of getting all the colonies to cooperate on issues of mutual concern. As far as defence was concerned they should agree on quotas of men to supply to an intercolonial army, while the governor of New York should be made chief commander of this force.[32] Again in 1700 he drew up another scheme of colonial cooperation. The central colonies which would spearhead the plan were New York, Virginia, Massachusetts, Maryland, and Pennsylvania. The meeting amongst the governors of these colonies was planned for October 1700. In the end, Maryland's governor, Nathaniel Blakiston, was too ill to attend. Nevertheless, the meeting went ahead in New York, and from it a number of proposals were put together for the Board of Trade. Penn's plan was to unite the colonies under one currency, to confirm the northern boundaries of the English colonies so as to avoid conflict with the French, to have reciprocal laws in the colonies over fugitives, and a common naturalization law emanating from England, to make legal practices and law intelligible for the common man, to erect a more efficient transatlantic postal service, and to provide more financial encouragement to the apprehension of pirates.[33]

Penn had good reason to fear for his proprietorship at that time, because his neighbour, governor-general Richard Coote, earl of Bellomont, had already been put in charge of Massachusetts, New Hampshire, and New York, so that it did not take a great leap of imagination to see a pattern emerging. If William III had a scheme to revive James II's Dominion of New England in a different guise, his own plan of colonial union could effectively take better care of intercolonial defence.

When war broke out again in 1702 Penn had once more to ensure the safety of his colonists. Fortunately for him, during his lifetime the Pennsylvania colony was never under direct military threat. The only real problem he had was over the pleas of the Delaware inhabitants, mostly Anglicans, to provide for defence in such an exposed area. The Philadelphia assembly would not agree to such measures. Penn tried to resolve the dilemma by allowing the three lower counties to set up a separate assembly. However, this did not completely remove the tensions between the upper and lower counties over the issue of defence, as the experience of Penn's deputy governor John Evans was to demonstrate. Evans's appointment was an attempt to solve the problem over keeping the proprietor to the agreement to defend his colony which Penn had undertaken in return for his charter. But Evans's contempt for the Pennsylvania Quaker stronghold soon became evident, while his inclinations for the Anglican-dominated Delaware region resulted in more tensions between the two territories. He shared the fears of the lower counties that Delaware was exposed to attack through the failure of the upper counties to provide for their defence. Evans tried to get the Pennsylvania assembly to contribute towards defence, but, as usual, the assemblymen continued to be mean on this subject. He therefore created a fake crisis which he hoped would scare them into voting the money. In May 1706 he raised a false alarm, claiming that the French were sailing up the Delaware towards Philadelphia. He himself rode around on a horse waving a sword. His actions caused panic and pandemonium in the City of Brotherly Love. When they found the crisis served no purpose but to try and expose their 'nakedness', the citizens were outraged.[34]

In Anne's reign the duke of Marlborough took it upon himself to supervise imperial defence.[35] Marlborough's strategy of having military men as governors for the colonies was similar to that of the deceased king William.[36] The duke was no doubt aware of the stipulation in Penn's charter regarding the position of captain-general. Penn's choice of Governor Evans in 1703 could hardly have impressed the duke, for though Evans had a military background, his judgement concerning the defence of the colony was ill conceived. The proprietor's awareness of his deficiency on that score can be seen in his insistence in the instructions he gave to his deputy 'that nothing may lye at my door in reference to the Defence of the Country'.[37] Perhaps it was in an attempt to impress the English government that he was serious about defence that Evans dreamed up the false alarm of 1706. When he was replaced in 1708 it was by an army officer, Charles Gookin, recommended to Penn by Marlborough.[38]

The commitment of the proprietor of Pennsylvania to imperial defence qualified his commitment to pacifism considerably, for Penn had accepted the captain-general's nominee. But this was not the first time he had made strategic concerns a priority. He had, after all, made Blackwell, another military man, his deputy in 1689. The Quaker philosophy of pacifism did not exclude the use of such means to solve dilemmas over defence. Indeed, English Quakers were quite willing to leave the business of defence in the hands of the Crown. However, in Pennsylvania, Penn was, if not a monarch, the sole proprietor and responsible for decisions over military matters. Also, his acceptance of Gookin was not the only sign of military cooperation with the duke of Marlborough. On the contrary, Penn showed an enthusiasm for England's strategic concerns quite extraordinary for a Quaker. He had for some time entertained schemes of conquest in Spanish America, if an account of them given by Nathaniel Hooke is to be believed.[39] To realize the objective of gaining territory from the Bourbon claimant to the Spanish throne in the Yucatan peninsula would have involved the use, not only of English troops, but of friendly Indians and slaves, to take on the 5,000 men in the area who would fight for Philip V. Since the Habsburg claimant, Charles III, had agreed to concede any conquests from Spain in the New World to the English, this would have created a new English colony in central America from which they would have been able to control the whole continent. The whole idea could be dismissed as a fantasy dreamed up by a rabid Jacobite if Penn had not written directly to the duke of Marlborough about the role of the West Indies in the peace negotiations of 1709.[40] Penn showed himself to be more the son of an admiral than a Quaker pacifist when he addressed himself to the problems of imperial conflict.

. . .

NOTES AND REFERENCES

1. Merrill Jensen (ed.), *English Historical Documents: American Colonial Documents to 1776*, 2nd edn (1969), IX, p. 85.
2. Ibid., p. 94.
3. *PWP*, II, p. 36.
4. *PWP*, II, p. 112.
5. Claypoole Letterbook, fos. 51–2, 26 July 1681.
6. *PWP*, II, pp. 256–9.
7. *PWP*, II, p. 406.
8. Jeannette D. Black (ed.), *The Blathwayt Atlas: Commentary* (Providence, 1975), pp. 106–7.
9. *PWP*, II, pp. 431–5.
10. Friends House Library, Penn MSS, WP to Rochester, 24 July 1683 (*PWP* microfilm).
11. *PWP*, II, p. 534, Markham to WP, 27 Mar. 1684.
12. *PWP*, II, p. 518, WP to the duke of York, 2 Feb. 1684.
13. *PWP*, II, pp. 560–1.
14. *PWP*, III, p. 61, Report of Lords of Trade, 2 Sept. 1685.
15. HSP Acc. no. 202, Penn to the Provincial Council, 21 Oct. 1685 (*PWP* microfilm).
16. *PWP*, IV, pp. 635, 651–2.

17. Allen W. Trelease, *Indian Affairs in Colonial New York: The Seventeenth Century*, 2nd edn (London, 1997), pp. 228–53.

18. *PWP*, II, pp. 448–54.

19. HSP Acc. no. 273, WP to Henry Savile, 30 July 1683 (*PWP* microfilm).

20. Francis Jennings, 'Brother Miquon: Good Lord!', in Richard S. Dunn and Mary Maples Dunn (eds), *The World of William Penn* (University of Pennsylvania, 1986), pp. 195–214. Jennings notes that the Delaware 'Miquon', like the Iroquois name for Penn, 'Onas', meant 'feather', 'and since goose quills were used for writing, they punned on Penn' (p. 198).

21. *PWP*, microfilm 4:352, WP to the Indians, England, 21 Apr. 1682.

22. *PWP*, II, p. 491.

23. *PWP*, II, p. 492. When Penn negotiated a treaty with Indians in 1701 it included some who lived on the Potomac River 'within the bounds of his province' (*PWP*, IV, pp. 52–3). No stretch of the Potomac came within Penn's grant!

24. HSP, Society collection, John West to Penn, New York, 16 Oct. 1683; 28 Aug. 1683.

25. *PWP*, II, p. 261, 21 June 1682.

26. *PWP*, II, p. 487; microfilm 4:528.

27. *CSP Domestic 1681–85*, no. 1315, 1824; cf. Gary Nash, 'The Quest for the Susquehanna Valley: New York, Pennsylvania and the Seventeenth-Century Fur Trade', *Quarterly Journal of New York History*, 48 (Jan. 1967), pp. 3–27.

28. *PWP*, IV, pp. 477–8. Dongan leased the river to Penn for a thousand years on payment of £100.

29. Trelease, *Indian Affairs in Colonial New York*, pp. 254–7.

30. *PWP*, IV, pp. 51–3.

31. Jennings, 'Brother Miquon', pp. 204–5.

32. *PWP*, III, pp. 482–3.

33. *PWP*, IV, pp. 618–19.

34. Gary B. Nash, *Quakers and Politics: Pennsylvania 1681–1726* (Princeton, 1968), pp. 259–60.

35. See Stephen Saunders Webb, *Marlborough's America* (forthcoming). I am grateful to Professor Webb for sharing his conclusions with me.

36. Stephen Saunders Webb, *The Governors-General: The English Army and the Definition of Empire* (Chapel Hill, 1979), p. 463.

37. *PWP*, IV, p. 231.

38. Webb, *The Governors-General*, pp. 444, 463–4, 499.

39. Nathaniel Hooke's Memoir given to the marquis of Torcy, 18 Feb. 1703, *Correspondence of Colonel Hooke*, p. 8.

40. *PWP*, IV, pp. 644–5; J.D. Alsop, 'William Penn's West Indian Peace Aims of 1709', *Journal of Caribbean History*, 19 (1984), pp. 68–75.

Chapter 10

GOVERNOR

Whereas Penn moved from Country to Court in England, in his own colony he was, in a sense, the Court. Consequently, as governor he had to deal with other interests and even found himself facing anti-proprietorial factions.

Penn arrived in the New World in October 1682. He received a piece of turf, a twig, and some river water from the Delaware inhabitants to symbolize his authority over the new land. After a brief stay at New Castle, Delaware, he travelled up to Philadelphia. And so, for the next two years, Penn proceeded to get the new government in working order.

His first concern was to try to implement a land policy which would settle the colony in line with his ideal of developing it so that it would be filled with inhabitants spread over the whole, with no empty spaces as in other colonies. To this end he hoped to allot land on the basis that every five thousand acres should have ten families at least. Unfortunately for Penn, such a tidy chequerboard scheme came into contact with economic realities. It would have proved impossible to cope with the tidal wave of settlers that moved into Pennsylvania in the opening years of the 1680s, even if they had been content to conform to the proprietor's policy of land settlement. However, they wished to make their own arrangements, and more to the point were prepared to purchase plots from other purchasers and not just from Penn himself. The result was chaos even before Penn decided to return to England in 1684 to sort out his dispute with Lord Baltimore over the three lower counties. He set up a commission of propriety to administer his land policy in his absence.

* * *

Penn did his best to control the fractious colonists throughout the first two decades by making sure his desires were carried out through his deputy governors. At the same time, as we have seen, he kept in close contact with members of the privy council in hopes of offsetting the attack on his charter. For the moment, however, a new frame of government was negotiated and Penn sailed back to England to settle his boundary dispute with Baltimore.

For the time being, Penn was able to protect Pennsylvania by getting the *quo warranto* against it revoked. He wrote to the Pennsylvanians urging them to 'seek peace and pursue it' because 'many eyes are upon you, & any miscarriage is aggravated to a mountain; and 'tis not a faith without works that will remove it'. Nevertheless, the colony's governing body was disintegrating into factions. The result was unpaid debts, the increasing spread of foreign coinage, and land disputes. While Penn was at loggerheads with the colonists over unpaid quit-rents, that did not have a direct political effect, as did the unpaid debts to London investors, the very people who were giving political backing to Penn in his efforts at home. The shortage of English specie had the direct effect of creating unpaid bills or a shortfall from exchanging foreign currency so that debts were not fully satisfied.

Within the Pennsylvania assembly and council were factions which represented the struggle for power between merchants who sought to maintain control from London and the colonial merchants who saw the need for control to be kept in Philadelphia. Superficially, the split evolved into a contest between proprietorial and anti-proprietorial factions. The first indication of the split was the refusal to grant the Free Society of Traders legal status and the debate over the first frame of government.

The problems over the constitutional relationship between the assembly and the council were exacerbated by the tension between Pennsylvania and the three lower counties. Provincial meetings were generally held in Philadelphia, which was too far to travel, according to the members from Delaware. Since most of the Delaware members were non-Quakers, the struggle for control over legislation was heightened. Most of the first councillors from the lower counties had been residents under New York's jurisdiction and did not feel as committed as Pennsylvania was to the 'holy experiment'. Thus the divisions cut across religious affiliations. The assembly continued to encroach upon the council's initiatives through amendments made to the Continuation Act which required it to be passed each time the general assembly met.[1]

Penn as absentee proprietor was the loser in these contests. The council, under the presidency of a Welsh Quaker, Thomas Lloyd, encroached on his proprietorial power, for instance by appointing judges without reference to him. As a result 'by the end of 1686, Thomas Lloyd, in league with most of the merchants and an increasing number of the larger landowners, had taken the first steps toward dismantling the machinery of proprietary government'.[2] Penn tried to offset this trend by placing his executive power in the hands of a body known as the commissioners of state. But when the commissioners, so far from stopping the erosion of his powers, further undermined him he appointed a new deputy governor who could come to grips with the contentious colonists.

Captain John Blackwell's appointment as deputy governor resulted from several considerations: the insufficiency of coinage, the uncontrollable factiousness of the colonists and their refusal to pay Penn quitrents, boundary disputes, and the threat of resumption of the charter by the Crown. Part of the reason for James II's policy of centralization was the growing threat of the French on the boundaries of the English colonies. Thus centralizing them under the Crown, thereby providing a contiguous line of defence, was strategically sound. By appointing Blackwell, Penn presumably thought he could assuage the Crown's need to establish a military presence in his colony. At the same time he could satisfy London investors by employing somebody with the financial expertise needed to put the colony on a sound monetary footing. Blackwell seemed to suit both bills. He was an ex-Cromwellian soldier, and his *Discourse in Explanation of the Bank of Credit* was a canny tract which recognized the difficulties the colonies had over specie. It has been suggested that Blackwell sent this treatise to Penn in 1687 with a view to obtaining the governorship.[3] Certainly Penn referred to his having sought the post when he dismissed him from it.[4] It could be that this is why Penn made the otherwise surprising decision, when informing the commissioners of state in Pennsylvania of the appointment, that 'if he do not please you, he shall be lay'd aside'.[5]

Blackwell's commission was issued in July 1688, but it did not reach him in Boston, Massachusetts, where he then resided, until November. By then the political situation in England had changed dramatically. When Penn commissioned Blackwell James II felt that Providence had smiled upon him, blessing him with the birth of a son and heir. With God on his side he would achieve his aims. In November Providence seemed to have turned against him, with the Protestant wind conveying William of Orange to Torbay. The political wind was also changing, and with it Penn's fortunes.

Almost immediately upon Blackwell's arrival in Pennsylvania in December 1688, friction occurred between the new governor and the commissioners of state. Consequently the government split into pro-Blackwell and pro-Thomas Lloyd factions. Penn exhorted the commissioners to receive Blackwell, whom he described as 'a grave sober wise man', kindly.

He acknowledged that the old Puritan was no Quaker, assuming he was an Independent. But he tried to make a virtue of this, asking the commissioners to 'use his not being a Friend, to Friends advantage'.[6] Notwithstanding the proprietor's pleas, they made their objections clear when, upon Blackwell's arrival in the colony, they did not even send somebody to greet him, though they had been given notice of his travelling from New England to Penn's country seat at Pennsbury. He made his way to Philadelphia to wait upon them, where they let him cool his heels before meeting him. When he entered their presence they did not even offer him a seat. Blackwell wrote to Penn, complaining that when he told them of his commission Thomas Lloyd replied that he was not governor until they had surrendered their authority to Penn. When he produced his commission from Penn, Lloyd told him that they did not regard it as a sufficient authority until it had been sealed with the Great Seal of the colony, of which he was the keeper. Although on the following day the council accepted Blackwell's commission, he and Lloyd had got off to a bad start, and their relationship scarcely improved after their first meeting.[7]

The disputes between the two men polarized council and assembly. Blackwell insisted that he was upholding the rights of the proprietor which they had usurped. As he interpreted Penn's instructions, he had been appointed to sweep the proprietor's chimneys: 'to inspect the animosities, to use some expedient; And, if no way else, authoritatively to end them, at least suppress them.'[8] Instead he had fomented more. Lloyd's faction formed themselves into the Charter Club, claiming they were maintaining the rights granted by it to the settlers against Penn's arbitrariness. At one stage Blackwell even threatened Lloyd with impeachment. It is clear that Blackwell turned out to be an unfortunate choice of deputy. He was old and irascible. Although he accused the Quakers of being ungovernable, they complained that he was prejudiced against them from his experience in New England, where Friends had been persecuted.

When news of the Revolution in England reached Pennsylvania in the spring of 1689 Blackwell's days as governor were numbered. Several colonies experienced coups which have come to be seen as the Glorious Revolution in America. Thus New York and Maryland fell under the control of the leaders of the reaction, Jacob Leisler and John Coode, while Andros was clapped into jail in Massachusetts. Pennsylvania is not held to have undergone a similar upheaval. However, far from being the quiet colony it is usually portrayed as during the Revolution, it could also be described as experiencing a coup. The effect of the Revolution upon the colony was the virtual ousting of Blackwell from power. That spring, Lloyd absented himself from the council and went to New York. There is no evidence that he became involved in any of Leisler's actions, but the knowledge that Penn was charged with treason by the new regime in England could have had a bearing on what Lloyd did. Blackwell complained that Lloyd hid the Great Seal before sneaking off. For Lloyd's part, his motives are unclear. Perhaps he held the deputy governor to be guilty by association with Penn, so that the government could be taken out of his hands. But his subsequent actions do suggest Lloyd was mimicking Leisler.

For Blackwell's part, he continued to act in his capacity of deputy governor for the time being. Blackwell was instructed to let the present laws, which were due for revision after five years, lapse, unbeknown to the general assembly, and administer the colony in the name of English law until the legislation could be brought into line with the laws of England. The response by the colonists, led by Lloyd, was to subvert Blackwell in any way they could. It was more serious than mere tit-for-tat disputes. Another council member, Griffith Jones, noted that 'it was the king's authority that is opposed, & looks to me as if it were raysing a force to rebell'.[9] For the next seven months, Blackwell struggled on, despite the perfidiousness of the Pennsylvanians. When Penn received a whole series of complaints from them, however, he dismissed his deputy. He tried to sugar the pill by offering Blackwell the post of receiver-general of his quit-rents, but he declined and went back to New England. He had had enough of Pennsylvania, complaining of the weather as well as the mosquitoes and the Quakers.[10]

In his place, Blackwell's most virulent adversary, Thomas Lloyd, presided over the council and assumed the powers of the deputy governor. Lloyd's appointment only exacerbated problems within Pennsylvania. Blackwell supporters such as William Markham, John Claypoole, and Griffith Jones lost their positions in the new government and Lloyd supporters took their place.[11]

Penn's hold on his colony was slipping. The assembly was under the control of the rebellious Lloyd, who paid little attention to the proprietor. The government under Lloyd refused to contribute to the colonial defence. This was especially worrying since information from Maryland suggested that Pennsylvania might suddenly be attacked. When New York's governor, Fletcher, ordered Pennsylvania to contribute fifty men towards colonial defence, the assembly pleaded poverty. Thomas Lloyd wrote an emollient letter to Fletcher assuring him that he and his fellow assemblymen understood the needs of New York – nevertheless, at the moment, they could not help. Pending further information expected from Virginia, they would get back to Fletcher. Two months prior, in

June of 1691, a report by the lieutenant-governor of Virginia on the colonial situation had singled out Pennsylvania as being particularly vulnerable to enemy attack. In his letter to the Lords of Trade and Plantation, the lieutenant-governor stressed the accessibility of the Quaker colony, because of its pernicious principles, for the enemy to retreat to and communicate from.[12]

Defence problems also brought out the tension between the three lower counties and Pennsylvania. Delaware disputed Lloyd's appointment. Frustrated by their inability to influence the council because of the Quaker majority, the members for the lower counties protested, adding that the distance to Philadelphia was too great to travel. The conflict resulted in the lower counties seceding and setting up their own assembly with Markham as deputy governor.[13] So, while Markham assumed the responsibility for the three lower counties, Lloyd controlled the three in Pennsylvania. Accusations of loose and seditious behaviour flew back and forth. Thus the separation of the Delaware counties was described by one member of the Pennsylvania council as a 'Revolt'.[14]

The factiousness of the colony was given another dimension with a dispute between the orthodox Quakers and a new group led by a prominent Scottish Quaker, George Keith. The Keithian schism which erupted between 1690 and 1693 was an attempt by Keith to impose a rigorous orthodoxy on the Friends' faith. His 'Confession of Faith' caused a split among the colonists. Thomas Lloyd led the faction which eventually indicted and tried Keith and others on two charges of civil transgression.[15] Writing to his friend Theodore Eccleston, Keith described the problems in the colony and noted that the disputes were becoming common knowledge.[16] They were also becoming vituperative. To Keith's abusive language of 'fools, idiots, silly souls, hypocrites, heretics, heathens, rotten ranters, Tyrants, Popes, Cardinals' his opponents riposted with 'Brat of Babylon' and 'Pope Primate of Pennsylvania'.[17] Penn, who was literally sickened on hearing of the schism, put it down to the political rather than the religious situation in Pennsylvania, since 'as to Doctrines, they cannot but agree'. He took Keith's side in the controversy, and blamed Lloyd for pushing it to extremes.[18]

The 'animositys and divisions' which Penn lamented in the government of his colony led ministers in London to be concerned about it. As early as October 1691 the opinion of the privy council was that if Penn could not control his colony – and he certainly seemed to be having a difficult time of it – then the Crown should be advised to take over immediately. Moves to extend the authority of the governor of New York, Benjamin Fletcher, to Pennsylvania and Delaware began in 1692 when the colonists were charged with abusing the navigation laws and refusing to support their neighbours in the war. The secretary to the privy council, William Blathwayt, said their good wishes were not good enough, and the council proceeded on 21 October to include Pennsylvania under Fletcher's command.[19] Penn was convinced that the faction against Lloyd 'brought this to pass'.[20]

'Oh! sorrowful Conclusion of 8 or nine years Government' was Penn's reflection on his position at the end of 1693.[21] But his prospects were just about to improve. The government dropped charges that he was actively engaged in Jacobite conspiracy. And he regained the proprietorship of Pennsylvania.

He did this through the formation of a new company to be called the New Pennsylvania Company. This company, created out of the death throes of the Free Society of Traders and the attempted Susquehanna company, was distinct from the colony's former companies in two respects: its motive, and the residence qualification of its subscribers. As to the first, the Pennsylvania Merchants' Proposal clearly stated their intention to 'the making of pitch tarr . . . to plant hemp and flax for sail cloth to apply themselves to the building of ships . . . to deliver what quantities of plank shall be thought fit'.[22] They promised to do all of this within the space of three years, and by December of 1693 the charter was recommended for approval subject to a five-year limit. The fact that it was what amounted to a government contract is evidenced by its terms. Its members could not trade privately while under contract, therefore their agents and factors could only represent their employers within the context of the organization. As for residential qualification, this was limited to those potential investors who resided in England. By these terms, the decision-making power remained in England. This was made abundantly clear when the Pennsylvania laws were revised, prior to Penn getting back the charter, to disallow the Pennsylvania Act concerning rates. The Act was an attempt by the colonial legislature to inflate the value of foreign currency. While advantageous to the colonial merchants when paying off a debt, the real effect of the law was to shortchange the English creditor. This was part of a general problem over money that was experienced throughout the colonies for some time. The other law which was vetoed was the Act concerning agents or factors who owed debts. As the law stood, it required these men, who defrauded their employers, to pay for damages. However, the other side of this particular regulation was that merchants' estates could be sold off to pay for any debts incurred by their agents. As these laws stood, they were in conflict with English law and effectively moved the judicial authority from London to Philadelphia. Once these Acts were removed from the books, power resided once more in England.

By launching the New Pennsylvania Company Penn finally came in from the cold. He petitioned the queen in July 1693, praying that Fletcher's commission might be revoked and his government restored. Mary referred it to the attorney-general and solicitor-general and they reported favourably to the Lords of Trade, who in August recommended that Fletcher be deprived of his authority over Pennsylvania and that it should return to Penn. They did so, however, with the provision that he meet Fletcher's orders as governor of New York for his own colony's quota of men required for war service. The figure of eighty men was agreed to after an agent for Pennsylvania, William Salway, went to New York to 'concent and agree upon a quota of men and money for ye defence of ye ffrontiers'. Anxious to keep his charter, once he regained it, Penn wrote to his colony warning its inhabitants to obey the demands of the English government.[23] When he was asked to reside in Pennsylvania, however, he baulked, saying that there was no need, for as long as he had his deputy there, his personal presence was unnecessary. He claimed proof in the quietness with which the colonists behaved themselves at the Revolution. The curt reply to this fantastic assertion was that the problems in the colony had arisen, in fact, through his absence.[24] However, the demand was dropped.

Instead of returning to Pennsylvania Penn made William Markham his deputy there. It was Markham who had to implement the demand for the colony's quota of men. When he put this to the assembly in 1695 they responded by making their approval conditional upon the granting of a new frame of government. At the time he refused, not having any instructions from Penn, and dissolved the assembly. But when they renewed the demand the following year he felt obliged to yield. The new frame was passed on the coat-tails of two money bills which provided for military assistance to New York. The assembly knew Penn's keeping of the charter depended upon his agreement to assist in the defence of the colony. The pressure from Whitehall to comply with the demand for aid gave the negotiating edge to the members. They argued that they could do nothing without legally invoking the charter. To do so would mean passing legislation. Markham succumbed to the move in November and proposed a frame of government. A few weeks later he formally recommended two items for consideration: the late queen's letter ordering the colony to support New York financially, and the proprietor's agreement in return for his charter to help neighbouring colonies in the war effort.

Although Penn ignored the creation of the frame, claiming it did not have his approval, he did not veto it. By vetoing the frame, he would have had to refuse the attached money bills, thus running the risk of losing his charter again. The majority of the assembly was playing a ruthless game with the proprietor by reminding him of his duty and their willingness to assist him in that endeavour, provided they got what they wanted.

There was, however, a strong minority which objected to the changes made in the frame of government in 1696. Claiming that it was unconstitutional since it had not received Penn's assent, they held elections in Philadelphia on 10 March 1697 in accordance with the provisions of the frame. When their rivals held elections there under the new rules they petitioned Governor Markham to protest.[25] The signatories to the petition have been seen as an alliance of Keithian Quakers and non-Quakers, mainly Anglicans, against the hegemony of the Friends.[26] Certainly the electoral provisions of the new frame to which they were objecting, as we have seen, to some extent protected the rural Quaker vote against the non-Quaker electors in the city of Philadelphia. The disputes occurring over the terms of the settlement, however, were not simply colonists versus imperialists or Quaker versus non-Quaker. Rather, they represented subtler divisions across religious and political divides. Spearheading the move for a new frame were members of the assembly who had been excluded from the government under Fletcher. John Simcock, Samuel Richardson, Samuel Carpenter, and James Fox formed a nucleus which was determined to wrest as much control from London as possible. However, the Remonstrance of Philadelphia inhabitants against the new settlement reflected the struggle between political interests along lines similar to the Court and Country division in England. The religious cross-section of signers of the Remonstrance signified a deep political split within the Quaker, as well as between the Quaker and non-Quaker, parties. It was also more than an opposition to a Quaker-dominated assembly. The conflict centred around supporters of David Lloyd, a provincial councillor and recent convert to Quakerism, and anti-Lloydians who also opposed the new frame of government. Opponents of the frame who objected to the usurpation of legislative initiative by the assembly included Robert Turner, Francis Rawle, Griffith Jones, and Arthur Cook. Turner wrote to Penn expressing his worry that the sweeping powers of the assembly and the way in which laws were implemented by it would attract the unwanted critical attention of the English government.[27]

The Remonstrance also was representative of the county of Philadelphia only. International trading interests were at stake. The Lloyd faction represented the internal trading interests of the Country. Thus they were anti-proprietary in the sense that the proprietary represented the Court whose imperial politics interfered with intercolonial trade. The focal point for this split was the Board of Trade's colonial policy.

The creation of the Board of Trade in 1696 and its subsequent actions concerning the colonies only produced truculence from the colonists. The colonial reaction to policy emanating from London was seen in such political manoeuvring as the circumvention of the admiralty jurisdiction. Moreover, the conflict between Philadelphia and London over the extension of the powers of the vice-admiralty courts highlights a growing separation of interests. This was shown by the contempt with which the Pennsylvania assembly refused Randolph jurisdiction to prosecute an illegal ship. The governor for the upper counties, David Lloyd, claimed the role of attorney-general for the plantation and blocked Randolph's attempts by imprisoning him and fining him £46 for damages.

The Act for preventing frauds was a counter-offensive to the Board of Trade's demands that vice-admiralty courts be introduced into the colonies. By providing local jury trial for offenders charged with piracy, power was effectively taken from the metropolitan. Randolph was scathing about the colonial law. Writing to Blathwayt, he pointed out that the laws on trade and fraud were contrary to English law on these matters, further noting seven points in Pennsylvania laws which he found in contempt of English law and reason. On the surface, the colonial laws looked as though they dealt firmly with illegal trade by requiring severe punishment for unlawful traders. But, in reality, carrying out the laws was another matter. The condition that officers would be fined treble if vessels were stopped more than one tide, searched, and found to be clear of the law, created understandable hesitancy in waylaying any suspicious vessel. Furthermore, when vessels were seized and condemned in Pennsylvania, their goods were handed over to its government instead of His Majesty's customs officer. The reason, according to the Pennsylvania justices of the peace, was that they were not aware of any court of admiralty erected nor of anybody qualified to hold such courts.[28] This was clearly a slap in the metropolitan face.

Penn did not agree with the terms of the new settlement, but he could not afford to appear in conflict with his colony. The provincial government's introduction of a new settlement worked to his advantage by putting the burden of defence upon the general assembly. The right to initiate legislation by the assembly was a major shift of power within the colonial government. The right to sit on their own adjournments and reorganizing voting requirements to give equal representation to rural counties was a blow to Philadelphia merchants and factors who represented London interests. But their attempts to seize power from London were to prove abortive. For real power lay in the requirement that Pennsylvania laws be in accordance with English laws. Nevertheless,

Penn knew it was time to return to his colony to straighten out what was threatening to become chaos.

Along with his wife and family he set sail for Pennsylvania in September 1699. This time, Penn took with him his new Irish secretary, James Logan. Only 26 years old, Logan was energetic, extremely intelligent, and loyal to Penn. For the rest of Penn's life, Logan was, in effect, Penn's right-hand man in the colony. On the way over, an incident occurred which showed another side to Logan and at the same time pointed up the continuing dilemma over what pacifism actually meant. While at sea, there was an attempted seizure of the ship by pirates. A fight ensued in which Logan stayed above board brandishing his sword against the intruders. Meanwhile, Penn went below board rather than draw a sword.

Penn stayed in Pennsylvania for almost two years. In that time, he tried to tackle his colonial concerns, but with little success. To begin with, the legislature still had not resolved the disagreements over the revision of the 1683 constitution. Penn ignored the 1696 version, so from 1700 to 1701 the colony was without a constitution.

One of the serious concerns underlying the dispute over a new frame of government was the validity of existing land titles. At the end of the 1680s, Penn created a commission of property to address the problem of unseated lands or lands not yet improved. Also, there was some political manoeuvring going on in Philadelphia, in which Chester county, in a bid to increase its tax base, attempted to attach the Welsh Tract to itself. The tract which took up the area immediately west of the Schuylkill River in the area of Radnor and Haverford townships was carved out for Welsh immigrants so that they could 'live together & help one another & keep our language to hold corresponde[nce] with them in our Native land'. But because the surveys were not established until 1687, Chester was seizing the opportunity to claim some of the land with the inhabitants so as to bolster its political clout. There was also the ongoing problem of the boundary dispute with Maryland, to which Penn's response was to carve out 30,000 acres of land in the lower counties for the Welsh settlers, move them in, and thereby establish a barrier to Lord Baltimore's claims.[29] Another scheme to come to grips with boundaries was Penn's plan to settle the Susquehanna valley and stem the move northwards by Baltimore. For this, he claimed the land adjacent to the river all the way down through present-day Conestoga. But there was also another reason for staking his claim. Securing the adjacent lands would result in cornering the fur trade, which would flow down the river and out to the Chesapeake River. This was part of a bigger plan devised by Daniel Coxe to establish a company which would control trade out to the Pacific Ocean.

Most of the problems over territory were only partly solved by the time events from the Glorious Revolution overtook Penn's plans; at least he was able to get a release from Governor Dongan in 1697 of the land around the Susquehanna in the north of Pennsylvania bordering New York. Now, with Penn in the colony, his land policy could take shape. For one thing, Penn could pursue the plan to settle the Susquehanna region which was vital to his fur trade scheme. Once in the colony, he could negotiate treaties with the Iroquois in order to develop the region.[30] Over 300 subscribers, mostly from Chester county, which extended to the Susquehanna, were involved. It was particularly enticing for them because Penn proposed a second city in the area. This could only mean more political influence.[31]

Penn also tackled the problems which had arisen in his absence over his proprietorial lands in order to recoup part of his financial outlay. These were exacerbated by inaccurate surveys of land which resulted in more feuds and, ultimately, the refusal by the inhabitants to pay quitrents to Penn. Penn tried to resolve the land problem with a new plan by reorganizing the colony's management and delegating land queries to five commissioners. When some colonists strongly objected to what they regarded as a prerogative court, James Logan was put in charge of the operation. The only previous attempt at some kind of control over the land question had been made by Blackwell, but he had neither the time nor the wherewithal to come to grips with the problem. For one thing, Blackwell tried to establish a payment scheme based on a list of names which was incomplete. Logan was determined to tackle the confusion, and did so by noting every acre of land surveyed so as not to miss any area no matter what name was on the deed.[32]

Meanwhile, Penn had to generate ready money and tried to do so by meeting the assembly in the autumn of 1700, asking for a proprietary tax bill which would cover his debts. All that he got in the end was a promise of £2,000 by getting a supply bill passed. Other than that, he succeeded in angering the provincials with his high-handed tactics.[33] Years later, Logan remarked on the consequences of Penn's last trip to his colony when he described the resentment of the assembly upon hearing Penn's desire for money. He had been 'hard to the People; and thereby lost the affection of many who had almost ador'd him'.[34]

The euphoria surrounding Penn's arrival at New Castle was short-lived. Logan reported that it was virtually impossible to describe the enthusiastic welcome they received, but a cloud had passed over the day which portended trouble. Robert Quary did not greet Penn immediately. As vice-admiralty judge in North America, Quary was also an Anglican, and a leading member of the Anglican vestry in Pennsylvania.

His vision of metropolitan pre-eminence was coloured by the Anglican hegemony for the moment. He saw himself as an instrument to reclaim the colonies in the name of the Crown and he used all possible means to achieve this. His experiences as an office holder in Massachusetts added to his distaste for chartered governments run by dissenters. His contempt for the Quaker majority in Philadelphia and the timing of the renewal of the Affirmation Act gave him an opening with which he thought he could bring about the fall of the colonial government. Realizing Penn was the ringleader of the opposition, Quary knew that if he could get Pennsylvania to collapse into the Crown's lap, the rest of the proprietaries would follow. Behind Quary were former Quakers who had turned back to the Church. There were clearly, as Logan noted, two parties: the group led by Quary questioned the proprietorial powers without taking an oath and pushed for the removal of the colony's constitution. Charges of illegal trading and using the colony as a haven for pirates were the fuel that kept the Board of Trade concerned in the affairs of Pennsylvania. The other side, championed by the councilman and lawyer David Lloyd, defended their stand against imperial interference, but the manner in which they did so only exacerbated the problem for Penn.[35] Logan certainly took the view that Penn could brook no disrespect from either side, so when Lloyd behaved insolently towards the proprietor, he was rebuked. The group led by Quary grew suspicious of Penn's true motives shortly after his arrival. At first Penn appeared to act in accordance with Crown policy. He dismissed three of the most troublesome members of the government: William Markham, David Lloyd, and Anthony Morris. All three had not only ignored Crown authority: Lloyd had brazenly stood against it. William Markham was implicated in illegal trading practices, not least because his daughter married a suspected pirate. In fact, he was up to his ears in shady dealings. He admitted accepting 'presents', and flouting the law by allowing specie into the colony. Therefore, his position as governor was untenable, and Penn replaced him with John Evans. Morris was also accused of smuggling, in this case, exporting tobacco surreptitiously in flour barrels, thus avoiding paying duties. David Lloyd was seen as the most visible opponent of external authority. He not only opposed Penn's authority but stood against outside directives on such things as support for the war effort of the 1690s.

However, when Penn called for new elections, his direct involvement in the polling raised some eyebrows and sent fear through the Anglican community. He claimed that nobody who swore an oath was qualified to elect or be elected to the government, and he went as far as prohibiting large groups of Anglicans to congregate at the hustings. The quarter sessions were another point of conflict. Three Anglicans were included as justices in the sessions, with six 'strong Foxonian Quakers, one Swede, and one sweet singer of Isreall'. The problem occurred over the issuing of oaths. The members of the Church of England insisted upon swearing the oath of office while the Quaker contingent refused and threatened to walk out, thereby ending the sessions. Penn intervened, but grew exasperated with the situation and declared that the trouble resulted from the Anglican quarter. Quary's suspicions were somewhat justified because, in lashing out at the churchmen, Penn exhibited a side that his biographers tended to overlook. Penn 'declared that he was a palatinate, and therefore would exert this authority that his commission should go no more a begging, but that they should know that his power was far greater than any kings governor in America', and with that statement he dismissed the three Anglicans.[36] This, in a nutshell, was the essence of the man. Penn's view of toleration was not based upon any democratic principle but on a type of tolerance an enlightened monarch or autocrat would employ for the good of his realm. Penn was employing the same rule under which he had been influenced. The French under Louis XIV and the English under Charles and James operated upon the assumption of indulgences and political liberties, to a point. Likewise, Penn provided for religious toleration, but to a point, and when he perceived it as getting out of hand, he restricted it. He viewed the behaviour of the churchmen as destabilizing the political and religious fabric of the colony, and took seriously the threat to the relatively peaceful society which he had created. Ironically, Penn's response was not far off from the type of response the English government had shown in the past to what it perceived to be disruptive influences to English religious and political society. It must be remembered that Penn saw at first hand the behaviour of the Anglican Church towards dissent in England.

There was finally the ongoing problem of the constitution of the colony. Shortly after he arrived in the colony, Penn made known his objections to the 1696 frame of government which had been virtually foisted upon his deputy governor. He announced that the government was to revert to the 1683 version. Yet he realized there was really no going back to a constitution that had been controversial. A new frame of government, the Charter of Liberties, was hammered out in which the separation of the three lower counties, collectively known as Delaware, was recognized.

Penn was coming to the realization that as long as the Anglican-dominated three lower counties were forced to submit to laws favouring the Philadelphia representatives, there would be a continuing threat to the colony's political stability. The only solution, therefore, was to allow

Delaware to form a separate government. With that decision, and his agreement to the new charter for Pennsylvania, Penn left for England.[37] This raises an interesting query as to Penn's motives regarding Pennsylvania. It was clear that Penn had lost all patience with his fellow Quakers in the colony. They, in turn, had a right to be suspicious of Penn's aims for his proprietorship. Penn was indeed wishing to sell it, but he did not want to sell at a loss, or to have his territory taken from him by the Crown or by Ford. His inclination for Delaware to form its own government seems to indicate that he did not necessarily mean to include those counties with the sale of Pennsylvania. Why? Delaware was proving less factious, more inclined to abide by England's navigation laws, and it controlled the vital entrance and exit to and from the Atlantic Ocean. There was also the doubt in the back of Penn's mind and others in England as to whether or not he really did own the government of Delaware.

Penn spent less than two years in his colony, but in that relatively short time his attitude to power became manifest. The colonists felt the full impact of his authority. At the same time, the proprietor saw at first hand the deleterious effect of his absence. Yet he sensed that it was more than that and decided that the experiment was floundering. Though he created an environment where religious freedom could flourish, political factionalism had broken out. Adding to these problems was the factionalism within Quaker ranks because of the effect of the Keithian schism. The fragmentation was enhanced by the insurgence of Anglicanism in the colony. The Pennsylvania charter's requirement for an Anglican minister to be appointed once a minimum of twenty Anglicans petitioned for one was now fulfilled. However, a complication arose in the colony over the passing of the 1696 Affirmation Act, because the Anglican contingent in the colony was claiming that the colonial legislation was now outside English law. Moreover, the Affirmation Act did not include participation in the judiciary. Thus Anglicans were insisting upon the right to swear an oath and to have the power to exact oaths from others. This, Penn urged, would lead to putting the Quakers in the colony in the position of being dissenters, as they were in England. He found this particularly galling when at the colony's beginning the Anglican contingent did not even make up a third of the population. Penn argued that the colony's progress was threatened if its religious freedom was circumscribed, and pleaded with Harley to get somebody of influence, such as the bishop of London, to persuade the more zealous Anglicans in Pennsylvania, 'headed by a Flanders camp parson', to see reason.[38]

Just before Penn left his colony he appointed Andrew Hamilton, governor of New Jersey, as his deputy in Pennsylvania. This appointment had, however, to be ratified by the Board of Trade when he reached England. Meanwhile he was asked by the assembly to take 'due care . . . that he be represented here by persons of integrity and considerable estates'.[39] In the event he trusted in a coterie of cronies to rule on his behalf until Hamilton's appointment was confirmed. Chief among these was Logan, who was made provincial secretary, clerk of council, receiver-general, commissioner of propriety, and proprietary secretary.[40] When he reached England, Penn put forward to the Crown his nomination of Andrew Hamilton as his deputy, an appointment which was held up by the Board of Trade and challenged in Pennsylvania. Just as he was beginning to establish his government Hamilton died. In his place Penn appointed John Evans, a 26-year-old Welshman whose chief attraction, apart from his willingness to take on the job, was that he was an Anglican.

Evans acted as Penn's deputy between 1703 and 1708. He was instructed 'to take care in all things to keep within the compas of & to keep up the powers of my Graunts . . . & in no wise suffer them to be broaken in upon by any refractory or factious persons what ever'.[41] This was easier said than done, especially when it became known in the colony that the proprietor was trying to sell its government to the Crown. If it was to become a Crown colony anyway, then there seemed little incentive to pay any regard to Penn's commands. The anti-proprietary party, led by David Lloyd, got control of the assembly at the polls in 1704 and again in 1705 and proceeded to try further to reduce Penn's powers. An exasperated Evans admonished them that 'the privileges of the people do not consist in divesting the Governor of all power and support'.[42] The most contentious issue was a bill to establish courts, to which Penn wanted to appoint judges at his pleasure, while the anti-proprietary party wanted to appoint them on good behaviour. After the proprietor's supporters gained control of the assembly in 1706 Evans was able to get his way on this point.[43] At the next annual elections Lloyd's supporters again triumphed and used their victory to try to impeach Logan, whom they regarded as the *eminence grise* of the proprietary party. Evans was able to hoist them with their own petard when he pointed out that impeachment was a process whereby the lower house of a legislature charged somebody with high crimes and misdemeanours before the upper house, and that by the Charter of Privileges which they had wrested from Penn the council no longer acted as a second legislative chamber. Unfortunately Evans overreached himself when he gave his assent to a bill passed by the Delaware legislature claiming the right to collect duty from ships entering into its waters on the way to Philadelphia. When some Pennsylvanian ships refused to pay such imposts, cannons were fired upon them. The Pennsylvanians petitioned Evans and Penn against such an outrageous act. As Penn remarked to Evans on learning of this outrage, 'it seems to have united the several parties against thee and me, in consequence upon a common interest which indeed looks like a finishing stroke to thy unhappiness'.[44]

Penn had little option but to fire Evans, void the act, and replace him with Charles Gookin, an Irishman and army officer. Gookin too had to face hostile assemblies after he arrived in the colony in 1709. But at the elections in 1710 there occurred the unique phenomenon of a complete change in the membership. The purge of the anti-proprietary party at the polls that year was a turning point in Penn's fortunes in Pennsylvania. He himself had helped to bring this about by sending a letter to Friends in the colony which was published as *A Serious Expostulation with the Inhabitants of Pennsilvania.* 'The eyes of many people are upon you,' he wrote.[45]

> The People of many Nations in Europe look on that Countrey as a Land of Ease & Quiet, wishing to themselves in vain the same blessings they conceive you may enjoy: But to See the use you make of them is no less the cause of Surprise to others while such bitter Complaints & Reflections are seen to come from you of which it's difficult to conceive even the sense or meaning. Where are the Distresses Grievances & Oppresions that the Papers sent from thence so often say you languish under? while others have cause to believe you have hitherto lived or might live the happiest of any in the Queens Dominions.

He concluded by urging them to think seriously about the elections, since 'from the next Assembly I shall expect to know what you resolve, and what I may depend on'.

He was highly gratified at the outcome. In a letter to Friends the following February he thanked them for their eminent zeal and concurrence for the public good, and their 'noble endeavours to rescue your poor Governour & Government out of the fallen selfish & ungrateful practices of some men'.[46] It was a fitting finale to his involvement in Pennsylvania politics.

. . .

NOTES AND REFERENCES

1. Craig W. Horle and Marianne S. Wokeck (eds), *Lawmaking and Legislators in Pennsylvania: A Biographical Dictionary* (Philadelphia, 1991), I, pp. 34–5, 236–7, 247, 273.

2. Gary B. Nash, *Quakers and Politics: Pennsylvania 1681–1726* (1968), pp. 103–4.
3. Joseph Dorfman, 'Captain Blackwell: A Bibliographical Note', *PMHB*, 69 (1945), pp. 233–7.
4. *PWP*, III, p. 256.
5. *PWP*, III, p. 209. Penn later claimed that he would never have appointed Blackwell 'if all others had not refused who were fit for it'. *PWP*, III, p. 284.
6. *PWP*, III, p. 209. Penn apparently meant by this that he appointed Blackwell 'thinking thereby the better to curb those that were not frds, being nearer to them then frds, tho a Professor too'. *PWP*, III, p. 350.
7. *PWP*, III, p. 218.
8. *PWP* microfilm, Blackwell to WP, 13 Jan. 1690.
9. Minutes of provincial council, I, 255, 5 Mar. 1688/89.
10. *PWP*, III, pp. 255–8, WP to Blackwell, 25 Sept. 1689.
11. Nash, *Quakers and Politics*, p. 128.
12. *CSP Colonial 1689–92*, p. 525, no. 1708; p. 478, no. 1583.
13. *PWP*, III, pp. 276, 295–306; *PWP* microfilm 2925, Declaration by the lower counties; *PWP* microfilm 1098.
14. *PWP*, III, p. 307.
15. APS, Penn Papers, 1, fo. 216, 5 Oct. 1692.
16. Bedfordshire Record Office, How MS 85, Keith to Eccleston, 12 Apr. 1693.
17. Nash, *Quakers and Politics*, p. 148.
18. *PWP*, III, p. 354.
19. *PWP*, III, p. 376.
20. *PWP*, III, p. 376, Penn to the Deposed Members of the Provincial Council, 15 Sept. 1693.
21. *PWP*, III, p. 383.
22. PRO, CO, 389/13, fo. 48.
23. APS, Penn Papers, I, fo. 294; *PWP*, III, pp. 393, 397–8, 415–16.
24. PRO, CO, 5/1233, fo. 15. At the same time he did not scruple to assure the provincial council of Pennsylvania that he hoped to return there in a short time! *PWP*, III, p. 405.
25. *PWP*, III, pp. 499–500.
26. Nash, *Quakers and Politics*, pp. 209–10.
27. *PWP*, III, pp. 510–11.
28. APS, Penn Papers, II, fo. 370.
29. W. Cooch (ed.), *Delaware Historic Events*: 'Welsh Baptist Meeting House' (Newark, 1946).
30. G. Nash, 'The Quest for the Susquehanna Valley: New York, Pennsylvania, and the Seventeenth-Century Fur Trade', *New York History*, 48 (1967), pp. 19–27.
31. *PWP*, III, pp. 671–8.

32. Edward Armstrong (ed.), *Correspondence between William Penn and James Logan*, 2 vols (Philadelphia, 1872), II, p. 150, Logan to Penn, 10 Aug. 1706.
33. Ibid.
34. APS transcripts of Logan letters by Deborah Logan, Logan to John, Richard, and Thomas Penn, 14 Nov. 1731.
35. Armstrong (ed.), *Correspondence*, I, pp. 16–18, Logan to WP jr.
36. Huntington Library MS BL 4: A Brief Narrative of the proceedings of William Penn (n.d.) *c.* 3 Dec. 1699 (full transcription in William S. Perry (ed.), *Historical Collections Relating to the American Colonial Church* (Pennsylvania, 1871)), II, pp. 1–4.
37. Deborah Logan (ed.), *Penn–Logan Correspondence* (1819), p. 55, WP to JL.
38. *PWP*, IV, p. 45. The parson in question was Edward Pocock, minister at Christ Church, Philadelphia.
39. *Votes and Proceedings of the House of Representatives of the Province of Pennsylvania* (Philadelphia, 1762), I, p. 145: address to the Proprietary, 20 Sept. 1701.
40. Nash, *Quakers and Politics*, p. 139.
41. *PWP*, IV, p. 230.
42. *Minutes of the Provincial Council of Pennsylvania* (Philadelphia, 1852), II, p. 286.
43. Ibid., p. 306.
44. *PWP*, IV, p. 605.
45. *PWP*, IV, pp. 678–9. Nash claims that Penn's paper arrived in November, too late to influence the October election (*Quakers and Politics*, p. 309). But the editors of *William Penn's Published Writings 1660–1726: An Interpretive Bibliography* claim that it is possible that it arrived in time to be printed and circulated; *PWP*, V, p. 508.
46. *PWP*, IV, p. 687.

Chapter 11

LAST YEARS AND LEGACY

. . .

LAST YEARS

When Penn wrote to the Friends in Pennsylvania to thank them for their support in the election there in 1710, which had transformed the political situation in the colony, he informed them that there had been major changes in English politics that year too. The ministerial revolution in England had seen the ousting of Godolphin, the diminution of Marlborough's influence in the government, and the triumphal return to power of Robert Harley at the head of a Tory ministry. Penn expressed the hope that it would not 'turn to our prejudice, at least I shall use all my interest to turn [it] to our advantage'.[1] He had already contrived to turn it to his own advantage. As ever, Penn was a political weather vane, turning to the prevailing wind from Court. He made his peace with the incoming Harley in the summer of 1710, and tried to use his influence with the Quakers to support Tory candidates in the autumn election. His influence with Friends at home, however, had not been as persuasive as in Pennsylvania, for Tories grumbled that the Quakers had voted for their Whig rivals at the polls.

This did no harm to Penn's relationship with the new prime minister, even though he confessed to him that 'I am now Good for nothing'.[2] On the contrary he was able to use his influence with Harley to lobby for those Quakers who wished to alter the wording of the affirmation.[3] He also used it to try to smooth the final stages in his protracted surrender of the government of Pennsylvania.

When he had first proposed selling it he had needed the money, for he was in dire financial straits. This situation had arisen largely from his dealings with Philip Ford. Ford was initially hired by Penn in 1669 to assist him in his father's affairs in Ireland and later as his business agent in London. Essentially, Ford kept account of Penn's expenses that ranged from the cost of his visits to London to paying the servants' wages and providing pocket money for the Penn family. For this service, Ford was paid an annual salary of £40 plus expenses. Initially, there did not seem to be a cash flow problem, although the accounts showed that Penn was having trouble collecting rent from his Irish estates. There was enough cash on the credit side for Ford to use personally to start up his own dry goods business. There is no hard evidence that Ford was falsifying his bookkeeping, but by 1685 Penn was already in debt to Ford to the tune of £4,000, and by 1696 Ford claimed that Penn owed him over £10,000. Penn put his colony up as collateral and, in return, paid Ford an annual sum of £630 towards the debt. In 1702, Ford died, leaving the deed to the colony to his widow, Bridget, and two Quaker merchants as trustees for it. His will allowed Penn to redeem Pennsylvania if he paid £11,134 8s. 3d. within six months.

Probably the reason for the intensification of Penn's efforts to sell Pennsylvania in 1703 was so that he could settle his debt with the Ford family. His failure to do so led them to sue him in Chancery in 1705. The dispute dragged on until October 1708, when it was settled out of court. From January to August of 1708 Penn was actually in a debtors' prison. By that time the Fords were demanding over £14,000. But they eventually settled for £7,600, which was largely raised for the bankrupt Penn by wealthy Quaker merchants.[4]

The resolution of the dispute removed Penn's urgent need to sell the government of his colony. Nevertheless, he renewed his attempts in 1710, when he petitioned the queen. His petition asked for 'such a sum as may reimburse him of a reasonable part of his past Expences, and relieve him from the Necesities that his Engagement in that Province has plunged him into'. By the 'Province' Penn meant just Pennsylvania. Delaware was not part of the deal. On the contrary, he wished his claim to the lower counties to be 'fully settled and confirmed'.[5] An actual sum was not mentioned in the petition, but where previously he had asked for £30,000 he indicated to the Board of Trade that he was now pre-pared to settle for £20,000. He also offered to be paid over a seven-year period.[6] The Board responded sympathetically but insisted that Penn's surrender should be absolute, and he should renounce his claim to the government not only of Pennsylvania but also of Delaware.[7] The nego-tiations dragged on, a delay which Penn, perhaps charitably, attributed to the many other weighty matters which the ministry had to deal with.[8] The matter was referred to the attorney-general, who reported in Feb-ruary 1712 to Harley, who had become lord treasurer and earl of Oxford the previous year. By July Penn was able to report that he had made an end of the business with the lord treasurer. A possible payment of

£16,000 over seven years was now reduced to £12,000 over four.[9] Penn probably agreed to settle for this since he understood that a bill to resume proprietary colonies by the Crown was about to be presented to parliament.[10] This perhaps accounts for the inclusion of the powers of government granted to him by the duke of York as well as those over the colony granted by Charles II in the surrender which he agreed over the summer of 1712. In September the queen gave instructions to the Treasury to pay Penn the first instalment of £1,000. But that was the end of the matter, for the conveyance was not completed when Penn, who had suffered a minor stroke in April, was incapacitated by a second in October.

About the time of his first stroke Penn drew up his last will and testament. It left the government of Pennsylvania and the territories thereto belonging to the earl of Oxford and his friend Lord Poulet. Both were by then Anglican Tories. This shows how far Penn had gravitated into Harley's circle since 1710. The two peers were to act as trustees to dispose of his powers in America to the queen 'or to any other Person to the best advantage & profit they can'.[11] He bequeathed the territory of the colony to a trust with seven trustees in England, including his wife, and five in Pennsylvania, including Logan. They were to set aside 10,000 acres apiece for the three children of William junior, his son by his first wife, and Aubrey, their daughter. The rest was to go to his children by his second wife. The relatively meagre inheritance provided for his eldest son probably reflects Penn's disapproval of his behaviour. Even though William junior had been an able agent for his father in England, when he went to Pennsylvania his credibility collapsed. There were shadows over Penn's son's conduct in England which gained substance in the colony. He had a penchant for the good life and ran up debts to maintain his ostentatious lifestyle, which his father indulged him in. Even though William wrote to Logan on the eve of his departure for Pennsylvania, telling him not to believe all that was said about him, the gossip turned out to be only too true. After arriving in the colony, William's first letter to his father showed an interest more in keeping up his lifestyle than in the business of acting as heir apparent.[12] It soon became clear to Logan that Penn's son did not sit in the saddle of government as well as he sat in the equestrian one. His only success in the colony was to become involved in playing soldier with the local militia and get embroiled in a tavern brawl for which he barely escaped arrest. He returned to England in disgrace. He distanced himself from the Penn household, spending most of his time abroad. He was not at his father's deathbed in 1718 and he died two years later in France.[13]

William junior and his family were to dispute the inheritance with Penn's second wife Hannah and her sons, a dispute that was not resolved for a decade after Penn's death. At times it seemed as though the proprietorship would be wrested out of the hands of any of the Penns. But in the end the family quarrel was resolved in favour of the founder's second family. His colony remained in the control of Hannah's sons, John, Thomas, and Richard, until 1776. They all became Anglicans, a development perhaps foreshadowed by Penn's making Lords Oxford and Poulet executors of his will.

Although he lived until 1718 Penn was never again able to take care of business. His wife, Hannah, had to cope with the loose ends of his dealings with the government. These were never completely tied up. Just before his death his wife was able to draw on the influence he had so long cultivated at court to fend off a threat to his title to the three lower counties. By then the Whigs were once more in the ascendant following the death of Queen Anne in 1714 and the accession of the elector of Hanover, George I. The Scottish earl of Sutherland petitioned the king for the Delaware territory in 1716. The attorney-general and solicitor-general, to whom the petition was referred, were both of the opinion that title rested with the Crown rather than with Penn, but advised that it should be tested in Chancery. Upon this Hannah decided to approach James Craggs, the secretary of state concerned. But she did so through the earl of Sunderland, who was then prime minister, as she put it to him, 'through thy long friendship to my poor weak husband'.[14] As so often in the past, Penn's political clout at the very end of his life was more considerable than that of a rival, and Hannah's intercession saw off Lord Sutherland's challenge.

*   *   *

.   .   .

LEGACY

William Penn's statue stands atop Philadelphia's city hall, towering over the city, looking out towards Shackomaxon and the Delaware River. One hand holds the treaty signed there with the Indians, while the other reaches out in the direction of the river as if to suggest where his authority lay. What had started out as an investment for an English dissenter ended up as an experiment that succeeded beyond anybody's imagination. By the middle of the eighteenth century, Philadelphia became a major colonial port for North American trade, operating a surplus economy, rivalling New York and outstripping Boston. The experiment had paid off. Yet today the vision of Penn differs depending upon which side of the Atlantic Ocean one stands. In England he is a historical figure, while in America he is an icon. Aside from the portrait of Penn in armour hanging in Christ Church, Oxford, there is no famous pictorial representation of him in Britain. In America, he is revered through paintings and statues, albeit mainly in Pennsylvania and Delaware.

While Penn is something less than an icon in English eyes, nevertheless he influenced religious and political thought during a period of experimentation in which lived some of the greatest minds of the century. He drew from their philosophies what he felt was worthwhile for his colony. Thus he could profit from previous attempts to introduce governments into colonies, such as those of John Winthrop with his vision of a city upon a hill, and subsequent colonial ventures from Maryland to the Carolinas. However, unlike the Puritan Errand into the Wilderness, where man was looked upon as fallen from grace so that only a handful of visible saints could rule, Penn thought everyone had the light within, and therefore all men could participate in the political process. Hence the view that everyone should consent to laws. Another possible precedent is suggested by an intriguing parallel between his own title for his constitution for Pennsylvania, the Frame of Government, and that of the Cromwellian Protectorate, the Instrument of Government. Perhaps the echo was inspired by his association with Algernon Sidney. Certainly Sidney's ideas as well as Harrington's have been detected behind the original version of the Frame, the Fundamental Constitutions for Pennsylvania. However, as it evolved through various drafts into the final Frame of Government in 1682, Sidney, as we have seen, objected to the wording, saying that it gave more power to Penn than he felt was consistent with republican ideals.[15] A direct comparison between the Instrument of Government and any draft of the Frame of Government shows that they have little if anything in common. Penn was not really a republican, and Cromwellian precedents played little or no part in his constitutional thinking.

Political philosophies were fashioned by men like Sidney and Harrington, Hobbes and Locke. Penn was presumably referring to these when he observed that there was 'nothing the wits of men are more busie and divided upon' than ideas concerning government.[16]

* * *

While Penn did not share Hobbes's pessimism about human nature enough to create a Leviathan to keep men in awe, neither was he sanguine enough about human nature, as Locke was, to rely completely on man's goodwill. Locke believed that most men could recognize their enlightened self-interest, and that laws were necessary to deter a minority who allowed passion to overcome reason. Penn accepted that some people were good and others were bad and that there had to be some mechanism to safeguard society from a few corrupt individuals. The analogy of the clock, which he fondly inserted into the preface of his Frame of Government, implied more than just the notion of winding it up and setting it off on its own course. Within the mechanism were laws that would contain the passions of man. But it needed good men to work it.[17]

> I know some say, Let us have good laws, and no matter for the men that execute them: But let them consider, that though good laws do well good men do better; for good laws may want good men, and be abolished or evaded by ill men; but good men will never want good laws nor suffer ill ones . . . But a loose and deprav'd people (which is the question) love laws and administration like themselves. That therefore which makes a good constitution must keep it; (vizt.) men of wisdom and virtue . . .

Here was a man who espoused the ideals of virtue and wisdom as qualifications for office, qualities which he believed that 'because they descend not with worldly inheritances, must be carefully propagated by a virtuous education of youth; for which after-ages will owe more to the care and prudence of founders and the successive magistracy, than to their parents for their private patrimonies'. Yet, ironically, the belief that public office required qualities that could not be inherited, thus making office-holding an elected position rather than an inherited one, came from someone whose station in life was inherited.

His egalitarian approach extended, albeit in a limited way, to the native North Americans. There was no doubt in Penn's mind that the Indians were a conquered race, but his peaceful relationship became the touchstone of his approach in general. Penn was merely putting into practice English policy that had already been formed with regard to the Indians. His hopes that men of goodwill would continue to run his colony were to prove misplaced in this respect, for his successors did not respect his fair dealings with the natives. On the contrary, they were to alienate them by their wilful misrepresentation of a treaty he made which gave him as much land as a man could walk in a day. In 1739 his son Thomas and Logan implemented this in a way which, while it abided strictly by the letter, broke its spirit. They got men to walk as fast as possible to maximize the amount of land obtained in a transaction ever afterwards notorious as the 'Walking Purchase'. The friendly relations with the Indians thereafter rapidly deteriorated, culminating in open violence in the French and Indian war.

Until then the pacifist policies of the ruling Quakers had never really been put to the test. This was no doubt helped by the geographical position of Pennsylvania, which isolated the colony from hostilities in Penn's own lifetime. In 1755, however, war spilled over the western frontier of Pennsylvania, causing refugees to flee east over the Susquehanna River. Something had to be done to defend the frontier. Those Quakers who could not break with their pacifist principles even in a defensive war resigned from the government. Penn's experiment of placing the government in the hands of good men was again tested and found wanting.

Penn himself weighed into political discourse with a grand view of what could be. His plan for a Union of Colonies was a pragmatic approach to solving intercolonial problems over duties and defence, yet it was also forward-looking. The Albany Plan of Union of 1754 was an echo of Penn's proposal of 1697. In neither case could we say that there was an aspiration for independence from Britain. The schemes recognized a practical necessity. For Penn, there was the constant recognition that whatever he created in North America, and in Ireland for that matter, was done for the greatness of the English empire. In that respect, there was a limit to his motive for establishing a colony. Nonetheless, the Articles of Confederation and the Constitution of the United States made a reality out of the ideas put forward in the earlier proposals.

Penn's legacy extended beyond his involvement with Pennsylvania. As an Englishman and a politician, he kept an eye on the centre of action, which was Europe. He spent most of his life in a war-weary world. As a man of peace, he directed his political discourse to resolving the conflicts in Europe. What emerged was another far-sighted document, which put forward a model for future attempts at world peace. *An Essay Toward the Present and Future Peace of Europe*, published in 1693, showed Penn's commitment to peace rather than to war. It also illustrated his broad and forward-looking vision for mankind. The very use of the word 'Europe' showed that he was up-to-date in his thinking, as it had only recently replaced the older term 'Christendom' to describe the Continent. The tenets of today's European Union can be discerned in Penn's prospectus. His main theme was proportional representation of member countries in a federation based upon their economic power. The office of president would rotate, and in no way would domestic sovereignty be surrendered to international sovereignty. Penn's essay also reveals his political astuteness by recognizing that such a union, which included Turkey, would neutralize the alliance that France had hitherto had with the Turks.

Penn's impact on religious and legal thought was impressive enough to earn him the title of 'un veritable Lycurgue'.[18] As a dissenter, Penn worked untiringly for religious toleration where people could practise their beliefs without fear. If that was put into practice, the economy would flourish. As a businessman, Penn saw the sense of such a philosophy. With the creation of Pennsylvania, Penn produced an experiment in which the ingredients of religious and ethnic plurality were mixed together. This melting pot became the cauldron from which the American ethos grew. As Penn knew well, an experiment never really ends, nor did he intend for his colonial experiment to reach finality. Perhaps therein lay the essence of the American ideal or the American dream. Deborah Logan, writing a century later, was not too far off the mark when she suggested that 'perhaps it is not going too far to call the original frame of Government designed by William Penn for his Province, and the preliminary discourse affixed to it, the fountains from which have emanated most of those streams of political wisdom which now flow through every part of United America, defusing civil and religious liberty, and favoring the expansion of happiness and virtue'.[19]

. . .

NOTES AND REFERENCES

1. *PWP*, IV, p. 688.
2. *PWP*, IV, p. 710.
3. *PWP*, IV, p. 190, Penn to Harley, 6 Jan. or Feb. 1712. The Affirmation Act itself was not up for renewal until 1715, but some Quakers petitioned to change the actual words used when affirming in 1712. See J. William Frost, 'The Affirmation Controversy and Religious Liberty', in Richard S. Dunn and Mary Maples Dunn (eds), *The World of William Penn* (Philadelphia, 1986), pp. 314–15; Mary K. Geiter, 'Affirmation, Assassination, and Association: The Quakers, Parliament and the Court in 1696', *Parliamentary History*, 16 (1997), pp. 286–7.
4. The story of Penn's dispute with the Fords is told in Richard S. Dunn, 'Penny Wise and Pound Foolish: Penn as Businessman', in Richard S. Dunn and Mary Maples Dunn, *The World of William Penn* (University of Pennsylvania, 1986), pp. 37–54.
5. *PWP*, IV, p. 682.
6. *PWP*, IV, p. 686.
7. *PWP*, IV, pp. 689–91.
8. *PWP*, IV, p. 694.
9. *PWP*, IV, p. 722.
10. *PWP*, IV, p. 723. In fact no such bill was ever introduced.

11. *PWP*, IV, p. 716.
12. *PWP*, IV, pp. 261–2.
13. Sophie Hutchinson Drinker, *Hannah Penn and the Proprietorship of Pennsylvania* (Philadelphia, 1958), pp. 136–7.
14. *PWP*, IV, p. 747. Charles Spencer, third earl of Sunderland, was the son of the second earl, whom Penn had known since their days at Oxford. The third earl had been secretary of state from 1706 to 1710, and closely connected with Godolphin and Marlborough. Sunderland had helped Penn fend off Baltimore's claim to the lower counties in 1709.
15. *PWP*, II, p. 54.
16. *PWP*, II, p. 213.
17. *PWP*, II, p. 213.
18. Montesquieu in *Esprit des Lois*, I, IV, c. iv.
19. Deborah Logan (ed.), *Penn–Logan Correspondence* (1819), II, p. 10.

BIBLIOGRAPHICAL ESSAY

Before the publication of *The Papers of William Penn* by a team of scholars led by Richard S. Dunn and Mary Maples Dunn (4 vols, University of Pennsylvania, 1981–87), this study of Penn would have been almost impossible. The Herculean task of gathering material that had been scattered to the four winds resulted in a collection of manuscript sources in print. The four volumes range from 1644, the year of Penn's birth, to his death in 1718. There is a fifth and final volume, edited by Edwin D. Bronner and David Fraser, *William Penn's Published Writings 1660–1726: An Interpretive Bibliography* (Philadelphia, 1986). This is a wonderful guide to his publications. Although what was printed in the volumes was mainly Penn's correspondence concerning his colony, the series included a voluminous collection of microfilms which contain invaluable manuscripts pertaining to Penn's life in England. Since this study is of Penn's activities on both sides of the Atlantic, the microfilmed documents complement those published to provide the essential materials for a profile of Penn in power. *The Papers* will never be surpassed, only enhanced.

In order to put Penn's career into context, one has to forage around for other primary sources, which provide insight into what was going on in English politics and colonial circles. For this the *Calendar of State Papers Domestic*, together with the *Calendar of State Papers Colonial*, and *West Indies*, are a necessary starting point. The Reports of the Royal Commission on Historical Manuscripts conveniently calendar the correspondence of many of the politicians of the day. Those which calendar the papers of Robert Harley document the political career of arguably the most important politician to influence Penn's career: Historical Manuscripts Commission Report on the Papers of the Duke of Portland, vols 3–5.

For the colonial dimension, a major stopping-off point is the material in the relevant volumes of the series collected under the title of

Pennsylvania Archives. These are: Samuel Hazard (ed.), *Pennsylvania Archives: Selected and Arranged from Original Documents in the Office of the Secretary of the Commonwealth . . . 1664–1747*, 1st series, 12 vols (Philadelphia, 1852–56), I; John B. Linn and William H. Egle (eds), *Pennsylvania Archives*, 2nd series, 19 vols (Harrisburg, 1874–93); William H. Egle and George E. Reed (eds), *Pennsylvania Archives*, 3rd series, 30 vols (Harrisburg, 1894–99); Gertrude MacKinney (ed.), *Pennsylvania Archives*, 8th series: *Votes and Proceedings of the House of Representatives of the Province of Pennsylvania* (Harrisburg, 1931), I. When studying the history of North America, a map is essential. I have pored over the maps in Jeannette D. Black (ed.), *The Blathwayt Atlas: A Collection of Forty-eight Manuscript and Printed Maps of the Seventeenth Century Relating to the British Overseas Empire in That Era, Brought Together about 1683 for the Use of the Lords of Trade and Plantations by William Blathwayt, Secretary, I, The Maps; II, Commentary* (Providence: Brown University Press, 1970–75).

The secondary literature is vast. There are over thirty-five biographies of Penn emphasizing different aspects of his life. I have been amazed at how the early biographies of Penn were more tributes to the Quaker than objective studies of the man. Perhaps this was due to their authors' own religious leanings. One of the earliest works, by Joseph Besse, *A Collection of the Works of William Penn, of which is Prefaced a Journal of His Life With Many Letters and Papers Not Before Published*, set the tone of piety. His preface to the collection was in praise of Penn's struggles as a Quaker rather than a discussion of Penn's life and career as a man, husband, and politician. Not until Thomas Clarkson came along was there a genuine attempt to write a full biography of Penn. His *Memoirs of the Private and Public Life of William Penn* (2 vols, London, 1813), however, still lacked adequate documentation. Even though more biographies followed, Penn the man remained an enigma. Throughout the nineteenth century primary sources were becoming more available, and we see the results in works such as W. Hepworth Dixon's *History of William Penn, Founder of Pennsylvania* (London, 1851). Penn's stature as a hero of sorts was so entrenched that when Thomas Babington Macaulay questioned his motives behind the push for religious toleration, a debate ensued that continues to this day. Although Dixon vigorously defended Penn's integrity, questions over Penn's involvement with James II after the Glorious Revolution of 1688 remained. Macaulay's attack provided the impetus for future historians to consider wider aspects of Penn's life in order to solve the mysteries surrounding him. On the heels of Dixon's work, Samuel MacPherson Janney produced a scholarly investigation, *The Life of William Penn With Selections from his Correspondence and Autobiography* (Philadelphia, 1852), which was considered the best work to date.

Augustus C. Buell's biography *William Penn: Founder of Two Common-wealths* (New York, 1904) directed attention to the Quaker's colonial activities. It was also the beginning of a more professional and object-ive approach to an appreciation of Penn. William Isaac Hull produced a comparative work on eight earlier biographies, *Eight First Biographies of William Penn: In Seven Languages and Seven Lands* (Swarthmore, Pa., 1936), carefully analysed them, and offered his own contribution to the investigation.

The decades since the 1960s have seen a new onslaught on the life of Penn. Edwin B. Bronner questioned whether Penn's colony was a success and wrote *William Penn's Holy Experiment: The Founding of Pennsylvania, 1681–1701* (Temple University Press, 1962). Then a host of scholars poured out biographies of the man, each one trying to capture a different aspect. Vincent Buranelli, *The King and the Quaker: A Study of William Penn and James II* (University of Pennsylvania, 1962), concentrates on Penn's relationship with James in an attempt to explain Penn's reli-gious motives. Melvin B. Endy Jr., *William Penn and Early Quakerism* (Princeton, 1973), highlights Penn's spiritual purpose which guided him in the secular world. Joseph Illick tried to lift Penn out of the Quaker mould and point out his role as a politician: *William Penn the Politician* (Ithaca, 1965) places Penn's actions within an imperial context. Shortly after Illick's groundbreaking work, Mary Maples Dunn's *William Penn: Politics and Conscience* (Princeton, 1967) produced an analysis of Penn's career in politics, and looked for a satisfactory explanation for how he could combine his worldly activities and his religious philosophy. Most recently, Harry Emerson Wildes, *William Penn* (New York, 1974), re-verts to examining every aspect of Penn's life. The result is an in-depth approach which was helped by extensive use of Penn's correspondence. Overall, my favourite study of Penn is Catherine Owens Peare's *William Penn: A Biography* (New York, 1957), which gets the essence of the man. Another important path to understanding Penn's world is to appreciate the political and social milieu in which he lived. This was explored in Richard S. Dunn and Mary Maples Dunn (eds), *The World of William Penn* (University of Pennsylvania, 1986). The book is divided into four sections: Penn's life; Penn's Britain; Penn's America; and his business world. All of the essays are essential reading, but two are of particular interest because of their provocative and fresh qualities: Stephen Saunders Webb, '"The Peaceable Kingdom": Quaker Pennsylvania in the Stuart Empire', puts Penn and his colony within the imperial context, as does Nicholas Canny, 'The Irish Background to Penn's Experiment'.

I found that in order to understand Penn, in the political context at least, I needed to look at the English political scene and Penn's English peers. All of the following are indispensable reading when looking into Penn's world. Douglas R. Lacey, *Dissent and Parliament Politics in England, 1661–1689* (New Jersey, 1969) deals with years in which dissent struggled for relief. Ronald Hutton, *The Restoration: A Political and Religious History of England and Wales, 1658–1667* (Oxford University Press, 1985) is the best account of the period in terms of scholarship and readability. John Kenyon's *Robert Spencer, Earl of Sunderland, 1641–1702* (London, 1958) is written with authority and panache. K.D. Haley, *The First Earl of Shaftesbury* (Oxford: Clarendon Press, 1968) is another wonderful profile of a contemporary politician. Brian W. Hill, *Robert Harley: Speaker, Secretary of State and Premier Minister* (Yale University Press, 1988), is a good read for someone trying to get a grip on the man. There are several good biographies of Charles II. If I had to choose which I would prefer in terms of reading enjoyment, Antonia Fraser's *Royal Charles: Charles II and the Restoration* (New York, 1979), like all of her work, is a joy to read. Two other biographies, John Miller, *Charles II* (London, 1991), and Ronald Hutton, *Charles II* (London, 1991), are excellent scholarly accounts of his life.

As far as Pennsylvania is concerned, for a detailed but quick run down on political personalities in colonial Pennsylvania from 1682 to 1709, there is no better place to look than Craig W. Horle and Marianne S. Wokeck (eds), *Lawmaking and Legislators in Pennsylvania* (Philadelphia, 1991), Vol. I. Gary B. Nash, *Quakers and Politics: Pennsylvania 1681–1726* (Princeton, 1968) sets the scene of the colony's political development and Penn's relationship with his colonists. James T. Lemon, *Best Poor Man's Country: A Geographical Study of Early Southeastern Pennsylvania* (Johns Hopkins Press, 1972) extends the study of Pennsylvania from Philadelphia to the hinterland of the colony, examining its geography as a basis for its economic growth. During the first twenty years of Pennsylvania's development, the Delaware region was very much a part of the plantation. Barry Levy, *Quakers and the American Family: British Settlement in the Delaware Valley* (Oxford University Press, 1988) analyses the migration of Quaker families from Wales and the Midlands of England to the Delaware area. Also see C.S. Weslager, *The English on the Delaware* (New Jersey, 1967). Delaware in this period, however, remains under-researched. Much has been made of Penn's relationship with the native North Americans. Unfortunately, studies on Penn and the Indians are still susceptible to pious interpretations. A notable exception is Francis Jennings's essay, 'Brother Miquon: Good Lord!', in Richard S. Dunn and Mary Maples Dunn (eds), *The World of William Penn*, in which he gives an objective account of Penn's Indian policy. Gary Nash's *Red, White, and Black: The Peoples of Early*

America (3rd edn, Prentice Hall, 1991) is the best study of racial relations to date.

For the colonial context I found most useful: Lois Green Carr, Philip D. Morgan, and Jean B. Russo (eds), *Colonial Chesapeake Society* (Chapel Hill: University of North Carolina Press, 1988); Allan Kulikoff, *Tobacco and Slaves: The Development of Southern Cultures in the Chesapeake, 1680–1800* (Chapel Hill: University of North Carolina Press, 1986); Robert C. Ritchie, *The Duke's Province: A Study of New York Politics and Society, 1664–1691* (Chapel Hill: University of North Carolina Press, 1977). John E. Pomfret's *The Province of East New Jersey, 1609–1702* (Princeton, 1962) and *The Province of West New Jersey, 1609–1702* (Princeton, 1956) remain the essential reading on the development of New Jersey and its relationship with Pennsylvania.

To understand the imperial context requires another approach to the life and times of William Penn. Works on this theme are relatively few compared to imperial studies on the American Revolution of 1776. But they are increasing as the realization sinks in that colonial North America was very much a province of Britain. A good foundation for such a study can be obtained from a couple of classic works. Charles M. Andrews, *The Colonial Period of American History*, 4 vols (New Haven: Yale University Press, 1934–38) takes the imperial approach, one which still forms the basis for anyone studying Anglo-America. Winifred T. Root, *The Relations of Pennsylvania with the British Government, 1696–1765* (New York, 1912) points the way for a study of provincial Pennsylvania within the British imperial network. One of the first historians to resurrect the importance of the imperial context in recent years is W.A. Speck, who wrote a comparative essay, *British America, 1607–1776* (University of Sussex Press, 1985) in the pamphlet series of the British Association for American Studies. The comparative approach was also adopted by David Grayson Allen, *In English Ways: The Movement of Societies and the Transferral of English Local Law and Custom to Massachusetts Bay in the Seventeenth Century* (Chapel Hill: University of North Carolina Press, 1981), and Ned Landsman, *Scotland and its First American Colony, 1683–1765* (Princeton, 1985), a study of Scottish migration to New Jersey. There are quite a few analyses of migration to the New World, but the one I found most helpful and interesting is David Cressy, *Coming Over: Migration and Communication Between England and New England in the Seventeenth Century* (Cambridge University Press, 1987). Undoubtedly, the most controversial contribution to the comparative history of Britain and its American colonies is David Hackett Fischer's *Albion's Seed: Four British Folkways in America* (Oxford University Press, 1989). The best studies of the imperial political connection are: I.K. Steele, *Politics of*

Colonial Policy: The Board of Trade in Colonial Administration, 1696–1720 (New York: Oxford University Press, 1986); Alison Gilbert Olson, *Anglo-American Politics, 1660–1775: The Relationship between Parties in England and Colonial America* (New York: Oxford University Press, 1973), and her later study, *Making the Empire Work: London and American Interest Groups, 1690–1790* (London, 1992). A good study of problems concerning the navigation laws and the men who enforced them is Michael Garibaldi Hall, *Edward Randolph and the American Colonies, 1676–1703* (Chapel Hill: IEAHC, University of North Carolina Press, 1960). Another 'imperial fixer' was investigated by Stephen Saunders Webb, 'William Blathwayt', *William and Mary Quarterly*, 25 (1968), pp. 3–21. A provocative approach by Webb, *The Governors-General: The English Army and the Definition of Empire, 1569–1681* (Chapel Hill: University of North Carolina Press, 1979) made me realize that Pennsylvania's place in England's military strategy needed explanation. Studying the economics of the imperial world takes courage and perseverance. It is greatly helped by John H. McCusker and Russell R. Menard, *The Economy of British America, 1607–1789* (Chapel Hill, 1985) and Henry Roseveare, *The Treasury 1660–1870: The Foundations of Control* (London, 1973).

INDEX

. . . .

Note: WP in the index stands for William Penn.